HOT-WIRING
YOUR CREATIVE PROCESS

STRATEGIES FOR PRINT AND NEW MEDIA DESIGNERS

New
Riders

CURT CLONINGER

Hot-Wiring Your Creative Process: Strategies for print and new media designers
Curt Cloninger

New Riders
1249 Eighth Street
Berkeley, CA 94710
510/524-2178
800/283-9444
510/524-2221 (fax)

Find us on the Web at www.newriders.com

To report errors, please send a note to errata@peachpit.com

New Riders is an imprint of Peachpit, a division of Pearson Education

Project Editor: Alison Kelley
Development Editor: Camille Peri
Production Editor: Hilal Sala
Copyeditor: Liz Welch
Proofreader: Haig MacGregor
Compositor: Kim Scott, Bumpy Design
Indexer: Valerie Perry
Cover design: Mimi Heft
Cover Illustrator: iStockphoto.com
Interior design: Mimi Heft

ISBN 0-321-35024-3

9 8 7 6 5 4 3 2 1

Printed and bound in the United States of America

For Julie.

You give me light; you are my day.

Contents

INVENTION, MY DEAR FRIENDS,
IS 93 PERCENT PERSPIRATION,
6 PERCENT ELECTRICITY,
4 PERCENT EVAPORATION,
AND 2 PERCENT
BUTTERSCOTCH RIPPLE.

—WILLY WONKA

INTRODUCTION

WHAT THIS BOOK IS AND IS NOT ABOUT

Supreme Court Justice Potter Stewart was once charged with determining whether or not a film was pornographic. In his ruling, Potter said he wouldn't even attempt to define pornography—"but," he added, "I know it when I see it." Many people feel the same way about creativity. They can't explain exactly what constitutes creative visual communication, but they know it when they see it.

If merely defining creativity is tricky, teaching creativity is even trickier; teaching creative design is downright challenging; and teaching creative graphic design is veritably daunting. One can be creative in business, homemaking, diplomacy, community living, and the like by developing underutilized cognitive thinking skills that function irrespective of the media or communication genre. Creativity in product design and architecture is constrained by real-world technical specifications that mercifully limit the number of possible solutions, since a chair must support a person's weight and a building must not collapse in a storm. But creativity in graphic design can be a very subjective, elusive goal because it is constrained only by the open-ended nature of human visual communication, in which there are as many exceptions as there are rules.

The problem, in other words, is that creative graphic design is not like algebra. There's no single right solution to any given design problem. There are a handful of best solutions, hundreds of fairly decent solutions, and millions of bad solutions. Not that graphic design is without its handbooks of principles, systems, laws, doctrines, rules, and regulations. All are valuable and have their place in design education. But at the end of the day, knowing grid systems, color theory, and the history of typography doesn't necessarily make you a creative designer any more than knowing a pinch from a pint and how to operate a Cuisinart makes you a creative chef.

Literally hundreds of books are available that cover the basic principles of graphic design. This is not one of them. I will revisit some fundamental design principles in order to tease out various creative solutions, but this book is not a graphic design primer. Instead, it tactically applies various design principles within the context of the creative process.

This book does not champion any single design philosophy or school. Instead, it shows you how to balance and apply various approaches based on your own personal strengths and the particular requirements of each individual project.

Modernist design expounds a set of principles that are self-assured, utilitarian, and codified. In many ways, Bauhaus-inspired modernism has dominated twentieth-century design. Yet its success and proliferation may have less to do with its objective correctness than with the fact that it is quantifiably teachable—there are right ways and wrong ways and not a lot of in-between. Usability and information architecture have inherited modernism's self-assuredness and quasi-scientific/psychological methodologies. But just because something is systematically teachable and comprehendible doesn't mean it's necessarily the best approach to a given problem. Any design problem includes stages that require a more intuitive, less systematic approach.

All that is to say, this is by no means a modernist or neomodernist design book. Nor is it an antimodernist book. (I love grid systems, and the work of my students consistently improves once they learn grid systems.) This book strives to do more than dogmatically support or systematically refute any single historical design approach. It strives to inspire creativity.

Hot-Wiring Your Creative Process: Strategies for Print and New Media Designers is a notebook of methods, tools, habits, and paradigms that various successful designers use. They range from what might be considered best practices and trade secrets to some pretty wild experiments to just plain common sense. Some may drastically alter the way you see your role as a

THIS BOOK STRIVES TO DO MORE THAN DOGMATICALLY SUPPORT OR SYSTEMATICALLY REFUTE ANY SINGLE HISTORICAL DESIGN APPROACH. IT STRIVES TO INSPIRE CREATIVITY.

designer. Others may affirm your current methodology. Taken as a whole, these approaches are meant to supplement, inspire, spark, rev up, and otherwise hot-wire your current creative process.

As such, this book is less of a "how-to" technical manual and more of a sourcebook for creative approaches. Art, philosophy, history, play, discipline, balance, chance, passion, and hiking will all be involved. This book proposes to be of real, practical use to the working designer. As design historian Philip Meggs observed, "A design philosophy is merely an idle vision until someone creates artifacts that make it a real force in the world." In other words, theory alone is useless apart from the working creativity of individual designers. My goal is simply to increase your creativity.

If creativity is ultimately something that transcends textual instructions, the idea of a book instructing you how to be more creative may seem paradoxical—a bit like teaching jazz improvisation. Yet music departments do offer courses in jazz improvisation. Improvisation is learnable, but it requires a less pedantic approach than merely memorizing and practicing scales. Likewise, creativity can be taught and learned. It's just that sometimes you have to go the long way around something in order to get at the heart of it, and creativity is one of those somethings.

What's So Great About This Book?

I am not the only person in the history of the civilization to have thought a bit about creativity. My research has taken me from Jungian psychology to post–World War I Soviet engineering, from aleatoric music to the elongated illustrations of Margaret Macdonald Mackintosh, from hacktivist tactical media to the handcrafted symmetry of Celtic illumination, and to a good number of points in between. I've tried to distill all this research and thinking into a useful book with several salient advantages. Here are a few of them.

This Book Contains Applicable Interviews

In his 1999 book *Why Are You Creative?* advertising agent Hermann Vaske conducted a series of interviews with famous "creatives" (the adjective that has become a noun). He asked them all, "Why are you creative?" David Bowie said he likes being creative because it allows him to crash his proverbial airplane; Mel Gibson likes it because it's a form of psychotherapy for him, like basket weaving; and so on. Their answers are all interesting, but none of them practically helps me become any more creative at Web design, new media art, multimedia education, pop music journalism, or any of the other creative things I do. They tell me more about the individual artists than they do about a universal path toward creativity.

THIS BOOK IS NOT A GUARANTEED PRESCRIPTION FOR MAXIMUM INCREASED

CREATIVITY. INSTEAD, IT FUNCTIONS LIKE THE 12-STEP PROGRAM OF ALCOHOLICS

ANONYMOUS: "IT WORKS IF YOU WORK IT, AND IT DOESN'T IF YOU DON'T."

Likewise, most creative people find that certain things help them get in a creative frame of mind. Personally, I love Stereolab. I love maroon. I love wandering the back roads of western North Carolina. I love the all-you-can-eat sushi bar at the Asiana Oriental Buffet. I love a bracingly cold shower after a long, hot run. And honestly, who really cares? What do these personal preferences have to do with hot-wiring *your* creative process? It would be presumptuous and foolish to assume that a bunch of subjective things that work for me are going to work for you.

At best following such advice is like wearing a lucky hat—merely a kind of psychological placebo. At worst, it can interfere with your own creative process. It's much more advantageous to hear from creative experts in your own field talking in detail about specific practical issues they have wrestled with.

Consequently, *Hot-Wiring Your Creative Process* is not a compendium of interviews with a bunch of creative people sharing their own abstract thoughts and idiosyncrasies—things that don't directly relate to your daily creative process. This book does contain occasional interviews with designers, but the interviews are about specific facets of the design process and not about basket weaving or metaphoric airplanes.

This Book Helps You Rock the Creative Process, Not Just Follow It

You can't really hot-wire your creative process until you have one. (In a sentence, the creative process is all the phases of a project: predesign, design, development, and implementation.) The way in which a designer approaches a project has a profound impact on its success or failure, and following a clearly defined creative process is much better than flailing about aimlessly—putting the cart before the horse, putting the design before the concept, and generally behaving like a freelance designer on her first gig. Intentionally following a clearly defined (or even loosely defined) creative process may be the single most useful practice in any designer's arsenal, and this book will show you how to do that.

Nevertheless, a creative process can't design a project for you. *You* still have to design the project. Although I will go over the fundamentals of the creative process in the first chapter, this book is less about project management and more about how to inject creativity into various phases of your project.

My main concern here is how you work the process. *Having* a creative process and *following* a creative process (even *working* a creative process) are not the same as *rocking* a creative process. It's easy to learn guitar chords and scales; it's much more difficult to rock. It's easy to learn color theory and grid systems; it's much more difficult to consistently find the quintessential heart of each design problem and address it with a solution that satisfies, surprises, and invigorates.

I do believe creativity can be imparted. The problem is that most teachers vacillate between abstract philosophical theory (like "the ramifications of deconstruction on interactive narrative") and practical how-to minutiae (like "creating custom Adobe Photoshop color swatches"), and never bridge the gap between the two. The key to rocking something is bridging that gap. This book broaches some heady, big-picture topics like semiotics and dialectics, but I try to translate each theory into practical approaches that you can apply to specific aspects of the design process.

This Book Gets You Unstuck

All designers occasionally get stuck at some point in their process. It can be in the predesign phase when you're trying to generate concepts. More often than not, it's at the beginning of the design phase when you're staring at a blank page or screen, trying to give visible form to the invisible concepts and goals of your project. Sometimes you get stuck in your ability to usefully delimit the nature of a design problem, to assess the scope of a project, or to collaborate with a client. You may even be stuck in your

career, dreading yet another client interview, wondering how you're going to convince them of the value of your input—that you're more than just a glorified cake decorator, that you actually want to get in on the ground level with the marketing team or product development team and help bake the whole cake.

There are dozens of obstacles to creative design that perpetually threaten to bog you down and get you stuck. Wherever you find yourself stuck, this book is full of ways to get you unstuck. It is true what they say: You can't steer a parked car. Once you come unstuck and regain the confidence to move your project forward, connections begin to emerge, ideas begin to flow, and you're back on track. While you're stuck, all you are is stuck.

This Book Is Full of Creative Yeast

Think of the creative process as a bread recipe. You can follow it to the letter, but if you leave out the yeast, the bread comes out flat. These strategies, tools, habits, and paradigms are like the yeast—active ingredients that help your creativity rise so that the project comes out plump and tasty. These approaches are not merely the butter on top of the bread. They are more integral and fundamental to the creative process than just finishing touches.

IT'S NOT CHEATING TO USE OTHER PEOPLE'S STRATEGIES, TOOLS, HABITS,

AND PARADIGMS. NOBODY WILL KNOW YOU USED THEM.

Yeast in a great bread recipe gives rise to delicious bread.
Hot-wiring a great creative process gives rise to tasty design.

Each strategy and tool should be applied during the appropriate phase of the creative process. Some paradigms are to be continually revisited and balanced throughout the entire process. Others will affect the overall way you think and work as a designer. This book is not a guaranteed prescription for maximum increased creativity. (Any author who makes such a guarantee is deluded or lying.) Instead, it functions more like the 12-step program of Alcoholics Anonymous: "It works if you work it, and it doesn't if you don't."

How to Use This Book

You don't need to read this book sequentially or in its entirety to get something out of it. Having said that, here are some things to keep in mind as you proceed.

Take What You Can Use and Leave the Rest

Each design project is different, and each designer is different, so take what you need for each project and leave the rest for later—or never. One approach may work for you on one project and be totally inappropriate for another. One may work for you as a designer and another may never work. You probably won't agree with everything in this book. It doesn't matter. My goal is not to start a historical design movement or put forth an irrefutably cohesive design methodology; my goal is to help you do better design work.

Will these approaches help you be a more creative CEO, software developer, sculptor, or entrepreneur? Some of them will, and some of them will be largely irrelevant. Take what you can use and leave the rest.

Leave Your "Designer As Hero" Badge at the Door

There will probably be some proud and defiant souls who shun this book. They don't need templates. They don't need advice. They don't need help. All they need is their own personal experience and their thrice-blessed muse. But the rest of us (and even those self-styled heroic designers) need help from time to time.

It's not cheating to use other people's strategies, tools, habits, and paradigms. Nobody will know you used them. Nobody will know your work is not from scratch, pure and unadulterated from the wellspring of your prodigious creative soul. Great design is solving a problem gracefully, humanely, and always with that inexplicable something extra.

There's no shame in being influenced by others, anyway, because we're all influenced by others in some capacity. It's simply unavoidable. Better to admit the inherently derivative nature of design and begin devising intentional strategies for coming under the positive influence of work we admire. Ultimately, you're still the one who has to come up with the design solution to a particular problem and execute it. You still have to decide how to balance your influences and incorporate them into your working process. As long as you're not outright plagiarizing, your work will be judged on its effectiveness alone, not on how much of it was influenced by someone else's input.

LIFE IS TOO SHORT TO KEEP CRANKING OUT MEDIOCRE CRAP. ASK ANY COMMERCIAL DESIGNER, "WHY DID YOU GET INTO DESIGN?" AND NONE OF THEM ARE GOING TO ANSWER, "I GOT INTO IT SO I COULD CRANK OUT MEDIOCRE CRAP."

Go Overboard

Simply put, don't be afraid to do whatever it takes to design your best. If it takes a book or a seminar or a degree or balancing an egg on your head while reciting the Declaration of Independence from memory in order to design greatly, then that's what it takes.

Everyone fears failure, and designers are no exception. But fear is the mind killer. It paralyzes. The approaches in this book may challenge you. They may take you out of your comfort zone. They may cause you to modify your familiar practices. They may cause you to risk. They may cause you to reengage and get passionate about a career that you've taken for granted and no longer really care about. Excellent! Welcome back to life.

Honestly, life is too short to keep cranking out mediocre crap. Ask any commercial designer, "Why did you get into design?" and none of them are going to answer, "I got into it so I could crank out mediocre crap." Rediscover the love you originally had for design. Go for it. It works if you work it.

Embrace the Fact That Design Is Freaking Sexy

Design is sexy. It just is. End of story. You know this intuitively. Every designer knows it. Granted, all of us have our own particular fetishes. For some it is the tactile sensuality of embossed cardstock. Others get off on the seamless staccato cadences of jump-cut motion graphics. For others, it's the irreverent, irregular, distressed textures of grunge typography. For the hardcore design fetishist, a generous use of white space in conjunction with an expanded Futura light typeface may be all it takes to illicit serious arousal.

In 1887, Arts & Crafts designer Selwyn Image wrote, "When you begin to realize, that all kinds of invented Form, and Tone, and Colour, are alike true and honorable aspects of Art, you see something very much like a revolution looming ahead of you." We need to stop thinking of design as the trailer-park cousin of art.

I have a friend, a great designer, who is going through a crisis of faith in the value of design. "I can make it look good. I can crank out working solution after working solution. But what's the point? Can design make any real difference in people's lives?" I believe great design can make a difference in people's lives. Design is applied human creativity in the service of human communication, in the service of human use, and that is worth something. And creation, any form of creation, can be a celebration of existence, a kind of fulfillment of purpose, even a communion with the Divine.

As you apply the principles and approaches in this book, don't just seek to do passable work. Make it your goal to create something extraordinary. The craftsmen of Bali have a wonderful saying: "We have no art. We do everything as well as possible." Such a holistic attitude doesn't distinguish between "high art" and "applied art." Anything worth making is worth making as well as possible.

■ ■ ■

DESIGN IS SEXY

Even the most minimal typographic treatment can elicit
a sensual response from the hardcore design fetishist.

PROCESS IS MORE IMPORTANT
THAN OUTCOME. WHEN THE
OUTCOME DRIVES THE PROCESS
WE WILL ONLY EVER GO TO
WHERE WE'VE ALREADY BEEN.
IF PROCESS DRIVES OUTCOME
WE MAY NOT KNOW WHERE
WE'RE GOING, BUT WE WILL
KNOW WE WANT TO BE THERE.

—BRUCE MAU, "AN INCOMPLETE MANIFESTO FOR GROWTH"

1 | A PROCESS PRIMER

All designers follow some sort of creative process, whether they know it or not. It's like church. Every church from high Catholic to nondenominational charismatic has some sort of liturgy—a form and order that it follows, strictly or loosely, every service. Likewise, every designer, even the most spontaneous and unintentional designer, has a creative process.

Your creative process may look something like this:

1. Get the gig.
2. Stuff creative brief in bottom drawer.
3. Avoid client's phone calls.
4. Drink 'n' think.
5. Stay up all night before the deadline, designing and developing the deliverables.

That's still a creative process—just not a very good one.

As long as you're going to have a creative process, you might as well be intentional about it. There are hundreds of books and articles on the creative process (some of which are listed in this book's bibliography). Its proponents break it up into all sorts of different steps and stages, but basically the creative process, particularly as it relates to graphic design, looks something like this:

1. Predesign
2. Design
3. Develop
4. Implement

That's it, and believe it or not, it will get you pretty far.

Designer Bruce Mau's declaration that "process is more important than outcome" may seem fairly extreme. Of course, from a client's perspective, it seems backward. But from a designer's perspective, it makes sense. As a designer, if you only pursue what seems right to you at first, if you jump right into the development phase without first researching the problem, if you never explore alternative design solutions, you will always wind up with a similar outcome. Assuming you're some sort of creative uber-god with Jedi designer instincts, an uncanny intuitive sense of market clairvoyance, and catlike visual communication reflexes, well and good. Otherwise, you'd better work the process. Even if you are a natural-born "elite" designer, you should still work the process because it can take anyone's designs to a broader, richer, more conceptually intriguing level.

A Brief Guide to the Creative Process

The four phases of the creative process are fairly straightforward and sensible. In this section we'll take a closer look.

1. Predesign

Predesign is the language, research, and interpersonal phase. It results in a written creative brief agreed upon by the designer and the client. This is the phase that most design students rush through, if they go through it at all. But it is arguably the most important phase of the whole project. Muddle the predesign phase and your conceptual approach will be skewed—a fundamental flaw that no amount of design-phase Photoshop voodoo will be able to hide.

Skipping the predesign phase and diving straight into the design phase is like taking a hasty, blurry snapshot of a still life and then devoting weeks meticulously painting from that blurry snapshot. Even if you reproduce the snapshot exquisitely, you'll end up with a blurry painting that misses the mark. As Joe Jackson sang, "You can't get what you want till you know what you want." The predesign phase involves figuring out what you want.

It breaks up into four sequential steps.

EYEBALL THE BIG PICTURE
Prior to doing any deep research, prior to even signing a contract, you want to get an overview of the nature and scope of the problem, as well as the nature of the client. Try to be as accurate as possible, realizing that at this point there's no way you can understand all the nuances of

Skipping the predesign phase
is like taking a blurry snapshot
and then spending weeks
meticulously painting it.

the whole picture. Requests for proposals (RFPs)
and initial client interviews occur during this
step. Even if you are doing subcontract work
for a large firm that you trust, and that firm is
working for a client that it trusts, you still want
to try to understand as much as you can about
the project before committing to it.

At the heart of every design project is a
problem. Cognitive studies expert Edward De
Bono concisely defines a problem as "the difference between what we have and what we
want." If there is no problem, then no solution
is required, in which case no design work is
required. You are free to make art or go to the
beach.

AT THE HEART OF EVERY DESIGN PROJECT IS A PROBLEM. IF THERE IS NO

PROBLEM, THEN NO SOLUTION IS REQUIRED, IN WHICH CASE NO DESIGN

WORK IS REQUIRED. YOU ARE FREE TO MAKE ART OR GO TO THE BEACH.

Try to get a handle on the problem from the start. You will refine your understanding throughout the creative process, but the sooner you define the problem, the more thoroughly your final solution will address it. The problem is not your enemy; it is your guide to the solution. As media theorist Marshall McLuhan observed, "The answers are always inside the problem, not outside."

RESEARCH

In the research phase, you research clients, their products or services, their competition, and their target audiences. With well-known clients, some of this research can be done via regular channels such as magazines, books, newspapers, libraries, and the Internet. Even then, all the specific information about your project will come directly from your clients.

Compare your standard research with the information they give you. Perhaps there are discrepancies between what the public thinks about your clients and what they think about themselves. Perhaps this discrepancy is relevant to how you solve their problem. For example, your chicken client may think its mascot, Clucky the Chicken, is beloved by customers. The problem is that Clucky may be too beloved, and nobody wants to eat Clucky.

Fast-food restaurant Chick-Fil-A needed a marketing angle when they sought the advice of Dallas-based ad agency The Richards Group. Rather than steer them toward a fowl mascot that would be advertising its own demise, the agency came up with a brilliantly unorthodox conceptual solution: get cows to market chicken. It makes perfect sense in a "Far Side" kind of way. The cows want to put fast-food burger joints out of business, so they drive consumers to Chick-Fil-A to save their own hides. The campaign has been immensely successful, as well as immensely amusing.

With a lesser-known client, you'll have to get most of your background information from the client interview. Try to understand the personality of the company and the personality of the product or service. Clients may tell you, "We want to take this exact visual approach," but they are actually paying you to advise them on what visual approach is best. Understand their larger goals, and not just their proposed solutions.

If your interview questions are thoughtful and probing, if you're able to get at the heart of the problem, smaller clients may actually learn more about their own companies from your interview. Asking the right questions forces clients to reconsider their companies from consumers' perspectives through the lens of your particular communications medium—print, Web, video, whatever. This can give a company new insight into its overall mission.

Client interviewing requires verbal communication skills and interpersonal skills; what country folks simply call "social skills." At this stage in the process, you are acting more like a visual communications consultant. You will fail in this role if you think of yourself only as someone who designs pretty stuff. Your services are valuable to the client even at this stage, before any "designing" has begun.

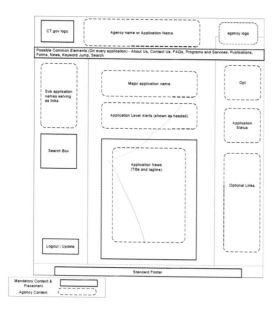

Design specs vs. Caroline Cloninger: It's better to design with a specific customer in mind than toward a set of impersonal specifications.

ANALYZE

Take all the research you've gathered and revisit it from various analytical perspectives. What is the crux of the problem? What were the weaknesses of any previous design solutions? Are there other successful design solutions by competitors? How might you incorporate those solutions into your approach? How will the limitations of the medium for which you are designing affect the way in which you solve the problem?

What is the aggregate personality of the primary, secondary, and tertiary audiences? Move from the abstract to the specific: Construct a hypothetical profile person for each audience, including name, occupation, income, age, gender, interests, and other relevant information.

What is the personality of the company? Give the company a name and pretend it's a person. Describe that person. If your client is Burger King, for example, maybe you decide that Burger King's name is King Edward, but his friends call him Ed. Ed is fun, jovial, and patient with children. Is there anything regal about him at all?

What is the personality of the product or service? Give the product or service a name and pretend it's a person. Describe that person. Perhaps the service that FedEx provides is named Jerry. Is Jerry an athletic college graduate with a crew cut and a courteous yet anal-retentive work ethic? Or is Jerry a slightly graying MIT engineer with a can-do attitude and a pocket-protector full of mechanical pencils? Does Jerry bear any resemblance to an actual FedEx courier? Should he?

If all this seems a bit poetic, it is. The goal is to move from raw statistics toward language that is evocative and descriptive. You are literally trying to put a face on all aspects of the project by creating a written "image" that will translate readily into graphic design. Don't discard any project specifications; obviously you'll need them. But it is easier to design for a face than for a set of specifications.

APPROVE A CREATIVE BRIEF

The creative brief is a short written document outlining the problems, goals, strategies, and challenges of the project. Whether the client or the designer generates the creative brief, it should be agreed upon by both. Signing off on a boilerplate, client-generated creative brief that goes against your own research and analysis will probably lead to a mediocre, inadequate design solution. Working from your own creative brief without getting the client to sign off on it will result in miscommunication and probably extra design revisions on your part. The goal is for everybody to be on the same page, and the creative brief is that same page.

Having said that, don't place an inordinate amount of faith in the creative brief. Language is slippery and highly subjective, particularly when describing the goals of a visual medium like design. If a picture is worth a thousand words, a mock-up is worth ten creative briefs. Breathe easier later, when your clients sign off on one of your design mock-ups, not when they sign off on your amendments to the creative brief. Don't spend an inordinate amount of time wrangling about the subtle nuances of the brief. It is not the final product; it's simply a vague but necessary starting point.

Having drafted a creative brief doesn't automatically ensure its implementation. The further along you get in the creative process, the easier it is to get engrossed in details and overlook your original research and goals. Once you agree upon the brief, revisit it throughout the creative process, checking your direction against it. This way, your decisions throughout will be informed and directed by your original goals. You may come across new information along the way that causes you to deviate from your original creative brief. If this happens, you should probably sit down with the client and approve a new creative brief.

2. Design

The lion's share of the creative work is done in the design phase. This is where you invent visual solutions, where your predesign research takes on actual visual form. New media designer Hillman Curtis says designers are like translators: They take ideas expressed in words and translate them into visual language. He calls this process "making the invisible visible." The design phase is where this occurs. The vague ideas of the creative brief are gradually translated into mock-ups that the client can see.

There is no substitute for the actual design phase. Predesign leads into design, and development fleshes out design, but neither is design. In this sense, graphic design is a bit like creative writing. In the creative writing process, you start with an outline and you finish with editing, but at some point you have to sit down and actually craft the prose itself. Gertrude Stein said of the process, "Creation must take place between the pen and the paper, not before in a thought or afterwards in a recasting." Likewise, your actual graphic design solutions are created during the design phase, once you begin sketching in physical or digital design space.

Despite the crucial function of the design phase, it is frequently rushed: You are on a tight deadline and the development is going to take a lot of time, so you rush through design and dive into development as quickly as possible. This is a bad idea. Your design will only be as strong as your design concept, and your design concept is often discovered and refined during design phase explorations.

The design phase breaks up into three sequential steps.

SKETCH

Before you even turn on a computer, take out your pencil and flip open a sketchbook. Return to your creative brief and explore core themes and concepts that arise. Feel free to go back and forth in your sketchbook between descriptive words and visual concepts. You are moving from thinking textually to thinking visually. Depending on your medium, make thumbnail sketches, draw storyboards, sketch logo marks.

This step of the design phase is largely personal. You probably won't show these sketches to the client. If you're not a great illustrator, don't worry about beautiful draftsmanship. These are rough sketches for your own personal reference, a low-pressure way of easing into the actual design process.

ASSEMBLE

Based on ideas and concepts that arise from your rough sketches, begin to get more specific. Turn on a computer and open up your design software of choice. Use type studies to try out different typefaces applied to the text you know you want to use. Do color scheme studies in which you choose a palette. In your software or notebook, do form studies that balance shapes, lines, textures, positive and negative space, and other design elements. Shoot or acquire imagery and begin combining it with your color scheme and your typefaces. Alter your color scheme to fit the imagery. Experiment with composition and balance. Explore various layouts.

All these approaches will vary depending on your medium and the nature of the project. Don't worry about editing at this point. The more paths you explore, the more source material you'll have available for later use.

MOCK UP

In the mock-up step, you are working toward a design or several designs that you will present to the client. Some designers allow their client to review their work during the sketching and assembling steps—the argument being that the more you involve the client throughout the process, the less chance there is for miscommunication and misunderstanding. Other designers don't show the client any visual work until the mock-up phase.

There are two arguments for this approach:
1. Sketching and assembling are private

processes for the designer's own brain, and the client would only be micromanaging during those steps. 2. Sketching and assembling are by necessity incomplete. The client is likely to confuse such work with finished mock-ups and judge it harshly, based on its level of incompletion rather than its conceptual merit.

How many mock-ups do you show the client? This is the million-dollar question. Legend has it that design master Paul Rand only showed one logo mock-up to his clients. This approach makes some sense. The client is hiring you to do the best work possible. Presenting them with three mock-ups suggests that you can't tell which is best. Just pick the best one and show it to them.

On the other hand, for my last book, *Fresh Styles for Web Designers*, for New Riders (2002), design firm Segura Inc. presented us with 20 mock-ups of the cover. This approach makes some sense as well. You're telling the client, "We're so creative we can come up with 20 approaches, one of which you'll surely like. We trust your judgment. Whichever one you choose, it's going to be good."

Conventional wisdom is that you should show clients three mock-ups—one they'll probably choose, one a bit more conservative, and one a bit more daring. That way, you cover a range somewhere near where you think they want to be. But even if you show only three final mock-ups, you are free to make as many preliminary mock-ups as it takes to arrive at those three.

However you decide to present your mock-ups, be prepared to explain your design decisions to your clients. Here again, developing your social skills is worthwhile. Amazing as it may seem, clients are not always able to immediately intuit the sheer unadulterated genius of every design you present.

I require my multimedia design students to turn in lots of "threes" (or multiples thereof) throughout the creative process—three written ideas for a project, nine sketches of a logo, three refined variations of a logo in digital form, three mock-ups of a magazine advertisement, nine thumbnail sketches of a web page layout, three mock-ups of an interactive navigation solution, and so on. Invariably a student protests, "But I already know *exactly* what I want to do." I answer, "Great, you've got your first mock-up. Now do two more." More often than not, the second and third mock-ups are better than the first.

There is something liberating about getting that first idea out of your mental space and into design space. It clears out your head so that you can consider the problem from a different perspective. It also takes the pressure off. You've got at least one solution if nothing else works. Now you are free to explore, play, and risk more daring solutions.

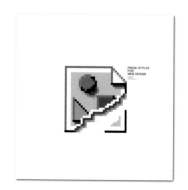

Segura Inc. presented 20 mock-ups for the cover of *Fresh Styles for Web Designers*. The empty refrigerator was the one chosen.

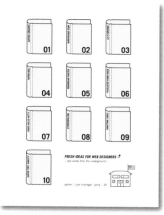

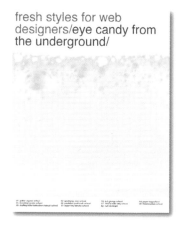

TITLE	FRESH STYLES
	FOR WEB DESIGNERS
SUBTITLE	EYE CANDY FROM THE UNDERGROUND
AUTHOR	CURT CLONINGER
ISBN	0 7897 640 7
UPC CODE	6 60355 33392 7
PRICE	$35.00
TRIM SIZE	7 3/8 X 9 1/8
PAGE	144
PUB DATE	03 2001
COLOR	4 COLOR
USER LEVEL	INTERMEDIATE/ADVANCED
CATEGORY	WEB DESIGN

fresh styles for web
designers/eye candy from
the underground/

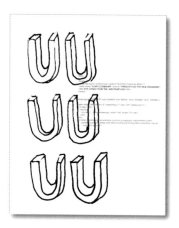

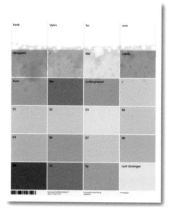

fresh styles for web
designers/eye candy from
the underground/

3. Develop

This phase varies greatly from medium to medium. For a two-dimensional CD cover or poster, the difference between your digital mock-up and your developed piece might not be much. In that case, this is the paper selection, prepress, and color correction phase. However, in interactive media, video, book production, architecture, corporate identity—any media of scale, movement, or function—the development phase is critical because you have something that must work or move or stand up or be applied interpretively.

In these media, there is still plenty of room—and need—for creativity in the development phase. It's just a different kind of creativity than in the design phase. The way a Web site rollover functions, the way a scene is lit, the manner in which a book is composited—all are areas that require a creative eye that is in sync with the overall goals of the project. Even in this phase, it is prudent to revisit the creative brief.

The development phase breaks up into three iterative steps.

BUILD

Develop the project to completion. Build it. Make it. Shoot it. Postproduce it. Code it. Composite it. Whatever. There may be interim, semifunctional demo versions along the way, but ultimately this step results in a final functional version that (according to your best guess) is ready to be distributed.

TEST

Show your built project to a user test group and assess its feedback. Experts are forever debating what constitutes optimal user testing. Probably the test audience doesn't have to be that large, but it should represent your target demographic as precisely as possible. The challenge is to create a test environment that accurately simulates the real world and then interpret your user response data in a useful way. (What constitutes "useful" is the key question.) This is practically impossible, since the very act of testing creates an artificial environment different from a real-world environment. However, imperfect and inexact as user testing may be (despite a myriad of rigorous "expert" methodologies), some form of user testing is better than no testing at all.

REVISE

Since user testing is at best a simulated situation, you're not obliged to take every bit of unfiltered user feedback as gospel truth. Assess the feedback and improve upon the aspects of your design that you agree are problematic based on your broader understanding of the project's goals. Revise the design and rebuild.

4. Implement

You can repeat the steps of the development phase forever, but at some point you will have to abandon your quest for hypothetical perfection, go with your best guess, and proceed to the implementation phase. As Apple CEO Steve Jobs famously observed, "Real artists ship." An

DESIGNERS WHO EMPHASIZE MAINTENANCE AND IMPROVEMENT AS PART OF THEIR

OVERALL DESIGN PROCESS ARE THE ONES WHO MAINTAIN A STABLE OF REGULAR

CLIENTS BECAUSE THEIR JOB FOR THESE CLIENTS IS NEVER FINISHED.

architect who never gets hired to design any actual 3D buildings is called a "paper architect." It doesn't matter how ingenious his blueprints are: unless he actually gets some buildings built, the history of architecture will not remember him. By the same token, real designers implement. It doesn't matter how well the design succeeds in the hypothetical test environment of the development phase. How a design weathers the implementation phase is the true test of its success.

The implementation phase breaks up into three nonsequential, iterative steps.

DISTRIBUTE PUBLICLY

Publish, go live, launch, or screen. Your client puts the work out there to be seen and used.

MARKET

Prior to and during distribution, your design solution is marketed. Sometimes your graphic design itself does the marketing, but often this happens in conjunction with press releases, reviews, or other types of collateral marketing. If you work for a marketing firm, you are in charge of the marketing. If you work at a graphic design company subcontracted by a marketing firm, the details of the marketing are out of your hands. In either case, make sure your design solution dovetails with your client's collateral marketing approach.

MAINTAIN AND IMPROVE

A Web site requires maintenance and improvement. Even a print campaign can benefit from ongoing maintenance and regular improvement.

Designers who incorporate maintenance and improvement into their overall design process are the ones who maintain a stable of regular clients because their job for these clients is never finished. Such designers practice design as an ongoing process. They are always chatting up future ad campaigns, 2.0 versions, and perpetual branding.

If improvement is required in the implementation phase, does this mean the design failed? Not at all. The only way to learn whether a solution actually works is to implement it and see if it does. With this in mind, Web design companies such as Chicago's 37 Signals have begun to fold the testing and revision of development into the maintenance and improvement steps of the implementation phase. The idea is to move from hypothetical prototype testing to working product as quickly as possible.

With Basecamp, a 37 Signals online software product, the company has remained nimble enough to respond to user feedback and implement ongoing improvements during distribution. Instead of receiving hypothetical feedback from a test group that may not represent its actual target audience, the company receives feedback from real users of its product. In this paradigm, the user is much more involved in the development of the product. The target audience is not a group to be manipulated and feared, but an advocate whose critical feedback is solicited and encouraged. In order to succeed with this open development approach, the design firm must be honest, transparent, and vulnerable. A huge helping of customer service social skills also comes in handy.

Variations on the Creative Process

Although every creative process can be reduced to the four simple phases of *predesign*, *design*, *development*, and *implementation*, some designers have discovered that tweaking the process can make it better fit individual projects or media. Some variations on the creative process are particularly ingenious because of the novelty of their approach. Others are remarkably suited to a particular task. What follows is a brief consideration of some of them. I've highlighted the aspects of each process that make it unique.

AIGA: Designing Solutions

AIGA (the professional association for design) has developed a three-step process that is intentionally generalized so that it can be applied to almost any medium: *define the problem*, *innovate*, and *create value*. Nowhere in this process is any type of media deliverable mentioned. The AIGA paradigm is particularly instructive. You are designing a *solution*. You are not designing a video spot or a poster or a Web site. Those are merely the media through which your *solution* may be expressed. This way of

WHEN YOU UNITE YOUR CREATIVE TEAM AROUND THE PROJECT, THINK OF YOUR CLIENT AS A MEMBER OF THAT TEAM. YOUR CLIENT IS NOT THE "NONCREATIVE ENTITY," THE "OTHER," OR THE "NECESSARY EVIL."

thinking puts the emphasis on conceptual problem solving throughout the process.

For example, in the standard four-step design process, you build your project in the development phase. In the AIGA process, you "activate your solution" in the "value generation" phase. The actions taken are the same in both processes, but the wording of the AIGA process intentionally foregrounds solutions and value generation rather than simply talking about building stuff.

The AIGA process also places a unique emphasis on team leadership. At the end of each phase, there is a managerial step. At the end of the first phase (define the problem), the team leader incites support and action. At the end of the second phase (innovate), she enables the team to work as a team. At the end of the third phase (generate value), her team "tacks," based on its successes and failures.

Hillman Curtis: New Media Design

In his book *MTIV (Making the Invisible Visible)*, new media designer Hillman Curtis proposes a seven-step process: *listen*, *unite*, *theme*, *concept*, *eat the audience* (figure out what makes the audience tick), *filter*, and *justify*. Although each of these steps folds into the standard four-step creative process well enough, Curtis's model emphasizes two particularly useful elements.

When you unite your creative team around the project, think of your client as a member of that team. Your client is not the "noncreative entity," the "other, " or the "necessary evil. "

Instead, your client is a member of the creative team with unique insight due to his intimate knowledge of his own product, company, and market.

"Filter" simply means to consider the limitations of your medium and let them inform your design approach. This is particularly necessary when you're designing low-bandwidth, online media because it has such stringent resolution limitations. But every medium has its own limitations. For example, print is limited compared to video in that print can't move. Furthermore, all communications media are limited compared to existence itself because all deliver mediated experiences rather than actual experiences. How you approach the inherent limitations of your medium can determine the success of your project.

Jesse James Garrett: User-Centered Web Design

User experience consultant Jesse James Garrett's creative process is novel, refreshing, and useful. Garrett first describes the five "planes" of a Web site, from front-end interface to back-end strategy. Then these planes become the actual chronological phases of his Web design process. From bottom to top, the planes/phases are: *strategy*, *scope*, *structure*, *skeleton*, and *surface*. Any decision you make at the strategy plane necessarily limits the decisions you are able to make at the subsequent scope plane, and so on.

By relating the "architecture" of your actual media to the chronology of your process, this model forces your graphics decisions to be based on your layout decisions, which in turn are based on your information architecture decisions, which in turn are based on your functional requirements, which in turn are based on your strategic goals. Garrett's process is not merely a series of chronological phases. Instead, each phase is structurally related to the phases that precede and follow it, and to the functional structure of the site itself.

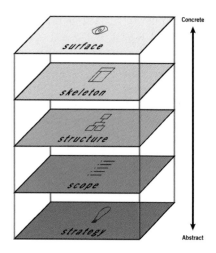

Jesse James Garrett's model for the five elements of user experience: The bottom layers correspond to the back-end functionality of the Web site and to the beginning of the creative process. The top layers correspond to the front-end design of the Web site, and to the end of the creative process.

Tony Spaeth: Corporate Identity

Corporate identity expert Tony Spaeth has developed an involved creative process for corporate identity development because it is a necessarily involved process. Two elements of Spaeth's process are particularly noteworthy for any designer.

It begins with a proposal phase. Before the contract is even signed, all the preliminary dialogue between the designer and the client is considered to be the first phase of the creative process. If the client doesn't hire the designer, the process is aborted or shelved. If the client does hire the designer, the proposal phase leads directly into the rest of the process. This formalizes and includes an important but often overlooked phase of the process—the precontract dialogue between client and designer. Once you are hired, you don't have to revisit everything that was discussed prior to your being hired.

Prior to Spaeth's implementation phase, an entire phase is devoted to implementation planning. Since corporate identity is more holistic than merely designing a logo, the implementation phase is planned in great detail—from how the new identity will be applied across corporate media such as stationery, Web sites, vehicles, building signage, and marketing materials, to how the new identity will be introduced to the public. This additional planning phase illustrates the fact that different design disciplines require different creative processes.

Strengths and Weaknesses of the Creative Process

The creative process is great as far as it goes, but it doesn't automatically make you creative. As an idea-generating tool, it has its share of strengths and weaknesses. Its basic strength is that it gives you something to hot-wire. Its basic weakness is that it doesn't come pre-hot-wired.

Strengths

It saves energy. Adherence to a creative process keeps you from having to reinvent the wheel every time you tackle a new design project.

It results in consistency of design work. If you adhere to the same creative process, your work will be more consistent from project to project. This doesn't mean that your work will be identical because the process allows for variation as dictated by the particular needs of the project.

It results in consistency of design practice. By adhering to the same creative process, repeat clients and referred clients will know what to expect from you. This will make them more comfortable, which will lead to better communication, which will lead to better work.

It gives you something to "work" when you are creatively dry. The creative process is a way to prime your creative pump. Simply by going through the motions of the process, you eventually fall into a familiar, creative groove that allows work to flow. Even designers who are skeptical of the practical, analytical benefits of the predesign phase will still go through it, almost as a ritualistic warm-up exercise for the

IF THE DESIGN PHASE IS LIKE SEX, THEN THE PREDESIGN PHASE IS LIKE FOREPLAY—

A WAY TO GET IN THE MOOD BEFORE THE CREATIVE FIREWORKS ACTUALLY BEGIN.

design phase. If the design phase is like sex, then the predesign phase is like foreplay—a way to get in the mood before the creative fireworks actually begin.

It can lead to unforeseen places. This is a huge strength. As Bruce Mau observed, you may not know where you are going when you start out, but you'll know that you want to be there.

Weaknesses

One size does not fit all. No single creative process perfectly suits every design project. You want to be flexible and have a backup plan when you run into a wall. You could transition to an entirely different creative process, or you could simply supplement your process with various strategies and approaches that have proved useful in the past. This book presents a number of such supplemental approaches.

It doesn't automatically generate quality design. The process can suggest a creative solution, but it doesn't automatically generate one. The themes and goals of your predesign phase don't magically transform themselves into compelling visual concepts simply because you follow the creative process. Otherwise, anybody could be a great designer, and we know this is not the case. Creative processes don't generate design; you do.

It doesn't automatically generate "art." Graphic design pioneer El Lissitzky claimed that design = problem + invention + art. The problem and invention components are dealt with

directly in the creative process. The creative process can literally be thought of as problem assessment followed by solution invention. So where does the art come in? The art is that extra, special, unnameable something that transforms a serviceable design into a resonant, memorable design. It has less to do with *which* process you work and more to do with *how* you work it. Lissitzky probably never would have phrased it this way, but the art is a function of hot-wiring.

■ ■ ■

CREATING IS THE MOST INTENSE EXCITEMENT ONE CAN COME TO KNOW.

—TEXTILE DESIGNER ANNI ALBERS

2 | BASIC CREATIVE WISDOM

Before we delve into specific design approaches, useful paradigms, best practices, tips, tricks, and hacks, let's begin with some fundamental, across-the-board wisdom that every creative maker of stuff should possess. This wisdom in and of itself won't make you a great designer, but without it, you will never become a great designer. If these pieces of advice aren't your style, then you should probably change your style. If these pieces of advice don't seem to apply to you, then you should probably apply them to you. Or may I suggest an exciting career in chartered accountancy?

To design something, to put it out there and say, "I did this and I stand by it"— that's scary business. Public creativity is exciting, but it is fraught with risks and anxieties. Designers fall prey to any number of personal pitfalls—from self-doubt to unfounded egotism (which is usually just a front for self-doubt), from workaholism to slackerism, from craving total anonymity to entering every design contest in existence (at $50 per entry). It's not easy being a designer, but the following bits of basic creative wisdom can at least ease some of the pain. Each of these pieces of advice is applicable throughout the entire creative process, and probably throughout life in general.

Believe in Your Creative Powers

Mystery Men is a film comedy about a motley crew of unlikely superheroes led by a pontificating mystic known as "the Sphinx." The Sphinx is full of paradoxical advice that he dispenses freely throughout the film. "In order to learn my teachings, I must first teach you how to learn." "You must be like the wolf pack, not like the six pack." And my personal favorite: "If you can balance a tack hammer on your head, you will head off your foes with a balanced attack."

Before the climactic showdown, the rag-tag superheroes have a crisis of faith and some even begin to doubt their superpowers. The Sphinx bolsters their resolve with this pearl of wisdom: "When you doubt your powers, you give power to your doubts." They buck up and go on to defeat evil and win the day.

Simple as this advice is, the Sphinx is right. A modicum of objective self-criticism is always useful, but full-on, overblown self-doubt is absolutely crippling to a graphic designer. Why? Because success in graphic design requires risk taking, and risk taking requires self-confidence. Playing it safe throughout the entire creative process can deal a deathblow to your project. For a stockbroker, safe, passable investing usually leads to a modest, acceptable return on investments. Fine. But for a graphic designer, safe, passable designing usually leads to a poorly designed project. Like comedy, graphic design is a field in which merely average work actually fails. Who's going to pay money to see a comedian who is more or less funny? Likewise, who's going to pay a graphic designer to more or less communicate their message? As a graphic designer, you have to nail the message, and to nail the message you have to go for it, and to go for it you have to have self-confidence.

But what if your worst fears are true? What if your work sucks, you don't have what it takes, and you should never have gotten into graphic design in the first place? All of this may well be true. If so, you may want to take some time to search your heart, ask advice from friends you trust, and reassess your career path. But the time to do all this soul-searching is in-between gigs, *not* during them. Once you say "yes" to a client and you sign the contract, you are the *man* or *woman* for the job. You are a professional designer. You are creative. You know your medium. You understand the principles of visual communication. You ask penetrating questions that get at the heart of the project. You shepherd your client's goals through a creative process that results in a unique, appropriate, successful design solution.

CONFIDENCE EMPOWERS RISK TAKING, AND RISK TAKING LEADS TO BETTER DESIGN. DOUBT BEGETS MORE DOUBT AND SECOND-GUESSING, WHICH LEAD TO FALSE STARTS AND TIMIDITY, WHICH LEAD TO LAME DESIGN.

Isn't this all just a bunch of mumbo-jumbo self-talk? Will it really make any practical difference? It will make more of a difference if you actually believe it. But even if you don't, it will still have a positive effect on your project. Let's take the worst-case scenario and assume that you actually do suck. You should get out while the getting is good. Chartered accountancy awaits. But instead you agree to do one last design project. How is thinking that you suck going to make the project any better? Believing in your creative powers can turn a sucky designer into a less-than-sucky designer. It can turn a competent designer into a good designer. And it can turn a good designer into a great designer. Because confidence empowers risk taking, and risk taking leads to better design. Doubt begets more doubt and second-guessing, which lead to false starts and timidity, which lead to lame design.

Don't misunderstand me. Self-confidence does not mean that you think of yourself as an immortal design god who can do no wrong. That's just delusional and harmful. It leads to lazy conceptualizing, slipshod execution, and a stank attitude that alienates all but the most masochistic of clients. Nor does self-confidence mean trying to bluff your way through the project on bravado and duct tape alone. If you take pride in advancing mediocre visual solutions on sheer force of personal will, then you probably missed your calling as a contemporary conceptual artist. Don't simply apply your self-confidence to self-marketing; apply it to the actual design problem.

On the whole, most designers seem to suffer more from self-doubt than from blind overconfidence. If you've got to err in one direction or the other, better to risk too much self-confidence. If your design solutions are too risky and brash, it's not rocket science to tone them down a bit. On the other hand, if your design solutions are too safe and timid, it's much more difficult to ramp them up a bit. To use a baseball metaphor, it's easier to hit a long triple and stop short at second base than it is to turn a bunt into anything more than a single. A bunt will only ever be a bunt.

Freshman design students are inordinately plagued by self-doubt. It can lead to a kind of timidity that focuses on minutiae at the expense of the big picture. It's not uncommon for a freshman student to spend an entire evening fretting over whether a border should be 2 pixels or 3 pixels thick, whether a font should be 11 points or 12 points. As if a single technical decision might somehow magically lead to the "correct" design. This is just timidity manifesting itself as anal-retentive perfectionism. With practice and experience, most freshman designers graduate to greater levels of self-confidence. The ones who don't are the ones who don't practice, the ones afraid to fail.

In this book we'll examine several approaches—from exploratory sketching to maintaining a design playground—that build self-confidence and can help you overcome self-doubt. Almost all involve risk, practice, and exploration. The best Olympic gymnasts fall thousands of times in practice over the course

OWN THE DESIGN SPACE. IT BELONGS TO YOU. DON'T LET IT PUSH YOU AROUND. PUSH IT AROUND.

YOUR CLIENT MAY BE THE BOSS OF THE ENTIRE PROJECT, BUT YOU ARE THE BOSS OF THE DESIGN PHASE.

of their careers. The more you push it, the more you fall, the better you get, the more you push it, the more you fall, and onward and upward, bruises and all.

To reiterate the classic mantra of design educator Robin Williams, "Don't be a wimp!" Own the design space. It belongs to you. Don't let it push you around. Push it around. Your client may be the boss of the entire project, but you are the boss of the design phase. Nothing is more harmful than a chorus of competing critical voices in your head when you're trying to explore innovative solutions. Peers, higher-ups, competitors, heroes, clients, design critics, teachers, your audience—these voices often cancel each other out, leaving you paralyzed and inert, drowning in a din of conflicting internal criticism, unable to step out and risk exploration. Silence these voices. You are in control, remember? Later it will be beneficial to hear from some of these voices, in orderly turn. But not now.

There is one group of voices that you should silence forever—the turkeys. Peter Lord, a Christian pastor and author, tells the fable of a baby eagle who fell in among some turkeys. Like the ugly duckling, he didn't quite fit in. He hated the taste of acorns and he hated scratching around on the ground. But he was assured by the turkeys that he would never amount to anything greater, so he gradually acclimated himself to the mediocrity of turkeydom. You don't have to look very far to find such turkeys in our gloriously cynical, posteverything era. Turkeys particularly abound in the world

of design and art, where there is this wrong-headed idea that the more you hate, the better your taste.

By definition, you will never please the turkeys (unless you are Paul Rand, Massimo Vignelli, or whichever design master they happen to worship). So don't even try. Fly above them and let them throw acorns. Who cares? This is not an excuse to dismiss valid criticism from people who care about your professional growth. It's just an excuse to dismiss criticism from people who criticize everything anyway.

Self-confidence is crucial in graphic design precisely because there is no single right answer to any given design problem. The more confidence you have, the more you are free to pursue widely divergent paths of exploration, the less dependent you are on rote formulas, and the closer you are to arriving at a unique design solution.

Don't Wait Around for "Eureka!"

We've all had our share of "eureka" experiences. Suddenly the solution to a problem presents itself to us, and intuitively we know that this is the way the design *must* proceed. In his pithy collection of essays titled *Understanding Design*, design educator Kees Dorst says these eureka experiences are actually mirages of hindsight. Nobody ever had a design epiphany without first working the creative process. You do the predesign research, you lock in on the theme of the project, you conceptualize the theme via sketching and designing. At some point along the way, your subconscious mind—which is churning nonstop—pieces together a solution, things click, and your conscious mind experiences this event as, "Eureka! I've found it!" (Your conscious mind always wants to take all the credit because it has an overdeveloped sense of its own importance.)

With this in mind, don't shortcut the creative design process. Don't get too specific too soon. Even with a tight deadline, allot an appropriate percentage of time to the early, preparatory phases of the creative process. This is not wasted time. It is start-up time. It is necessary time to fill your mind with lots of applicable content to chew on.

There is a popular image of the artist lounging around melancholically pondering existence, waiting for her muse to whisper revelation into her ear. Unfortunately (or fortunately), professional creators rarely have such luxury. My mother, Claire Cloninger, is a writer and lyricist with several books and hit songs to her credit. She writes for a living, usually with deadlines looming. Her tried-and-true cure for writer's block: "If your muse won't work for you, kick her in the ass and get her going." The same cure may be applied to graphic design. Your entire time can't be spent sitting around musing. Instead, work the process. This is not to say you can't take a break and go for a walk, but even that is part of the creative process. Creative work is still work, so work at it.

A GOOD CONCEPT POORLY EXECUTED IS MORE COMPELLING THAN A POOR CONCEPT WELL EXECUTED. IF I'M FORCED TO CHOOSE BETWEEN CRAFTY DESIGN EXECUTION AND CLEVER DESIGN CONCEPT, I'LL CHOOSE THE LATTER EVERY TIME.

Overvalue the Conceptual

If I had to give just one piece of advice, this would be it. You can't value the conceptual enough. Modernist architect Mies van der Rohe famously said, "God is in the details." Easy enough for God, who is able to keep track of a pretty decent amount of information at any given time: concepts, details, and all. But since we're not God, we'd better start off with the concepts and work our way into the details. Not that detail and execution are unimportant; it's just that they are always subordinate to the concept.

A good concept poorly executed is more compelling than a poor concept well executed. Of course, the ultimate goal is an amazing concept immaculately executed. But if I'm forced to choose between crafty design execution and clever design concept, I'll choose the latter every time. The market agrees with me. Who makes more money—the marketing executive who comes up with the advertising concept or the junior designer who executes the concept? Again, it need not be an either-or situation. There is room for creativity at all phases of the design process. But skip creativity in the conceptual phase, and the rest of the project will be like gilding a turd.

A Good Concept Doesn't Have to Be Complicated

In graphic design, the best concepts are rarely complicated because there is only so much complexity you can inject into a billboard or a Web site without overwhelming the viewer. By definition, a concept is an abstraction, a metaphor, a simplification of some larger, more complex, immaterial theme. As cognitive studies expert Edward de Bono observes, "You need to use concepts. Concepts are the human mind's way of simplifying the world around. Warning: If you do not use concepts, then you are working with detail."

The Nike logo is a classic example of a simple concept. It looks fast and active, like victory being won. It makes you want to say, "swoosh." It's been branded so well it doesn't even need accompanying type. What could be simpler than that? Absolut Vodka's branding campaign. For goodness sake, Absolut branded the shape of a freaking bottle! How clever is that? Remove all the markings from the bottle and you still recognize it. Because the logo is so primordial and flexible (while still being distinctive), it can be applied almost limitlessly in Absolut's advertising campaigns. The designers have made the bottle shape out of taxicabs and even water in a canal. Such is the power of a strong, simple concept.

This classic Bic pen advertisement is all concept. Granted, it is implemented well. The white ground with just a hint of dimensionality added by the pen's shadow creates intrigue and draws us into an otherwise flat space. The execution of the infinity symbol is not so sloppy that it detracts from the punch line of the concept, yet still sloppy enough to look hand drawn. We are meant to think that a person just recently drew this symbol and set the pen down. A great expanse of time is evoked in this otherwise static, nonsequential image. Even if

Simple solutions are versatile. Absolut's brand is a simple bottle shape, which can be applied to anything from yellow taxis to water.

In this Bic pen advertisement, the simplicity of the design foregrounds the genius of the concept.

Paula Scher's Citi logo is deceptively ingenious in its simplicity. The best design solutions often seem effortless, but they rarely are.

this ad had been executed in a less aesthetically pleasing manner, it would still work, based on the strength of the concept alone.

Finally, consider Paula Scher's design for the Citibank logo. Citicorp bank and Travelers Group insurance had merged, and their new logo needed to combine aspects of each of their previous identities—the letters "citi" and the red Travelers Group umbrella—in a way that didn't seem like a logo train wreck. Not an easy task, but Scher arrived at a simple conceptual solution to a complicated design challenge. The dots of the i's became endpoints for an umbrella hood, and the "t" looks like an umbrella handle. The solution is obvious enough now, but nobody saw it until she showed it to us.

A Good Concept Focuses and Drives Good Design

A good concept acts as a sensible anchor, a touchstone that unifies and directs every other design decision. A good concept can give the project a unified narrative voice. Every aspect of the design—image, type, grid, proportion, copy, illustration—should contribute to the overall tone. Even if it involves a large team of designers, the whole project should feel as if only one person is speaking—the voice of the project. Such unity is impossible with a vague central concept, or no central concept at all.

The first page of Genesis in the Doves Press Bible is a famous example of multiple design elements pulling in the same conceptual direction to form a unified whole. Edward Johnston

drew the almost alarmingly bold, austere calligraphy of the first line. Emery Walker designed the handsome body type, inspired by a classic fifteenth-century Nicolas Jenson typeface. Doves Press partners Walker and T. J. Cobden-Sanderson arrived at the balanced layout and meticulous letter spacing. Shunning the Arts & Crafts ornamentation of the era, Doves Press pioneered a minimalist approach free of figures and ornaments. The glory of this page is the unity and balance of all its elements: the proportional margins, the even texture of the type, the structural symmetry between the calligraphic letters and the letterpress letters. What is the central concept that unifies this approach? The contents of the text itself. This is an account of the beginning of time, space, and existence as we know it. The design is fittingly potent and confident. In the beginning was the word, and the Doves Press Bible subordinates every other element to it.

T. J. Cobden-Sanderson and Emery Walker: page from Doves Press Bible (1903). The confidence of the Genesis creation account is the central concept that unifies the various elements—type, texture, calligraphy, color, and space—of this remarkable design.

IN THE BEGINNING

GOD CREATED THE HEAVEN AND THE EARTH. ❡AND THE EARTH WAS WITHOUT FORM, AND VOID; AND DARKNESS WAS UPON THE FACE OF THE DEEP, & THE SPIRIT OF GOD MOVED UPON THE FACE OF THE WATERS. ❡And God said, Let there be light: & there was light. And God saw the light, that it was good: & God divided the light from the darkness. And God called the light Day, and the darkness he called Night. And the evening and the morning were the first day. ❡And God said, Let there be a firmament in the midst of the waters, & let it divide the waters from the waters. And God made the firmament, and divided the waters which were under the firmament from the waters which were above the firmament: & it was so. And God called the firmament Heaven. And the evening & the morning were the second day. ❡And God said, Let the waters under the heaven be gathered together unto one place, and let the dry land appear: and it was so. And God called the dry land Earth; and the gathering together of the waters called he Seas: and God saw that it was good. And God said, Let the earth bring forth grass, the herb yielding seed, and the fruit tree yielding fruit after his kind, whose seed is in itself, upon the earth: & it was so. And the earth brought forth grass, & herb yielding seed after his kind, & the tree yielding fruit, whose seed was in itself, after his kind: and God saw that it was good. And the evening & the morning were the third day. ❡And God said, Let there be lights in the firmament of the heaven to divide the day from the night; and let them be for signs, and for seasons, and for days, & years: and let them be for lights in the firmament of the heaven to give light upon the earth: & it was so. And God made two great lights; the greater light to rule the day, and the lesser light to rule the night: he made the stars also. And God set them in the firmament of the heaven to give light upon the earth, and to rule over the day and over the night, & to divide the light from the darkness: and God saw that it was good. And the evening and the morning were the fourth day. ❡And God said, Let the waters bring forth abundantly the moving creature that hath life, and fowl that may fly above the earth in the open firmament of heaven. And God created great whales, & every living creature that moveth, which the waters brought forth abundantly, after their kind, & every winged fowl after his kind: & God saw that it was good. And God blessed them, saying, Be fruitful, & multiply, and fill the waters in the seas, and let fowl multiply in the earth. And the evening & the morning were the fifth day. ❡And God said, Let the earth bring forth the living creature after his kind, cattle, and creeping thing, and beast of the earth after his kind: and it was so. And God made the beast of the earth after his kind, and cattle after their kind, and every thing that creepeth upon the

27

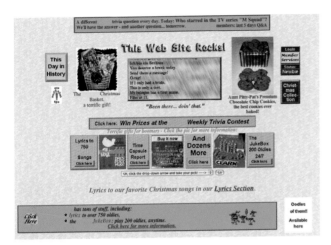

A classic case of "too many cooks spoil the broth." In this case, it appears that the cooks also have Attention Deficit Disorder and are on hallucinogens.

Compare that masterpiece to any of the thousands of pitifully designed, 1988-era Web sites with no conceptual direction whatsoever, and the disconnect can be physically nauseating. A clear, clever, appropriate concept acts like a central hat rack on which to hang all the design elements so that they aren't scattered about the room in a jumbled mess.

The concept needs to drive the design phase at every turn. If you skip the conceptual step and rush headlong into specific decisions about layout, typography, color, and imagery, you will be dealing with merely the sheen and surface of visual communication. This is graphic design as cake decorating. Such design reads like a play without a plot. Even an absurdist play like *Waiting for Godot* still has a plot (two guys wait for a third guy who never shows), which is based on a theme (life is absurd). Can meaningful dialogue truly exist apart from a plot that drives and anchors it? Can meaningful design truly exist apart from a concept that drives and anchors it?

A Good Concept Bridges the Gap

A good concept is rooted in and derived from the identified themes of the project. It acts as a bridge between predesign research and design execution. The transition between prose theme and visual concept is one of the most crucial phases of the creative process. It's easy enough to distill key themes from your predesign research. You start with objective prose and you end with subjective prose, but you're still moving in the realm of prose. Likewise it's easy enough to take a visual concept and develop it into a refined design. You start with sketchy design and you end with polished design, but you're still moving in the realm of design. The magic, the challenge, the work, the "art" of a conceptual designer is to bridge that dividing line between prose and visual communication. In so doing, you literally "materialize" the abstract themes, giving them form and substance in the realm of visual (and sometimes physical) space. We'll discuss this further in the "Exploratory Sketching" section of Chapter 3.

A Good Concept Is Dense

In addition to materializing prose themes, you are "densifying" them: making them denser. For example, identity designers take the complex, expansive personality of an entire company and condense it into a single logo. Great logos are dense. They pack a punch. They take a lot of thematic information and deliver it in one concise, terse, conceptual mark. Pow!

In this sense, designers are again like comedians. What makes a comedian's punch line cathartic and exhilarating is not just that it's funny. A punch line works because it lands on you all at once in one clever, terse, provocative, dense phrase. Laughter is simply the natural result of a dense punch line decompressing itself in your mind. The more a punch line sneaks up on you and takes you by surprise, the more likely you are to involuntarily laugh out loud.

A sunset view is much more breathtaking when you emerge from the woods and come upon it all at once. Winning a boxing match in 13 rounds by a split decision is not as dramatically decisive as winning in an instant with a knockout punch. The revelation in a whodunit movie is best delivered with a sudden pointing of the accusatory finger, a dramatic swelling of the soundtrack, and a tight zoom in on the wide-eyed face of the accused, furtively looking around the room for some means of escape. In *Psycho*, when we discover that Norman Bates' mother is no longer living as we had supposed, it is all the more disturbing because Hitchcock reveals it to us in a compact visual instant—a rotting corpse in an attic rocking chair. We are then left to decompress the ramifications of this dense revelation in horrific aftershock.

Density is the picture that's worth a thousand words. A strong visual concept has impact and punch that a prose essay simply cannot. Which is more dramatic: a thousand-word essay on the horrors of war or a powerfully conceptualized antiwar poster?

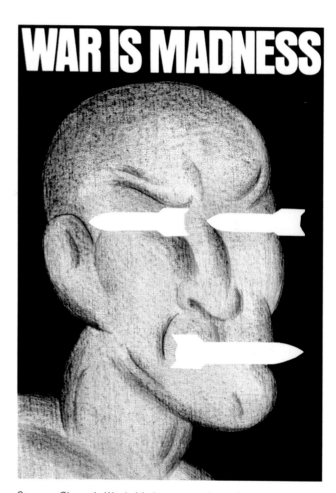

Seymour Chwast's *War Is Madness* poster is worth a thousand words and then some. Adding supplementary words to it would dissipate its impact.

A Great Concept Requires Sketching Time

Why do so many designers rush through the concept step? Perhaps this is because most of the conceptualizing involves sketching and doodling, neither of which adults take very seriously. Words? Yes, they are very serious and businesslike. Photoshop histogram levels and Illustrator Bézier curves? Yes, they are all very technical and professional. But just sketching and doodling with pencil and paper? It somehow doesn't seem like you can justify billing a client for that.

The goal of sketching is freedom and exploration, so it is actually counterproductive to focus on precise draftsmanship and logical progression. The goal is not the artistic quality of the sketches themselves, but the concepts that they tease out and develop. Sketch loosely. That's why it's called "sketching"—it's sketchy. You're trying to stay conceptual without getting too specific. The less specific your sketches, the more interpretations they will yield when you develop them in detail later on.

What's wrong with getting too specific too early? Why not "sketch" in Photoshop? Aren't pencil and paper antiquated and overrated? I'm not suggesting you use pencil and paper because they are nostalgic or "pure." I'm not one of those designers who has some great aesthetic love for X-Acto knives and rubber cement. Pencil and paper are simply the right tools for visual conceptualizing at an early stage for a number of reasons:

- They are less mediated. You can just grab them and push them around without having to shift-right-click or locate the pulldown menu. Software adds an extra level of objective technical interference between you and your intuitive, subjective conceptualizing.

- The area of your paper can be physically expanded and viewed simultaneously. (We'll talk more about this in the "Exploratory Sketching" section of Chapter 3.)

- Most importantly, pencil and paper focus you on the underlying visual concept and keep you from jumping ahead to the surface sheen. Pencil and paper force you to codify your concept in design space prior to developing it fully.

Conceptual sketching is necessarily different for different design disciplines. For video, conceptual sketching looks like rough plot outlines and loose storyboarding. For a poster, the concept sketches resemble the final poster in form and layout but lack illustrative details, photography, color, and refined typography. For Web

IF YOUR VISUAL CONCEPT CAN STAND ON ITS OWN WITHOUT COLOR, DIGITAL TYPE,

AND SPECIAL EFFECTS, YOU KNOW YOU'VE GOT A STRONG CONCEPT.

and interactive media, the sketching phase is necessarily less overtly visual and more functional and metaphorical. You've got to address not only look but also feel, hierarchy, and interactivity.

There are other analog ways to sketch besides with pencil and paper. You can sketch by cutting and pasting newspapers, collaging, painting; you can even use crayons. Each approach will lead you down a slightly different conceptual path, which is what you want. The more paths you explore, the more likely you are to come up with a winning concept.

You can always explore conceptual paths in your mind, away from your desk. But if you never begin the sketching process, your mental conceptualizing is likely to get stuck on the prose side of the prose/design divide. You want to conceptualize visually during this phase of the creative process, and sketching kicks that kind of thinking into gear.

There are a slew of technically skilled graphic designers who have mastered grid systems, typography, and the fundamental principles of modernist design. But if that's all you have, you will only be able to take your design so far. At some point, you will run into the dreaded wall of stylistic formalism. Ultimately graphic design is about visual communication, and communication is about the transference of ideas. To transfer ideas visually, you have to use concepts. As you begin to overvalue the conceptual, you will become a more holistic designer, and your work will improve exponentially.

Visit the "Zone" but Don't Live There

Some schools of method acting encourage the actor to "become" the character. Actors actually live as their characters in order to gain insight into them. Whether this approach is valuable or indulgent depends on whom you ask. Either way, even method actors have to translate the insights they've gained into an interpretive, intentional performance. Likewise, in graphic design, it is wonderful to get an intuitive feel for the "vibe" of a project, but you can't stay personally geared up in this "vibe" for the entire duration of the project. There are three key aspects of the project you want to understand: the product you are selling, the company you are representing, and the audience to whom you are speaking. Take some time to visit these three "zones," to see things from these three perspectives. Do it early on in the creative process and revisit each zone occasionally throughout.

- The product zone: "Be the ball," so to speak. Assign the product motivations and characteristics, as if it were a person. Pretend *you* are the product. What's your motivation?

IF YOU NEVER BEGIN THE SKETCHING PROCESS, YOUR MENTAL CONCEPTUALIZING IS LIKELY TO GET STUCK ON THE PROSE SIDE OF THE PROSE/DESIGN DIVIDE.

- The client zone: Become the client. What are you hoping will be the result of this ad campaign? What will please you? This is not a hard one to imagine, since the client has probably filled in all of these blanks himself.

- The audience zone: This is by far the most important of the three zones. Become your audience. In the early research and design phases, cut out pictures of your target audience and put them up around your workspace. Listen to the music they like. Eat at the restaurants they like. Go to the clubs they like (be they country clubs or rave clubs).

At some point, however, you have to drop the research, become yourself, and actually get back to the task of designing. Let's say you have to design a magazine advertisement for teen girls' jeans. Your research indicates that your target demographic is listening to Britney Spears that year. Unless I've grossly misjudged my readership, your work probably won't benefit from listening to Britney Spears for weeks on end. Too much role-playing eventually becomes counterproductive. You want to get into the heads of your audience to see things from their perspective, but you don't want to "become" a 14-year-old female graphic designer. You are you, and you function properly surrounded by things that work for you. Perhaps your target audience listens to a lot of Perry Como. Unless Perry Como is your crooner of choice, exposing yourself to his unique vocal stylings for an extended period of time is not really simulating the experience a Perry Como fan has listening to Perry Como. More likely, you are simulating the experience a Perry Como fan has listening to Meatloaf.

There is a fourth zone: your own inspired emotional zone. You may get into this zone by listening to music that gets you hyped, watching films that recharge your creative batteries, drinking too much coffee, doing push-ups, or whatever. There's nothing wrong with designing from a place of emotion, but you can't spend the entire project operating from that hyped-up zone. At some point you have to reenter a calm, analytical space. As fictitious golf legend "Chubbs" Peterson advises Happy in Adam Sandler's film *Happy Gilmore*, "[Golf] isn't hockey. You don't play with raw emotion." Much as it pains me to admit it, graphic design is probably more like golf than hockey. Or maybe it's somewhere in between.

Sculptor Gustav Rodin was asked, "What is the creative process from its beginning?" He

TOO OFTEN THE EXECUTION PHASE OF THE CREATIVE PROCESS BECOMES A

ROTE CHORE. THAT MIGHT BE THE PERFECT TIME TO REVISIT YOUR ORIGINAL

INSPIRATION AND LET IT ENLIVEN AND REILLUMINATE THE PROJECT.

replied, "First, I have an intense feeling which slowly becomes more concrete and asks me to give it a solid shape. Then I begin to plan and design. Finally, when it comes to execution, I again abandon myself to the feeling, which may prompt me to modify the plan." This seems like wise advice for designers as well. Too often the execution phase of the creative process becomes a rote chore. That might be the perfect time to revisit your original inspiration and let it enliven and reilluminate the project.

In his classic *Graphic Design Manual*, designer and educator Armin Hofmann writes of the balance between emotion and intellect: "There should be no separation between spontaneous work with an emotional tone and work directed by the intellect. Both are supplementary to each other and must be regarded as intimately connected. Discipline and freedom are thus to be seen as elements of equal weight, each partaking of the other."

The more adept you become at toggling back and forth between emotion and intellect, the more integrated and humanized your design work will be. If that means a playlist with half White Stripes and half Brian Eno, so be it. You may even want to mix some Perry Como in there too.

■ ■ ■

In this chapter, we'll examine four methods you can employ at various stages of the process to get "unstuck" and bypass the mire of indecision, stagnation, and inertia. One method, exploratory sketching, is for the "blank page" step at the beginning of the design phase. Another method, time-limited designing, can occur at various stages throughout the design phase. It's best to use scope plumbing if you're stuck at the very beginning of the development phase. And oblique strategizing can be used throughout the entire process, from predesign to implementation. If the creative process is a machine, then these methods grease the machine, moving it forward toward a final design solution.

EXPLORATORY SKETCHING IS SKETCHING IN ORDER TO EXTEND YOUR OWN THINKING ON THE MATTER. YOU ARE NOT DRAWING TO COMMUNICATE A WELL-FORMED IDEA. YOU DON'T YET HAVE A WELL-FORMED IDEA.

Exploratory Sketching

Exploratory sketching is sketching for yourself to generate ideas. It is entirely different from representational drawing, which is drawing to communicate your ideas to someone else. Yet many graphic designers function as if representational drawing were the only kind of sketching. We know that we have to show our client a mock-up, a form of representational drawing. So we begin our design phase by sketching thumbnails of what the mock-up might look like; then we refine them into polished mock-ups, and we feel we have properly worked the design phase. But such practice completely skips the important step of exploratory sketching.

In exploratory sketching, you are talking to yourself visually, jotting down ideas with images instead of words. You won't ever show these sketches to your client. Most of them will never figuratively appear in your final mock-up. Exploratory sketching has more to do with thinking than it does with art or graphic design. It is "visual thinking," to use art psychologist Rudolf Arnheim's term.

You are free to draw things that don't mean anything to anyone but you. You are free to explore dead-ends and abandon them without any obligation to tie them up. You are simply exploring the nature of the problem as you currently understand it. You are sketching in order to extend your own thinking on the matter. You are not drawing to communicate a well-formed idea. You don't yet have a well-formed idea. You are drawing in order to tease out ideas.

Engineers, inventors, and even mathematicians use exploratory sketching in their research as a form of visual thinking, with little difficulty and to great benefit. Why, then, is it so difficult for graphic designers to sketch this way? One reason is that our final output is also visual, and the two kinds of visual language get confused in our minds. It is difficult for us to disassociate our exploratory sketches from our final output because we are always thinking ahead, trying to shortcut a solution to the final representational design.

Thumbnail sketching, for example, does not count as exploratory sketching. Thumbnailing and storyboarding are looser, prototypical forms of representational sketching; they are still drawn with the final mock-up overtly in mind. In thumbnailing, you keep in mind the proportions of the final space—the composition and layout. Thumbnailing doesn't help you generate concepts or ideas; it simply leads you toward a representational mock-up. It is less like free-form visual exploration and more like an early stage of representational visual communication.

In his wonderful book *Experiences in Visual Thinking*, engineer and educator Robert McKim likens exploratory sketching to an idea factory. It's not a full-blown graphic design factory. It doesn't supply finished representational solutions but simply processes ideas in the visual realm.

As long as we are still dealing with ideas, then why not keep using prose? Because at some point, your project is going to have to transition from words to visual space. Exploratory sketching is a sensible way to gradually transition from abstract words to abstract visuals without having to abruptly and awkwardly jump directly from representational prose to representational visuals.

But why sketch at all? Why not just conceive visual solutions in our minds? Sketching, drawing, modeling—what McKim calls "externalized thinking"—has several advantages over "internalized thinking," or seeing the solution in your mind. One is that it releases you from having to keep so many images in your mind simultaneously. When you sketch, you empty your mind, storing its contents in a physical form and freeing it up to conceive other ideas.

Another advantage of externalized thinking is that it encourages contemplation and analysis. With internalized thinking, you must use your mind to do two things—store an image and analyze it. But when you put an image on paper, you can use your full mind to contemplate it, without having to visualize it internally. It's much easier. The medium of pen and paper becomes an extension of your mind. Once you sketch several things, you can begin grouping them and then analyzing them spatially—something you would be hard-pressed to do if they were all in your mind.

Finally, sketching is advantageous because it allows for happy accidents. In the process of drawing something, you may accidentally discover something else. Such accidental discovery is much less likely to happen by keeping the visual ideas inside your mind.

The following guidelines for exploratory sketching will lead you through the entire process.

Preparation: Purge

How do you prepare your mind for this type of sketching? One school of thought says that your first idea is probably your best idea; another says it's probably your worst. Those who say you should trust your first instinct are optimistic about the human spirit. Those who say you should doubt your first instinct have probably taught freshman design students. Having seen my share of similar first-try solutions to similar design problems over the years, I tend to believe that your first idea is probably not your strongest. If it fell right into your lap, it probably fell into everybody else's lap too.

If you agree with this logic, you'll want to purge your mind of obvious solutions before you start. Simply write down the first few ideas that immediately come to mind and set them aside. If they are actually brilliant and much better than your subsequent ideas, you can always return to them later.

Launch from Words

Our job as graphic designers is to take the technical, specialized language of various businesses and translate it into design. The creative design process is the *gradual* translation of stated goals into visual solutions. We shouldn't leap directly from creative brief to finished design.

The first step is to translate the language of the business memo into more sensory and poetic language that can serve as a launching pad for exploratory sketching. New media designer Hillman Curtis suggests a process called "targeting the theme." After you've researched the project, write down ten words or phrases that best sum up the theme of the project. They can be words like "beneficial" or phrases like "happy go lucky." Then draw a three-ringed target and put one word from your list in the center, one in the second ring, and a third in the outer ring. Just like a pop music lyric, a design project should only be about one theme. The secondary and tertiary themes shed light on the primary theme, but many themes are too divergent.

Building on Curtis's concept, you can begin exploratory sketching by riffing off of these three words or phrases. As you "visually think" them, sketch loosely and abstractly—figures, shapes, diagrams, connections. At this stage, feel free to mix words and images. Just make sure that you are not putting down all words.

After you've sketched a while from your three key words, try paraphrasing them to generate a new direction. For example, "happy go lucky" and "carefree" mean almost the same thing, but each phrase has subtle nuances that can lead down very different visual paths. "Happy go lucky" may suggest a smile, a four-leaf clover, a cartwheel, or a dance, whereas "carefree" may suggest sleeping, relaxing, floating, burdens falling away. Change the phrase to "devil may care" and head down an entirely different path. Get out a thesaurus and explore synonyms. Translate your key words into slang phrases and colloquialisms. Slang is usually much richer with visual overtones.

One of my students was designing a T-shirt for a local music club. He targeted the three themes "sex," "drugs," and "rock and roll," in that order of importance. I thought he was just being flippant, but he justified his decision by saying that the club was well known for its music (rock and roll), but not known as a place to have a beer (drugs) and socialize (sex). In rebranding the club, he wanted to somehow reverse this order of audience perception. The cliché key words he chose actually became a useful way to approach the design problem. Exploratory sketching that begins with "sex, drugs, and rock and roll" will probably be more interesting than exploratory sketching that begins with "music, beer, and socializing." Then again, maybe not. Explore both.

If you think all this sounds like a bunch of marketers brainstorming a new tagline, you're missing the point. The phrases are merely points of departure for exploratory sketching. The phrases may seem ridiculous. The sketches themselves may seem ridiculous. But you can evaluate them critically later. In this step, you are simply exploring where your targeted themes lead visually. The more freely you explore, the more raw material you give yourself to work with later.

You can also remix your thematic key words for a new exploratory-sketching launch by turning your original ten words into adjectives. Then come up with ten nouns derived from these adjectives. For instance, if the adjective is "playful," you might choose the noun "children." If another adjective is "solid," you might choose the noun "tank." Once you've come up with ten corresponding nouns, mix and match the original adjectives with the new nouns, and launch an exploratory-sketching session from each pair. You may wind up with a sketching run that launches from the idea of playful tanks and another that launches from the idea of solid children. The goal of this recombinatory text exercise is to spark promising combinations that may not occur to you otherwise.

Another launch strategy is proposed by cognitive studies expert Edward de Bono in his famous thinking course. (De Bono dares to suggest that thinking is actually a teachable skill.) Simply launch from any random noun. Open a dictionary to any page and scan down until you come to the first noun. Then launch your exploratory sketch from it, keeping the goals of your project in mind as you do. Let's say your design problem is how to make a hairspray product seem fresh and invigorating, and the first noun you come to is "cactus." In this sketching "experiment," you're trying to explore what a cactus has to do with your invigorating hairspray (an admitted challenge). Everything is

AFTER YOU'VE SKETCHED A WHILE FROM THREE KEY WORDS, TRY PARAPHRASING THEM TO GENERATE A NEW DIRECTION. TRANSLATE THEM INTO SLANG PHRASES AND COLLOQUIALISMS.

DON'T USE THE COMPUTER FOR EXPLORATORY SKETCHING. THERE IS TOO MUCH OF AN

INTERFACE BARRIER BETWEEN YOUR HEAD, YOUR HAND, AND THE DIGITAL IMAGE THAT RESULTS.

related to everything else in some way. Starting from "cactus," try to "sketch your way home" to your original design problem. Your design problem is the control; your random word is the variable. It doesn't matter what random word you choose—it will always connect to your design problem in some way, providing a back-door into it. This approach may seem bizarre, but it can yield original results. Always starting with and ending with the problem can put you in a mental closed circuit. The random noun strategy pulls random aspects of existence into dialogue with your problem—aspects that can invigorate your understanding of the problem and your current approach to it.

Along the same lines, graphic design innovator Stefan Sagmeister sometimes thumbs through his old sketchbooks looking for previous ideas that he can apply to a current project. His reasoning is similar to de Bono's: When an idea comes from completely beyond the parameters of a current project, it can spark a novel and interesting approach. In Sagmeister's strategy, as in de Bono's, no matter where you begin your exploratory sketching, you can usually relate it to your current project, and often with refreshing results.

Sketch Laterally (But Stay Grounded)

Edward de Bono famously coined the now ubiquitous phrase "lateral thinking." It basically means: Don't fix on a single solution too soon. Early in your design phase, explore wide rather than deep. Come up with several possible solutions to a given problem before fixing on one and developing it "vertically" into a finished design. The obvious advantage of lateral thinking is that it lets you compare the merits of various solutions before committing to one. A less obvious advantage is that it allows you to synthesize multiple solutions into an even better solution. A third advantage is that one idea can lead to another. When you sketch laterally, you don't have a specific agenda for where your sketching explorations should lead. The whole sketching process is eventually heading toward order and synthesis, but sometimes the chaos of a system must increase before it can realize its ideal state of balance. So don't be afraid to "get on out there" with your sketches—break the rules, be outlandish, reach, drift. Later in the process, when the time does comes to evaluate, it will be much easier to reel in crazy ideas than to extend tame/lame/safe ideas.

The danger of a too-loose approach is that you will fall into rote and unfruitful sketching ruts. If you find your mind regularly wandering toward pineapples, Hawaii, and hula skirts, recognize this as a dead-end and nip it in the bud. To keep these ruts from forming, stay grounded in the goals of the project. Keep them always in the back of your mind. This requires balance. Too much conscious focus on the problem at hand defeats the exploratory purpose of sketching. No focus at all on the problem at hand can lead to repetitive forays into your own idiosyncratic unconscious fixations. Such forays may be psychologically therapeutic for you, but they won't do your client much good.

Sketch with Intuitive Tools

The specific tools you use for sketching are a matter of personal preference. The goal is to choose tools that are intuitive to you, tools that don't place a technical barrier between your thinking and your sketching. Don't use the computer for exploratory sketching. Even with a responsive pen pad, there is currently too much of an interface barrier between your head, your hand, and the digital image that results. Focusing on pressure settings and keystroke shortcuts interferes with the kind of spatial, intuitive thinking that exploratory sketching seeks to promote.

Whatever materials you use, they should be as cheap as reasonably possible. Choose inexpensive newsprint over heavy watercolor paper. Choose good, serviceable pens but not top-of-the-line pens. You are going for quantity, not masterpiece quality. Think of your materials as practical and disposable—simply tools to get the sketching job done. Perhaps you have a fetish for exquisite art supplies. Get over it when it comes to this kind of sketching. Unless you are phenomenally wealthy, expensive materials inhibit risk-taking in exploratory sketching.

Try out a variety of pens and pencils to see which ones suit you best. A nylon-tip art pen draws a more painterly, less exact line than a fine-point fiber-tip pen. A charcoal stick feels different in your hand than a No. 2 pencil and will result in a more loosely drawn line. In other words, the nature of your materials has a bearing on the way you approach your sketching, both formally and psychologically.

I enjoy sketching with a wonderful Chinese calligraphy brush that was a gift from a colleague whose father is a renowned calligraphy artist. The brush radically alters my approach to sketching, making my line—and my thinking—very fluid and abstract. A calligraphy teaching says, "Emancipation of mind and freedom of

Suggested Sketching Materials

For Drawing With:

- Fine-point black fiber-tip pen
- Medium black ballpoint pen
- Three nylon-tip pens in grayscale range
- Three felt-tip markers in grayscale range
- Black charcoal stick
- No. 2 pencil
- Pink Pearl eraser
- Three prismacolor pencils in your choice of colors

For Drawing On:

- 5" x 8" moleskin notebook with plain pages
- 18" x 24" newsprint pad
- Roll of newsprint or shelf paper (18" or however wide you can get it)
- Roll of tracing paper (however wide you can get it)

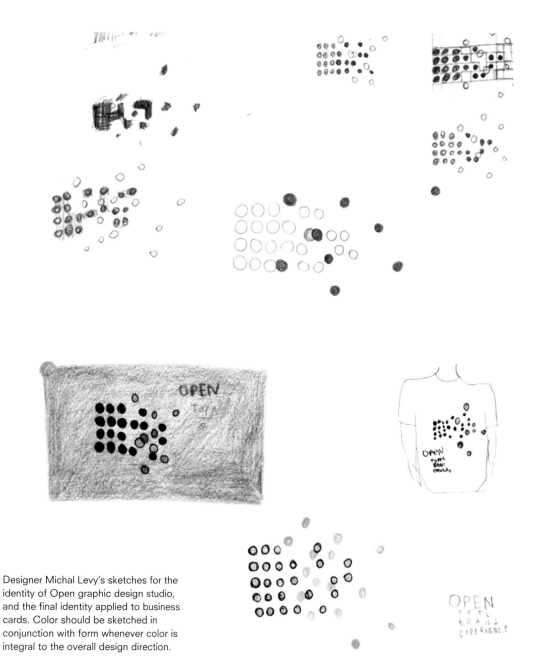

Designer Michal Levy's sketches for the identity of Open graphic design studio, and the final identity applied to business cards. Color should be sketched in conjunction with form whenever color is integral to the overall design direction.

gesture are in effect identical." And freedom of gesture is greatly influenced by the tools you use. You could launch the same exploratory-sketching exercise using different drawing media and arrive at radically different results.

Tracing paper and prismacolor pencils come into play during the evaluation and integration stage, which will be discussed later in this chapter. As a general rule, don't use color in your initial exploratory sketches. It introduces a level of detail that is too specific for this

early stage. As with every rule, there are exceptions. Use of color is applicable in exploratory sketching when color is integral to the concept you are exploring. Even then, you want to use color as an abstract, indicative element, and not fuss over precise Pantone values or even specific hues.

A moleskin notebook is useful for portable and perpetual sketching, which will also be discussed later. A large roll of newsprint is for spatial sketching.

Sketch Spatially

Rather than sketching sequentially, page by page in a notebook, do your exploratory sketching on large rolls of newsprint. This allows you to think spatially rather than linearly. Ideas are able to branch, loop backward, and continue forward in a holistic fashion. During a single sketching run, you will have immediate visual access to all that has gone before, and you will be able to draw inferences and see connections on the fly—something you couldn't do flipping back and forth through pages of a notebook.

Linguistic thinking tends to be linear because spoken language proceeds linearly, one word after another. Writing reflects this linearity. Words start at the top-left corner of the page and march in sequential rows toward the bottom-right corner of the page. But sketching need not be that way; it is inherently spatial and nonlinear. Sketching on scrolls is a fluid way to explore ideas. It allows unorthodox juxtapositions that can lead to more inventive solutions.

THINK FORWARD. DON'T EVALUATE IN TERMS OF WHAT WORKS NOW, BUT IN TERMS OF WHAT MIGHT LEAD SOMEWHERE.

Sketch Fast and Continuously

Limit your exploratory-sketching runs to anywhere between 5 and 15 minutes. This will focus you and keep you attentive as you sketch. It will also remove the pressure of having to come up with a good idea. As you sketch, don't think of yourself as a creator, an ingenious problem solver, or even a great drawer. Those roles place an undue burden on you to come up with something immediately clever. They tempt you to shortcut the exploratory process.

Instead, think of yourself as an explorer. You are striving for many different ideas; you are not striving for quality. Don't stop to assess the quality of your ideas. Sketch quickly and keep sketching until your time is up.

Transition Between Abstract and Concrete Sketching

In your exploratory sketching, feel free to use abstract forms. Much more than photographers or even illustrators, graphic designers are allowed to venture into the realm of pure abstraction. Abstract lines, shapes, and patterns are particularly appropriate in exploratory sketching when your ultimate goal is something iconic like a logo. It may feel like doodling, but that's fine as long as you're doodling with the goals of the project in the back of your mind.

Conversely, don't shy away from the desire to draw more concretely, as long as such concrete representation is useful in visually exploring your ideas. Transition between concrete and abstract sketching as needed. Different drawing modes result in different kinds of exploration and enforce different kinds of thinking.

Sketch Perpetually

Regardless of how good your drawing skills are, you can always improve them. The better your drawing skills, the more effective you will be at exploratory sketching. I keep a Moleskin sketchbook (5 by 8 inches) of guided drawing exercises, and I try to do one a day.

In his book *Conceptual Blockbusting*, engineer and educator James Adams suggests another way to improve your improvisational sketching skills. Carry a pocket sketchbook with you everywhere. Instead of explaining your ideas and thoughts verbally (to coworkers, your spouse, your kids), practice explaining your ideas by sketching them. You are allowed to use words but only in conjunction with your sketches. This exercise will eventually drive your friends and loved ones insane, so you may want to practice it for limited periods of time.

Evaluate and Integrate

Once you have completed several exploratory-sketching runs, it's time to tack them up next to each other, step back, and begin evaluating and integrating them. How many runs should you complete before this step? There is no magic number. You don't want to sketch forever and do fifty 15-minute sketching runs before integrating them, but this is rarely the problem. The temptation is to complete two or three 5-minute sketching runs and then jump straight into evaluation and integration.

Once you have enough raw sketching to evaluate and integrate, it's time to switch thinking modes. You are no longer exploring, sketching anything that comes to mind. You are now evaluating, reeling things back in, and synthesizing them. You are not evaluating the aesthetic quality of the sketches—you are evaluating the potential usefulness of the forms and ideas they represent. And you are looking for forms and ideas that can be combined in interesting ways.

PHYSICAL LOGISTICS OF EVALUATION AND INTEGRATION

What does evaluation and integration literally look like? How do you do it? First, tack or tape all your scrolls onto a wall next to each other. Then cut up your scrolls into smaller pieces and rearrange them based on any number of criteria—complexity, conceptual meaning, formal similarity, ways in which they relate to the design problem. You are looking to make connections between the different parts of your sketches.

As you rearrange things, make notes on the sketches. Use a colored pencil to distinguish your new notes from your original black and grayscale notes. If a single sketch fits into multiple categories, simply copy it on tracing paper or a Xerox machine and distribute the copies.

Use other colors to indicate additional layers of meaningful relationship. One color might highlight similar forms, another might highlight your best ideas, and a third might highlight ideas that challenge your original understanding of the design problem.

To discover and create meaningful relationships, try the following tips:

- Squint and look for similar patterns.

- Return to words and let them help. Choose a promising sketch section and write down adjectives that describe it. Then scan the rest of your sketches for sections that those adjectives also describe.

- Categorize the objects you've sketched based on real world criteria. Size, shape, weight, hardness, speed, man-made, organic, pretty, ugly, common, rare—the list is endless.

"Synectics"—the brainchild of design consultants William J.J. Gordon and George Prince—is a formal method of bringing diverse elements into harmony. In his book *Design Synectics*, design educator Nicholas Roukes suggests several other ways to group things based on synectic principles:

- Functionally: according to what they do.

- Structurally: according to how they are built.

- Kinetically: according to how they move.

- Irrationally: according to your intuitive feelings, not a rational scheme.

- Randomly: according to chance. Shuffle a bunch of your sketch sections and deal them out randomly into groups.

Once you have evaluated and grouped your sketches, it's time to integrate them. You are trying to come up with synergies—combinations that are more than merely the sum of their parts.

Roukes suggests several "*synectic* trigger mechanisms," or ways of integrating disparate source material in hopes of triggering interesting results: subtract, repeat, combine, add, transfer, empathize, animate, superimpose, change scale, substitute, fragment, isolate, distort, disguise, contradict, parody, prevaricate, analogize, hybridize, metamorphose, symbolize, mythologize, fantasize.

Some of these trigger mechanisms are mechanical. For instance, merely rescaling a sketch and superimposing it onto another sketch can yield suggestive results. Others are more conceptual. Hybridizing a sketch of color bars and traffic signs, for example, might lead to the idea of replacing all traffic sign symbols with abstract color bars.

A related list of trigger mechanisms is called SCAMPERR, an acronym coined by creative-thinking educator Bob Eberle. SCAMPERR stands for: substitute/simplify, combine, adapt, modify/magnify, put to other uses, eliminate, rearrange/reverse.

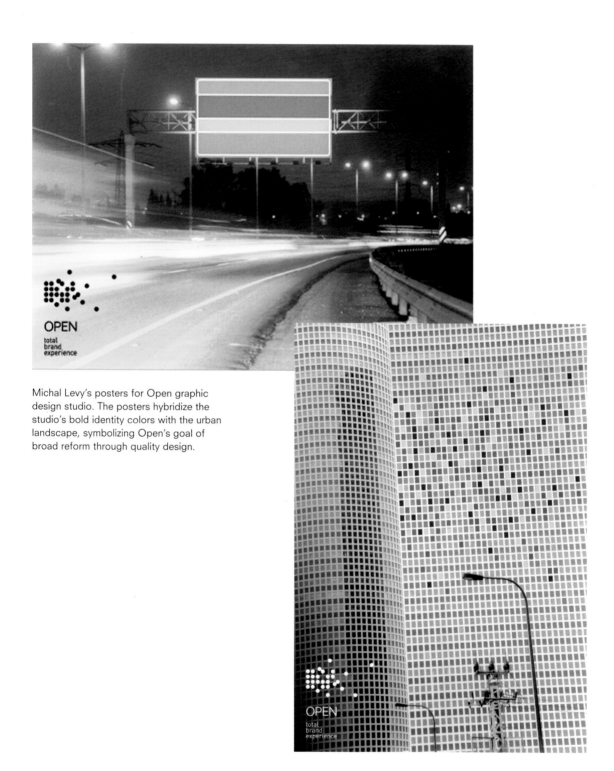

Michal Levy's posters for Open graphic design studio. The posters hybridize the studio's bold identity colors with the urban landscape, symbolizing Open's goal of broad reform through quality design.

SCAMPERR and synectic trigger mechanisms are just tools to get you going. You'll also develop your own methods of integration.

CONCEPTUAL GOALS OF EVALUATION AND INTEGRATION

What are you trying to achieve in the evaluation/integration phase? You are gearing up for a second round of exploratory sketching. You are trying to amass interesting, provocative, and relevant starting points that will lead to even more fruitful sketching explorations. With this goal in mind, the following approaches to evaluation and integration are crucial:

Look for raw potential, not finished perfection. You're not trying to shred these sketches and dismiss them completely. That would produce nothing. You're trying to identify the potentially useful elements, reassemble them, and riff off them. Think forward. Don't evaluate in terms of what works now, but in terms of what might lead somewhere. Several future directions will usually reveal themselves if you are looking from a positive critical perspective.

Look for things that can be combined. The writer of *Ecclesiastes* famously asserts, "There is nothing new under the sun." What is new is finding connections between things that previously had no relationship. Indeed, some cognitive scientists define creativity as nothing more than the process of combining ordinary things in novel and transformative ways.

Allow your results to redefine your understanding of the problem. The problem as stated in the creative brief is simply a best guess, given information known by you and your client at that time. You then try to solve the problem as you understand it. At the same time, your exploratory sketching may unearth aspects of the problem you hadn't thought about before. Don't be afraid to reformulate the problem, to widen the scope of the project, to establish new goals, and to change your perspective on the project. Just make sure your client agrees with your reassessment.

One of the goals of exploratory sketching is simply to better understand the nature of the project. Frequently the problem posed in the creative brief is too narrow and rigorous in its scope and formulation. Or it may be too broad and vague. If you simply seek to solve the problem as stated, you may miss solving the problem that actually exists.

Iterate

Once you have evaluated and integrated your first round of raw sketches, begin a second round of exploratory sketching based on insights you have gained. Once this second round of sketching is complete, begin a second round of evaluation and integration. How many times should you cycle through this process? It depends on what kind of results you are getting. You don't want to stop too soon while good ideas are still surfacing, but you don't want to continue until you've run the project into the ground. Two times through may be enough; five times may be too many.

Leave some time in between iterations to chew the cud. Put the project on the back burner and let it simmer for a while. Give your mind time to make its own connections.

Mix It Up

As methodically as I've described this process, it can actually be very loose, idiosyncratic, and personal. Don't feel obliged to proceed cookbook fashion. Mix up your approach, experiment, and observe the results.

Vary the time of each sketching run. Vary the number of sketching runs per cycle. Vary the number of overall cycles. Try different methods of evaluation and integration. Try launching your sketches from different word combinations. Sketch more abstractly. Sketch more concretely. Alter your drawing surface (scroll, notebook, note cards). Alter your drawing tools (brushes, finger paints, ripped construction paper, photographic elements). Subdivide the overall project and explore different aspects of it in turn. Discover what works for you and stick with it. Or better yet, constantly adapt and improve your approach. The goal is to get to the point where you are consistently able to birth and refine a set of intelligent visual ideas.

Time-Limited Designing

Time-limited designing, a technique developed by Stefan Sagmeister, pushes you to transition from creative brief to polished mock-up in a very limited time, rather than easing into the process gradually. In this sense, it may seem the exact opposite of exploratory sketching. But your goal is not to shortcut the creative process and come up with a finished product quickly. Your goal is to design within extreme constraints in order to generate unique results. If you do your best work at the last minute (or, in this case, 30 minutes to 3 hours), this is a way to simulate the deadline experience without putting your project in actual jeopardy.

For most people, time-limited designing is more like a professional growth exercise than an actual tool for coming up with finished work. But you may discover that your time-limited designs are actually usable. Place your three-hour mock-up alongside one that took you much longer to develop, show both to a design critic you trust, and ask her which is better. If she can't tell the difference (or if she likes the time-limited design better), you may be onto something.

An improvisational boldness and bravura can enter your design when you are faced with strict time limitations. Design becomes less like a problem-solving intellectual exercise and more like a jazz performance. As such, time-limited designing is particularly appropriate for concert posters and CD covers, where the spirit of a performance is visually communicated.

Stefan Sagmeister's famous Cranbrook lecture poster. The letters were carved into his skin by an intern—a vivid way of symbolizing the dark, anxiety-ridden side of the creative process.

Interview: Stefan Sagmeister

In 2000 Stefan Sagmeister took a year off from his professional design practice to experiment, research, and reconsider his reasons for being a graphic designer. During that time he experimented regularly with time-limited designing. I asked Stefan about his approach to this practice.

A few years ago, you did an exercise in which you would design an entire CD cover in three hours. Did you ever revise the designs once your time was up?

On the CD exercise, there were no revisions. The result was a very finished-looking prototype.

Where did you get the idea for designing with time limitations?

I was influenced by the artist Allen Wechsler. He is doing all these wonderful pieces based on limitations. I met him at Yale, where we both gave a workshop, and we got along very well.

Do you still use this time-limited design strategy in your current process?

Yes, I do. I use some form of it on most projects. If I am looking for an idea, I usually give myself a very short time to work on it—say, 30 minutes. This is also to make sure I concentrate. I find it difficult to actually think for hours, but 30 minutes I can manage.

What are you trying to accomplish by limiting your time?

I'm trying to open up a new channel of idea generation.

Are you trying to force visual concepts to the surface? Or are you seeking to design in a way that is more intuitive and less concept-driven?

The latter.

When you design with time limits, have you already interviewed the client? Do you already have a visual concept in your head? Do you already have source elements (photography, typography) on hand?

These are very precise questions about a process that by its very nature is imprecise. I could answer "yes" and "no" to all of these questions because all instances have occurred.

When you're designing with time limits, do you use software or draw in a sketchbook?

In a sketchbook and using prototypes.

Most of your work strikes me as very personal. When you use your own body and handwriting, are you acting as a prop representing every man, or are you representing every creator, or are you just yourself?

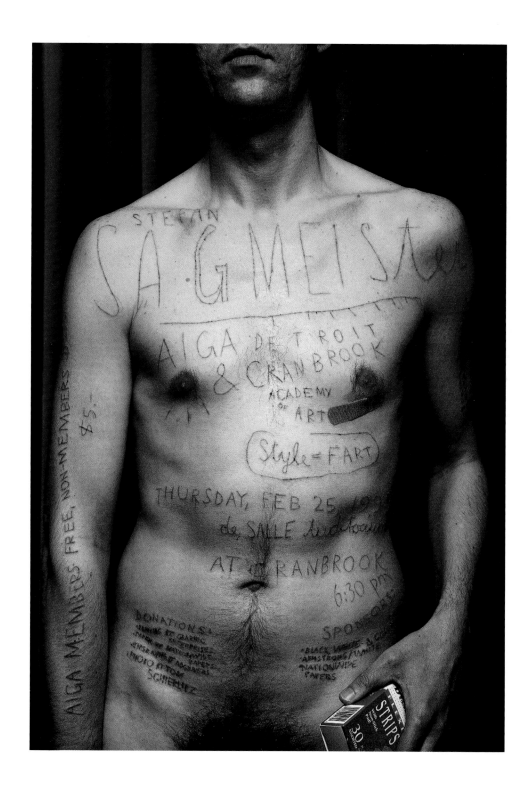

I only use myself when the project—either a talk or an exhibition of our work—wants it. In those instances, my body is just utilized like a product shot. I do think that, with so much cold fluff out there, a more personal strategy is legitimate.

There is a modernist notion of designers as transparent, voiceless engineers—working behind the scenes without injecting their personal "voices" into the mix. For such designers, is time-limited designing still a viable strategy?

Not being such a modernist designer myself, I have no clue, but I assume the strategy would still work. Besides being trendy again, modernism has so many problems right now. Just look at the Parisian suburbs.

Does time-limited designing work for projects other than CD covers?

As a generator of ideas and forms, it works on any project. But then, of course, many projects require very time-consuming postproduction work—securing copyrights, editing—which is one of the main reasons I never offer "speed" as a selling point to our clients.

How long does a client usually give you to complete a CD package?

We take three months, and most often work a good amount of that time. Our complete design time on a cover is between 100 and 400 hours.

If you nailed the majority of the design in three hours, would you feel sheepish about billing your client for the full amount?

I have never sold a three-hour design, but I would not feel badly about it. Paula Scher said she sketched the Citibank logo during the first meeting and had no problems charging them plenty. She says it took her 30 seconds and 30 years to design it.

Scope Plumbing

Scope plumbing is a simple project management strategy that you employ at the very beginning of the development phase. It boils down to an equation: breadth + depth = scope. If you know how wide your project is overall and how deep it is at an average point, then you know its scope. Scope plumbing doesn't really get you "unstuck" as much as it prevents you from getting very stuck further down the road.

First select a representative segment of your project and develop it until it is completely finished and ready for release. Note how much time this takes and what problems you encounter. Next develop your entire project but only at preproduction depth. Note how much time this takes and what problems you encounter. Now you have a fairly accurate assessment of how long the entire development phase will take and what problems you are likely to encounter. This foreknowledge can be a blessing as you proceed to develop the rest of the project.

Scope plumbing varies from medium to medium. Take video production as an example. Let's say you have to produce a 30-second commercial spot. You've storyboarded it, scripted it, booked your locations, and you're ready to start shooting. The general wisdom is to shoot all your footage, then edit it, then add visual effects, then add the soundtrack. Scope plumbing says to first choose a representative 5 seconds of the commercial and take it through the entire production phase.

Full-fledged scope plumbing is not always feasible—say, if you've got a single day to shoot your footage and your location is 400 miles from your studio. But once you have shot all your footage, you can apply a modified version of scope plumbing even with these limitations.

Scope plumbing makes sense for complex projects like corporate identity, book design, and large-scale Web site design. It is less helpful for producing a small run of 50 T-shirts. Yet even then, it's common wisdom to do a single test print, observe the results, and modify your design accordingly before you rush headlong into printing all 50 shirts.

SCOPE PLUMBING BOILS DOWN TO AN EQUATION: BREADTH + DEPTH = SCOPE.

IF YOU KNOW HOW WIDE YOUR PROJECT IS OVERALL AND HOW DEEP IT IS

AT AN AVERAGE POINT, THEN YOU KNOW ITS SCOPE.

Oblique Strategizing

In 1975 musician/producer Brian Eno and painter Peter Schmidt printed a pack of cards called *Oblique Strategies: Over One Hundred Worthwhile Dilemmas.* The word *oblique* literally means "slanting or inclined—neither parallel nor perpendicular nor right-angular." On each card was printed a brief creative strategy developed by Eno or Schmidt. The strategies themselves are oblique, and they suggest ways in which an artist may approach the creative process from a more oblique, less direct perspective. There are several ways to use the cards, but the most common is to work on a project until you get stuck, draw a card, and apply that strategy to your current situation.

History and Purpose of the Cards

In his article "A Primer on Oblique Strategizing," journalist Gregory Taylor describes how Eno and Schmidt developed a set of basic working principles—best practices discovered through creative experience. These strategies were written down in the form of oblique advice. Some were even devised intentionally for testing, to see whether or not they would prove practically useful. In times of pressure or intense concentration, such as expensive studio recording sessions or all-night painting sessions, Eno and Schmidt tended to forget the strategies. The cards became a practical way to keep the strategies in mind.

In a 1980 radio interview, Eno explained, "If you're in a panic, you tend to take the head-on approach because it seems to be the one that's going to yield the best results. Of course, that often isn't the case—it's just the most obvious and *apparently* reliable method. The function of the Oblique Strategies was, initially, to serve as a series of prompts which said, 'Don't forget that you could adopt *this* [alternative] attitude.'"

The cards themselves are a work in progress. At the time of this writing, five editions have been published, each a bit different. The first three editions included a few blank cards so that users could add their own strategies. With each new edition, some cards were added, others removed, and others reworded.

Eno and Schmidt's Oblique Strategy cards are not the only creativity cards in existence. Other sets include the Creative Whack Pack, IDEO Method Cards, the ThinkPak, BOFF-O! (Brain On Fast Forward) Cards, and Free the Genie Cards. While other card sets are meant to generate broadly applicable creative "ideas," the Oblique Strategy cards are unique because they were made by a musician and a painter with their specific audio/visual media in mind. As such, they are more directly applicable to graphic design, which is concerned with matters of visual form and creative composition. The Oblique Strategies are also less generic and more poetically evocative than other card sets in their idiosyncratic specificity.

The fifth edition of Oblique Strategies by Brian Eno and Peter Schmidt. Each card contains a different strategy for overcoming your current creative dilemma.

Using the Cards

The cards come with the following instructions from Eno and Schmidt: "[These cards] can be used as a pack (a set of possibilities being continuously reviewed in the mind) or by drawing a single card from the shuffled pack when a dilemma occurs in a working situation. In this case, the card is trusted even if its appropriateness is quite unclear."

Used in the latter manner, the cards incorporate an element of chance. Oblique strategizing is not about pure chance, however, because you are encouraged to modify the deck with your own strategies, and you are the one who ultimately interprets the meaning of each card and decides how to apply it to the problem at hand. Unlike I Ching, which is much more elaborate, or Tarot cards, which attempt to be oracular, there is no "magic" about oblique strategizing. It's more like prefabricated advice that you can access in the midst of a project and apply as you see fit.

What is the value of oblique strategizing? Edward de Bono's random word exercise provides an instructive analogy. When you start with a random word and relate it to your project, the word itself is not as important as the insight you gain about your project. Likewise each oblique strategy suggests a fresh approach to your current working situation. No matter what card I draw, I can always find some way of applying it to the problem I'm working on. In so doing, I'm forced to think about the problem from a different perspective.

I use the cards to get unstuck. Until I'm stuck, the cards are just so many vague pieces of advice without any practical application. When I'm stuck, I draw a card and apply it. Some people draw three cards at a time and choose the one that seems most applicable. I don't do that because it forces me to waste mental energy comparing and selecting. I'd rather focus all my mental energy on the current dilemma.

The Oblique Strategies are only as useful as your ability to apply them. Appropriate interpretation is the key. The cards are oblique for a reason. They are prompts, not detailed instructions. Don't feel enslaved by them. Simply use them to get unstuck. When you're stuck, sometimes all you need is the confidence to proceed in a direction. Oblique Strategy cards can give you that confidence.

THE OBLIQUE STRATEGIES ARE ONLY AS USEFUL AS YOUR ABILITY TO APPLY THEM. THE CARDS ARE OBLIQUE FOR A REASON. THEY ARE PROMPTS, NOT DETAILED INSTRUCTIONS.

Analyzing the Cards

I divide Eno/Schmidt's Oblique Strategies into four main categories: *formalist* (about structure), *procedural* (about process), *attitudinal* (about your mental outlook), and *contradictory* (about opposite extremes). Here is a sampling of Oblique Strategies subdivided into these four categories.

FORMALIST

- A line has two sides.

- Allow an easement (an easement is the abandonment of a stricture).

- Assemble some of the elements in a group and treat the group.

- Decorate, decorate.

- Define an area as "safe" and use it as an anchor.

- Instead of changing the thing, change the world around it.

- Make a blank valuable by putting it in an exquisite frame.

- Not building a wall but making a brick.

- Take away the important parts.

PROCEDURAL

- Back up a few steps. What else could you have done?

- Change nothing and continue with immaculate consistency.

- Don't avoid what is easy.

- Faced with a choice, do both.

- Go to an extreme, move back to a more comfortable place.

- Make an exhaustive list of everything you might do and do the last thing on the list.

- List the qualities it has. List those you'd like.

- Slow preparation, fast execution.

- What were the branch points in the evolution of this entity?

- Short-circuit (example: a man eating peas with the idea that they will improve his virility shovels them straight into his lap).

ATTITUDINAL

- Question the heroic approach.

- Be less critical more often.

- Disciplined self-indulgence.

- Emphasize the flaws.

- Give the game away.

- Into the impossible.

- Discover your formulas and abandon them.

- Lost in useless territory.

- Honor thy error as a secret intention.

CONTRADICTORY

- Change ambiguities to specifics. / Change specifics to ambiguities.

- Destroy nothing. / Destroy the most important thing.

- Do something boring. / Do something sudden, destructive, and unpredictable.

- How would someone else do it? / How would you have done it?

- Make what's perfect more human. / Mechanize something idiosyncratic.

Not all Oblique Strategies fit into these four categories. For example, one of my favorite strategies demands a category of its own: Call your mother and ask her what to do.

Acquiring the Cards

The first four editions of the Oblique Strategy cards are limited, and you can purchase them occasionally on eBay, usually for prohibitive sums of money. As I write this, the fifth edition of the cards is on sale at www.enoshop.co.uk for a very reasonable price. I highly recommend acquiring a set.

There are also several automated online versions that draw a random card for you at the click of your mouse. These versions are forever coming and going. Search "oblique strategies" on Google or visit Gregory Taylor's definitive Web site on the cards: www.rtqe.net/ObliqueStrategies. Among other things, Taylor's site contains a comprehensive list of the strategies and an admirably obsessive spreadsheet documenting their evolution from edition to edition.

Making Your Own Cards

The Oblique Strategy cards began as a personal creative aid for two artists. The cards were meant to evolve, improve, and adapt to meet the working needs of the artists over time. In that spirit, I invite you to make your own Oblique Strategy cards, tailor-made to your working process. Print them on tiny cards and call them MicrOblique! Print them oversized and call them MacrOblique! The possibilities are endless.

On the next few pages, I give several of my strategies to use as a springboard. Keep your strategies oblique, open to multiple interpretations. Discard those that don't work.

If you really want to get advanced, designate different cards for different phases of the creative process. Try using attitudinal strategies during predesign and formalist strategies during design. Then switch them around and see what happens.

Starter Strategies

These strategies are simply quotations that inspire me to approach creation from useful perspectives. They are from a variety of sources. I begin with quotations by Eno and Schmidt as a kind of homage. Some of the strategies are slogans of the Situationist art movement that were scrawled throughout the streets of Paris during the riots of May 1968.

Oblique Strategy cards are like stored-up nuggets of provocative wisdom from a centered, thoughtful perspective. Then, when you are engrossed in the minutiae of a project and you can't see the forest for the trees, you're able to draw on this wisdom and apply it accordingly. Oblique strategizing is a way of gaining a fresh perspective on your process while still remaining mentally engaged in the nuts and bolts of it.

[It] must accommodate many levels of... attention without enforcing one in particular; it must be as ignorable as it is interesting. (Brian Eno)

In a roomful of shouting people, the one who whispers becomes interesting. (Peter Schmidt)

No replastering, the structure is rotten. (Situationist graffiti)

Chance must be systematically explored. (Situationist graffiti)

Going through the motions kills the emotions. (Situationist graffiti)

Action must not be a reaction, but a creation. (Situationist graffiti)

Exaggeration is the beginning of invention. (Situationist graffiti)

Keep the irregularities inconsistent. (Edward Fella)

If the solution is not beautiful, I know it is wrong. (Buckminster Fuller)

If it works, it's obsolete. (Marshall McLuhan)

The answers are always inside the problem, not outside. (Marshall McLuhan)

Too much control kills anything. (Nicolas Roeg)

Total control can be the death of work. (Andy Goldsworthy)

Just enough is more. (Milton Glaser)

Does [the element] look as if it were *inevitable*, or would the page look as well or better for its omission? (Albert Bruce Rogers)

Beneath the pavement, the beach. (Situationist graffiti)

Frankness instead of persuasion. (Michel Foucault)

Act frankly. (William Henry Channing)

Await occasions. (William Henry Channing)

Smart/dumb: smart and dumb at the same time. (Van Dyke Parks)

Just waves in space. (Tommy Newton)

If the audience can understand every word, then you're singin' it wrong. (Muddy Waters)

I again abandon myself to the feeling, which may prompt me to modify the plan. (Gustav Rodin)

The slow motion moves me / The monologue means nothing to me. (Elliott Smith)

Art does not reproduce the visible; rather, it *makes* visible. (Paul Klee)

Without secrecy, there is no art. (Jan Svankmajer)

Surrealism exists *in* reality, not beside it. (Jan Svankmajer)

Get rid of your ambitions. (Alexei Shulgin)

Don't regard people as idiots [unfit] for creative communication. (Alexei Shulgin)

Even the simplest scribble... is... the bearer of psychic components, and the whole sphere of psychic life lies as if in perspective behind the most insignificant form element. (Hans Prinzhorn)

Darkness and light, strife and love. (James Jones)

All things shining. (James Jones)

Art is not there to be simply understood, or we would have no need of art. (Joseph Beuys)

The reason art exists is because its mode of operation does not take the mode of ideas. (Jean Dubuffet)

Imagine an eye unruled by man-made laws of perspective, an eye unprejudiced by compositional logic, an eye which does not respond to the name of everything. (Stan Brakhage)

My discipline... consists of reducing everything to a few steps. (Paul Klee)

We are far too easily pleased. (C.S. Lewis)

The concrete... may become a vehicle of mystery, beauty, and depth. (Oliver Sacks)

Addition by subtraction. (Karim Rashid)

[Art] is a question of producing our-selves, not things that enslave us. (Guy Debord)

[It] was intrinsic to me that the work show the human being that it had passed through in every conceivable way. (Stan Brakhage)

You might as well see humor as poten-tially revolutionary. (Hakim Bey)

'Tis a poor piece of cloth that can stand no embroidery. (Appalachian saying)

Style = Fart. (Stefan Sagmeister)

Beauty will be *convulsive* or it will not be at all. (André Breton)

Imagination is not a gift, it must be conquered. (André Breton)

Break it, stretch it, bend it, crush it, crack it, fold it. (Bruce Mau)

Graphic design is the spit and polish but not the shoe. (Ellen Lupton)

Think more, design less. (Ellen Lupton)

Talk less and draw more. (Johann Wolfgang von Goethe)

God is in the details. (Ludwig Mies Van Der Rohe)

God is in the concepts. (Curt Cloninger)

Don't Knock It Till You Try It

All of these methods—oblique strategizing, scope plumbing, time-limited designing, and exploratory sketching—take some getting used to. If you try them just once and give up on them, you really haven't given them a fair shot. New processes and tools can be awkward at first, but once you get past the initial learning curve, they can make you more productive and creative.

Don't try to evaluate the effectiveness of these methods in the midst of using them. Instead, commit to a method and let it run its course, then look back and assess its effectiveness. All of these methods will need some fine-tuning and customization before they suit your particular media and working practice.

At the same time, if you decide a method isn't working for you, shelve it. Perhaps you'll encounter a future project for which it is better suited. The more methods you have at your disposal, the more versatile you are, and the more likely you are to arrive at consistently elegant solutions for a variety of design problems.

■ ■ ■

IMMATURE ARTISTS IMITATE.
MATURE ARTISTS STEAL.

—LITERARY CRITIC LIONEL TRILLING, 1962

4 | MINING ART AND DESIGN HISTORY

From art nouveau in the late 1800s through the modernist movements of the early twentieth century up to the Swiss international style of late modernism in the 1950s and '60s, the goal was always to break from the forms of the past and speak in a design language that was new and forward looking. Still, this was always the ideal more than the reality. No matter how innovative and forward-looking some artists may seem, they are never without influences. Picasso was influenced by African art, Van Gogh by Asian art. I'd like to believe that the chaos of Dada had no historical precedent, but even if it was completely out of the blue, every movement since Dada that claims to be completely out of the blue has had its roots, ironically, in Dada.

It is natural for art to draw from the past, and even more so for design, which seeks to be original yet in a familiar way. (Industrial designer Raymond Loewy called this principle MAYA—"most advanced yet acceptable.") So when designers in the '60s and '70s began appropriating and remixing historical art and design influences, they weren't really doing anything new. It just seemed new compared to the forward-looking doctrines of modernism.

Look to Design History

Design historians have put forth all sorts of do's and don'ts regarding the proper way to appropriate historical influences. For me, the bottom line (with very few caveats) is, "Does it work visually? Does it solve the design problem?" My main caveat has to do with residual historical connotations that attach themselves to certain styles. Regardless of its iconic power, you wouldn't want to appropriate the black letter typography and historical realism of a Nazi propaganda poster to promote a church picnic. Yet you might want to reappropriate it to create an antiwar poster that portrays a contemporary politician as a neofascist. Be aware of the historical contexts from which you are drawing.

Another caveat is to avoid "eclectic historicism"—a mix 'n' match, hodge-podge design approach. Yet even a hybrid approach can work if the designer has a keen aesthetic eye and keeps the overall goals of the project in mind. For example, Paula Scher's 1979 "Best of Jazz" poster mixes colors and angular layouts from early-twentieth-century constructivism with Victorian-era woodblock display typefaces. This approach "breaks the rules," but it works because it solves her design problem—how to make a good-looking poster that prominently displays a lot of text in a little space, with no real budget for photography.

When mining visual history for inspiration, you can look to graphic design history itself or beyond graphic design history to more direct, less derivative influences.

New media designer Hillman Curtis suggests that designers should fall in love with a master: Find someone whose work resonates with you and learn all about his history and practice. I concur and also suggest you fall in love with a movement—constructivism, Bauhaus, new typography, art deco, 1950s Polish posters, or whatever—and inundate yourself with it. How is it situated historically? What movements preceded and influenced it? What movements followed and were influenced by it? What movements did it oppose? I particularly love the design and architecture of the Glasgow School.

There are several good histories of graphic design. *Graphic Style: From Victorian to Digital*, by Seymour Chwast and Steven Heller, is a popular one that begins with mid–nineteenth-century Victorian design and continues through the end of the twentieth century. Other design histories begin later, with the Arts & Crafts movement at the end of the nineteenth century, since it is in many ways the spiritual parent of the modern design movement.

Technically, the actual history of "graphic design" proper is relatively young. Book designer William Addison Dwiggins coined the term in 1922. Until then (and for decades following), graphic design was called "commercial art." But what we call graphic design can be traced back through Guttenberg printing to medieval manuscript illumination to Egyptian hieroglyphs. Philip Meggs attempts such a broad survey in his classic *Meggs' History of Graphic Design*. It is a precious resource because it discusses not only forms and methods but also conceptual motivations and historical contexts. And it reaches back well before the Victorian era.

Paula Scher's "Best of Jazz" series poster sets Victorian type in a constructivist style, achieving a memorable result that is both innovative and classic.

Look Beyond Design History

Even Meggs, comprehensive as he is, leaves out all sorts of visual forms of communication not in the direct lineage of graphic design. Outsider art, indigenous art, tribal art, Eastern art, and many movements within the European "fine" art tradition are not mentioned simply because they have no overt bearing on the evolution of graphic design as he perceives it. But you don't need anyone's permission to mine art history directly and make it part of your own design practice.

Design historian Steven Heller tells the story of *Esquire* magazine designer Helmut Krone, who greatly admired the work of legendary American designer Paul Rand. Krone surrounded his workspace with pictures of Rand designs. Louis Danziger, a fellow designer and colleague, advised Krone, "If you want to be as good as Rand, don't look at Rand; look at what Rand looks at." At the time, pictures of Egyptian and Chinese artwork surrounded Danziger's own workspace.

Multitalented designers Charles and Ray Eames amassed an amazing amount of inspirational ephemera during their design careers. The film *901: After 45 Years* documents the packing up of their workspace at 901 Washington Boulevard in Venice, California, after Ray's death in 1988. The space is full of *stuff*—shells, oversized metal letterforms, posters, an extensive antique toy collection, dolls, primitive sculptures, woven baskets, stamps, dried flowers, art from multiple cultures and eras, their own art, art by their friends and colleagues, children's art, dyed Easter eggs, photographs, flags, sketches, ceramic bird candleholders, a full library (not just of design books), a homemade audio toy tower, an eighteenth-century hand-cranked hurdy-gurdy organ, and, of course, the tools of their various trades (from furniture making to filmmaking). The documentary is simultaneously inspirational and humbling.

Go to the source for your inspirations. Choose work that resonates with you. Don't just look to the usual suspects, the same historically respected designers. With everyone reading the same design magazines and surfing the same Web sites, where do you look to find unique inspiration? As ironic as it seems, try your local library. It's amazing how much visual inspiration has been sitting on university library shelves, untouched for years. Paul Klee's Bauhaus Notebooks alone (*The Thinking Eye* and *The Nature of Nature*) have the potential to irrevocably change the way you think about design, form, art, and existence.

WITH EVERYONE READING THE SAME DESIGN MAGAZINES AND SURFING THE SAME WEB SITES, WHERE DO YOU LOOK TO FIND UNIQUE INSPIRATION? AS IRONIC AS IT SEEMS, TRY YOUR LOCAL LIBRARY.

Two Ways to Mine:
Forms and Concepts

There are two basic ways to mine art and design history:

- **Mine visual forms.** Focus on the surface styles and mechanical methods of past art and design.

- **Mine conceptual approaches.** Focus on the conceptual theories, underlying principles, and reasoning of past art and design.

Mine Visual Forms

When mining visual forms, you are most interested in visual solutions that might apply to your current design problem. Ask yourself, "What was the designer trying to accomplish? Why did this solution make sense from his perspective, in his particular historical context? Is there anything about this visual solution that still applies to my current design problem?" Even when mining visual forms, you still need to ask "why" in addition to "what" and "how."

Here are just a few visual forms from the past, with suggestions on how they might be applied usefully in a contemporary context. *Genius Moves*, by Steven Heller and Mirco Ilic, catalogs literally a hundred influential visual tropes, devices, and approaches from twentieth-century graphic design. If this section whets your appetite and makes you want to investigate further, their book is a logical next step. Ultimately you'll want to research your own primary sources and distill them in a way that best suits your particular practice.

SMOTHER THE SPACE

Some mental patients suffer from a psychological affliction called "horror vacui" —fear of empty spaces. There is an entire genre of art brut created by artists suffering from the compulsion to fill every available area of the canvas.

Mental patients are not the only ones who have made it a practice to smother the design space. In the 1500s printers used criblé (dots of black ink) to fill in margins and background space, adding a kind of weight and texture to what would otherwise have been flat black and white compositions. In the mid-1800s, Victorian designers went hog-wild incorporating newly available forms of Islamic ornamentation. Whether the ornamentation had anything to do with the subject of their advertisements was usually beside the point.

Arts & Crafts designer William Morris reacted against such ill-considered uses of ornamentation, but even he was near compulsive in his elaborate vine, thistle, flower, and bird patterns. His page layouts are far from minimal. Morris wasn't opposed to ornamentation—just to its tacky misapplication. Modernism attempted to banish ornamentation, but it resurfaced in the psychedelic, neonouveau poster art of the 1960s.

If you typically shy away from ornamentation and tend toward minimalism, try filling your entire design space. If it gets too cluttered, you can always back up. But you'll never know what kind of visual interest and texture can be achieved from this extreme approach if you never experiment with it.

YOU WOULDN'T WANT TO APPROPRIATE THE BLACK LETTER TYPOGRAPHY AND

HISTORICAL REALISM OF A NAZI PROPAGANDA POSTER TO PROMOTE A CHURCH PICNIC.

BE AWARE OF THE HISTORICAL CONTEXTS FROM WHICH YOU ARE DRAWING.

This page from William Morris's *The Works of Geoffrey Chaucer* abounds with rich ornamentation, harmonized into a baroque visual tapestry of line, tone, and form.

Web designers are constantly challenged by how to kill "extra" space on oversized monitors. Tiling Web backgrounds that appear behind the main content are one solution. Just make sure the tiling patterns are in visual continuity with the rest of your design.

"FRACTAL DESIGN"

A variation on smothering the space is what I call "fractal design." The more you zoom in on a fractal, the more its outer structure is repeated within its inner structure, creating symmetry between the macroscopic and the microscopic. The *tughra* of Sultan Sulaiman the Magnificent of the Ottoman dynasty is an excellent example of this kind of design. A *tughra* is like a signature or seal, unique to each sultan. The more ornate the *tughra*, the less likely it is to be counterfeited. The closer you look at Sulaiman's *tughra*, the more detail is revealed. The microscopic design reiterates motifs established in the macroscopic design.

Including extra detail at the microscopic level is most likely a stupid idea for an outdoor billboard, but not a bad idea for a CD or book cover because its owners will look at it frequently and discover its hidden details over time.

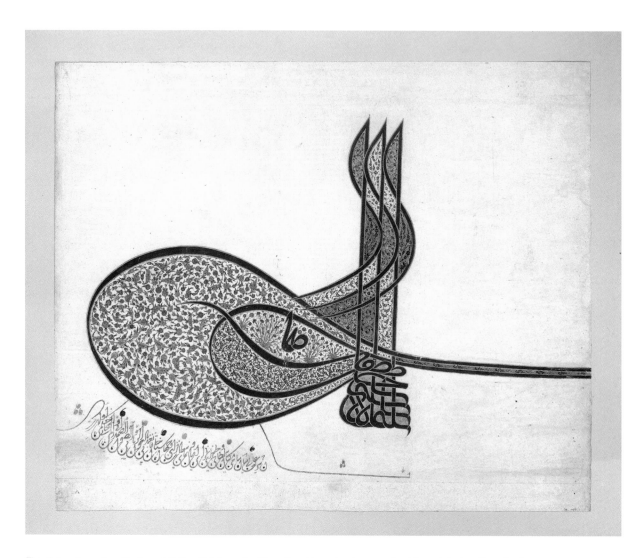

The sixteenth century *Tughra of Sultan Sulaiman the Magnificent* is a classic example of fractal design. Zooming in on the piece reveals microcosmic details that are in conscious dialogue with larger, macrocosmic patterns.

THE BLACK SPOT

The opposite of smothering the space is having a single, striking image floating in a world of negative space. Proto–art nouveau illustrator Aubrey Beardsley was known for "the black spot." His black-and-white illustrations portray the main figure as a heavy, solid black form, with the rest of the composition populated by thinner black lines and negative space.

Japanese *Ukiyo-e* art is similar in this respect, using a single dominant form and leaving a lot of negative space to balance it. (*Ukiyo-e* literally means "pictures of the floating world.") This approach has a number of advantages—it draws attention to the object you are silhouetting and creates interesting, organic, nongridded negative space in your composition.

Aubrey Beardsley's *Moska* contains a striking "black spot" figure surrounded by negative space. The figure immediately commands our attention.

THE ICON

Illustrators have long boiled down complex subjects to their iconic essences. The Lascaux cave paintings in southern France are an early example. Iconic illustration is a kind of reductionist shorthand, giving the maximum impact with the minimum line. Iconic illustration coupled with a "black spot" compositional approach can be particularly effective.

A master of the icon was art deco illustrator A. M. Cassandre. He didn't merely abstract his stylized subjects; he abstracted them in a way that made them seem epic. Cassandre transformed ships, trains, and buildings into strong geometric symbols of progress and luxury.

Designer Saul Bass was another master of the icon. His figures were even more abstract than Cassandre's, often represented by minimal forms created from torn paper. Bass was also an extraordinary logo designer, and he applied the principles of logo design (reduction, distinction, encapsulated essence) to his posters and animated movie titles.

Iconic design is particularly suited to poster and billboard design, where you have only a short amount of time to catch someone's eye and convey your message.

Saul Bass's movie poster for *The Man with the Golden Arm* frames a single, powerful icon of a grasping, crooked arm, which succinctly encapsulates the theme of this film about heroin addiction.

The Designers Republic album cover for the band Pop Will Eat Itself and Paula Scher's poster honoring the centenary of Henri de Toulouse-Lautrec's death both use type to create figurative forms. The former evokes an '80s futurism and the latter a Moulin Rouge nostalgia, but both owe a debt to Dada's playful reappropriation of letterforms.

TYPE AS FIGURE

The Dadaists and futurists both used type as form—not necessarily to write words but to make actual figures. They used the available tools of the trade (type, dingbats, and metal leading) in unorthodox and playful ways. More recently The Designers Republic and Paula Scher have both used typography to actually create figurative images.

Nouveau Salon des cent-exposition internationale d'affiches hommage à Toulouse Lautrec

TOULOUSE—SCHER 2001

The noble sculptural figures of Chartres Cathedral are given a sense of grandeur and otherworldly weightlessness by their strange elongation.

ANTI-FIGURE

Islamic society largely forbade drawing animal and human figures, so Islamic art developed an intense emphasis on abstract ornamentation. Arabic typography itself often doubles as abstract ornament. What if in your own work you were unable to use photography and illustration to represent figurative forms? What novel solutions might you be forced to pioneer simply by using typography and abstract ornamentation?

The Arts & Crafts designers of Doves Press took this antifigurative approach one step further—designing without even ornament, using only typography. Their designs relied entirely on letterform, typographic texture, and proportional balance between text area and margin. Try limiting yourself to a single typeface alone and see if you can still achieve visual interest in your design.

ELONGATED HUMAN FIGURES

On the portal of Chartres Cathedral stand what are known as the kings and queens—noble human forms given an unearthly sense of grandeur by their strange elongation. Romanesque manuscript illustrators used to stretch their human forms in order to fit their page design. At the end of the nineteenth century, the four designers of the Glasgow School incorporated abstract, elongated figures into their poster designs. And recently, director Tim Burton's animated characters in *The Nightmare Before Christmas* and *Corpse Bride* are given an ethereal, macabre essence by their elongation.

Don't feel constrained by the laws of gravity and the human physique. I'm not suggesting the creation of grotesque abominations, but this is graphic design, not science class. The figures are yours to reinterpret as you see fit.

Mining Conceptual Approaches

When mining conceptual approaches, you are more interested in the underlying principles that led to the production of a work than to its surface appearance. Conceptual approaches are much more versatile than visual forms. Oftentimes you can take a conceptual approach and reapply it to achieve a number of different stylistic outcomes. Mining conceptual approaches is a way to proceed "in the spirit" of an era without reappropriating its exact visual vocabulary.

WHAT IF YOU WERE UNABLE TO USE PHOTOGRAPHY AND ILLUSTRATION TO REPRESENT FIGURATIVE FORMS? WHAT NOVEL SOLUTIONS MIGHT YOU BE FORCED TO PIONEER SIMPLY BY USING TYPOGRAPHY AND ABSTRACT ORNAMENTATION?

Here are just a few conceptual approaches from the past, with suggestions for how to apply them in a contemporary context. Again, do your own research and unearth concepts that complement and enhance your personal design.

HYPERTROPHY

"Hypertrophy" is the term for oversized growth of a body organ or muscle. (Think weight lifters on steroids.) In media theory, the term refers to the practice of pushing a medium beyond its ability to cope sensibly. Cubists pushed two-dimensional painting into a state of hypertrophy by trying to represent multiple perspectives in a single picture plane. Futurists pushed painting into a state of hypertrophy by attempting to represent motion in static 2D space. Graphic designers inspired by deconstruction tried to push print design into hypertrophy by introducing multiple layers of meaning into a single composition.

Try to make your medium express qualities it is not meant to express. Use typography to convey the nuances of the spoken word via expressive letterform, rhythm, size, weight, and color. Try to get the flat picture plane to express dimensionality without resorting to Renaissance perspective. By pushing your medium beyond its ability to function comfortably, you enter a more expressive realm of visual communication.

Marcel Duchamp's *Nude Descending a Staircase, No. 3* and Katherine McCoy's Cranbrook Graduate Design poster both employ different forms of hypertrophy. Duchamp pushes the frozen canvas to display time-based movement and McCoy pushes the flat picture plane to display multiple layers of meaning.

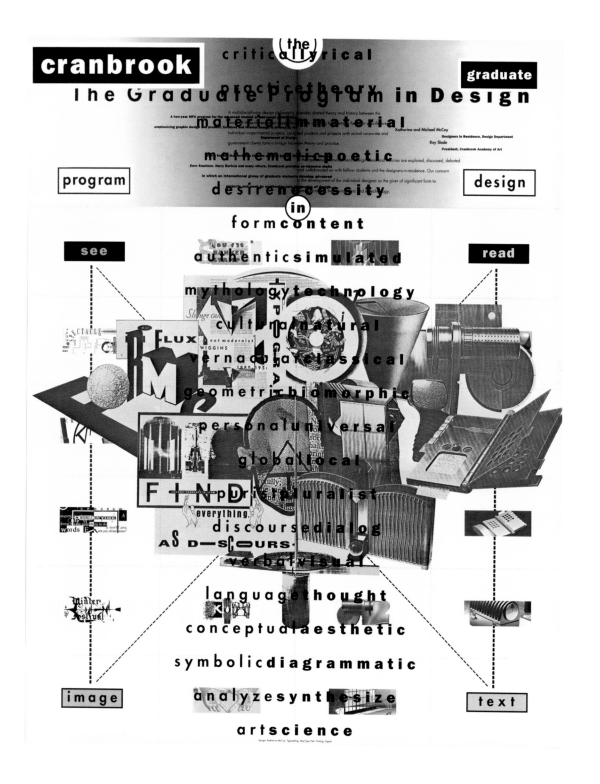

MNEMONIC DESIGN

Mnemonic design is simply design used in the service of memorization or orientation. Celtic monks incorporated mnemonic design in their illumination of the *Book of Kells*, a manuscript of the Four Gospels. There are over 2,100 unique capital letterforms in the manuscript. Scholars believe that the unique design of these letters served as a kind of way-finding device. The *Book of Kells* was penned hundreds of years before the Bible was divided into chapter and verse, and its readers needed to easily locate specific passages. Each letterform was drawn in a way that related to the section of the gospels it introduced. The monks could scan through the manuscript and find the passages they were looking for by recognizing these unique capital letterforms.

Today mnemonic design is frequently used as a way-finding device in magazines and on Web sites. This makes it possible to maintain design continuity throughout the magazine or site while allowing each section to have visual characteristics that are specific to its contents.

PUNK D.I.Y. / READYMADE DESIGN

German designer Kurt Schwitters developed his own personal flavor of Dada that he named *merz*. He would collect garbage and use it to create design collages. In the 1970s punk designers applied this same readymade, found-object approach to their poster designs, album covers, clothing, and yes, even personal hygiene (such as self-piercings with safety pins). The resultant visual style accurately represented the immediacy and anarchy of punk.

But not all do-it-yourself approaches result in the same grungy style. What if your found objects are bold Helvetica, flat computer-screen colors, and tiling backgrounds? Contemporary Dutch designer Mieke Gerritzen incorporates such elements to arrive at a kind of neopunk style for the Power Point era. Ultimately, the spirit of punk is less about distressed typefaces and more about a cut-and-paste conceptual approach toward materials and production.

Instead of collecting physical ephemera like Schwitters, why not collect and collage Internet ephemera—badly enlarged and overly compressed JPEGs; chunky, bit-rotted GIFs? There is plenty of readymade digital garbage out there just waiting to be collaged and recontextualized.

TRUTH TO MATERIALS

Reacting against the shoddy, mechanically produced goods of the Victorian era, Arts & Crafts designer William Morris advocated a return to hand-craftsmanship and "truth to materials." If furniture was meant to *appear* hand-made, it should actually *be* hand-made. The influential architect and designer Henri van de Velde took this ethic and applied it to manufactured goods. Van de Velde argued that machine-made objects could still be true to their materials, as long as the objects intentionally reveal their manufactured nature. If an object is plastic, it should look plastic instead of being made to look marble or wooden. If a chair is bolted together,

Mieke Gerritzen's brochure for the Fourth International Browserday uses bold sans-serif type, basic black-and-white contrasts, and off-the-shelf icons to achieve a kind of anti-designed information overload. Although Gerritzen doesn't use torn paper or Xeroxed photographs, her readymade approach is conceptually punk.

let the bolts show and make them part of the design. "Truth to materials" became a foundational tenet of modern design.

Later, deconstruction critiqued modernism, yet even it adhered to its own strange version of "truth to materials." Deconstruction sought to dismantle the finished product (text, art object, architecture, design) in order to lay bare the way in which it was constructed. As graphic designer Edward Fella observes, "Deconstruction is a way of exposing the glue that holds together Western culture." Exposed bolts or exposed glue, both modernism and deconstruction were interested in the role that source materials play in the final design. Modernism sought to construct things "truthfully"; deconstruction sought to deconstruct things in order to reveal the absence of "truth."

But what happens when your "material" is primarily digital, or simply a laser-printed piece of paper? How do you stay "true" to virtual, immaterial materials? In such cases, the creative process itself becomes your material. Contemporary designer Stefan Sagmeister says, "I always try to go in a direction where the final piece will incorporate the process visibly." His hand, his process, and his thinking are frequently evident in his final design.

Digital tools are so good at eradicating imperfections that they can result in immaculately slick work that starts to feels false. Like the Wizard of Oz, our challenge as designers is to come out from behind our digital curtain and allow the seams of our process to show.

CONTROLLED IMPROVISATION

There is much to be said for allowing at least a modicum of improvisation into your design process. Lithographers Henri de Toulouse-Lautrec and Louis Prang both drew their illustrations directly onto their final lithographic plates without any presketching. William Morris was known for his fastidiousness and craftsmanship, yet even he incorporated an improvisational hand during his execution phase. He still did preliminary sketches of his page layouts, but he drew his final pages freehand, without copying or tracing. He claimed it made the final work more vigorous and less mechanical. Allow space in your process for the idiosyncrasies of the human hand to surface, particularly in a digital environment.

TOTAL DESIGN

Design historian Philip Meggs said of the great early modern designer El Lissitzky, "[He] did not decorate the book—he constructed the book by visually programming the total object." Contemporary designer Clement Mok suggests a similar approach regarding information architecture and corporate identity. Graphic designers today are often seen as cake

WHAT HAPPENS WHEN YOUR "MATERIAL" IS PRIMARILY DIGITAL, OR SIMPLY A LASER-PRINTED

PIECE OF PAPER? HOW DO YOU STAY "TRUE" TO VIRTUAL, IMMATERIAL MATERIALS?

Stefan Sagmeister's 1997 AIGA New Orleans poster intentionally reveals the intuitive process that created it. Sagmeister forgot to include the design credits in the original layout, so he simply wrote the credits on a yellow sticky note and stuck them to the poster.

Know Why and Internalize

decorators, called in at the last minute to add some finishing, cosmetic touches to a cake that has already been baked by the client. Yet design has historically meant much more than this. The great teachers of the Bauhaus were also architects, painters, furniture designers, interior designers, city planners, and social visionaries. As a designer, the more you can be involved in the entire creative process (from product development through packaging and marketing), the better the overall design will be. This is particularly evident with Web design, where the cake decorators have literally become the "information architects." Quality graphic design is always more than a visual cherry on top.

When distilling influences from the past, you need to know why you are doing what you are doing. Be at least somewhat conversant with graphic design history. Otherwise, things can get strange. For example, 1980s "postmodern" designers revived art deco to connote the elegance of the 1930s. But what happens if I make something neo–art deco in 2006? Does it still connote the 1930s, or does it now connote the 1980s? If the latter, then *yikes!* I could be striving for the elegance of the Empire State Building and accidentally wind up invoking the spirit of Duran Duran.

Here is another dilemma: According to modernists, modernism is supposed to be a universal, eternal approach rather than an era-bound visual style. Can you reappropriate modernism as a visual style simply to connote the era of modernism? Can you design a Müller-Brockmann-esque poster solely to connote the Swiss grid era without coming across as an earnest disciple of contemporary modernism?

Like telling a joke, it's all in the tone of your delivery. There is a deft way to handle design allusions and a ham-fisted way to handle them, so know why you are doing what you are doing. Are you borrowing a recognizable style in order to intentionally connote an era? Are you borrowing a visual form without any intention of

THE ULTIMATE GOAL OF ALL THIS INFLUENCE MINING IS TO INTERNALIZE YOUR

INFLUENCES AND MAKE THEM A PART OF WHO YOU ARE AS A DESIGNER.

connoting an era? Are you borrowing a conceptual approach, a general philosophy, an ethic, or a process?

You will likely combine old visual forms with new conceptual approaches and old conceptual approaches with new visual forms. Such is the nature of influence. The ultimate goal of all this influence mining is to internalize your influences and make them a part of who you are as a designer. Internalization is like baking a cake. You can throw all the ingredients together, but until you bake them, it's not really a cake.

If you find yourself modifying arbitrary aspects of your design to avoid being accused of plagiarizing your influences, then you haven't internalized them well enough. Copying confines; influence liberates. Someone once said, "Creativity is forgetting your sources." I forget exactly who.

I do remember that designer Milton Glaser said this: "Every generation has to make its own discoveries, even if they are old discoveries." In this chapter, I've mined a few conceptual approaches and visual forms to get you started. Continue your own research. Mine your own forms and concepts. Make your own old discoveries and internalize them into something new.

■ ■ ■

UP AMONG THE FIRS WHERE
IT SMELLS SO SWEET

OR DOWN IN THE VALLEY
WHERE THE RIVER USED TO BE

I GOT MY MIND ON ETERNITY

SOME KIND OF ECSTASY
GOT A HOLD ON ME

—SONGWRITER BRUCE COCKBURN

5 | VARYING DEGREES OF DERIVATION

One of my goals as a creative person is to balance my input and output. If I never output any original media, then I'm merely a consumer. But if all I do is work, without taking time to receive inspirational input, then eventually my output begins to go stale and dry up. So I read books, look at artwork, watch movies, go hiking, have conversations with friends and family, and generally live my life.

The truth is this: Unless you live quarantined in a white room, you are perpetually exposed to input—whether from graffiti on a subway or Picasso in a gallery. The challenge is to control the nature of your input. If you live in a city, most of your input is derivative. By *derivative*, I mean you're not directly observing nature. You are generally observing man-made stuff once or twice removed from the source inspiration of nature. You look at buildings made by humans, navigate city streets laid out by humans, and experience a variety of media created by humans.

There's nothing wrong with this, but if your creative output begins to stagnate, one way you can remedy it is by modifying the nature of your input. You can either turn the man-made input up and get oversaturated in the derivative, or you can turn the man-made input down and expose yourself to nature. Neither solution is ideal. Overexposure to nature can lead to the same kind of stagnation as over-exposure to man-made things. I recommend alternating back and forth between these two extremes, with extended periods of "normal" living in between. By varying your input, your output is more likely to avoid stagnation and complacency.

YOU'D BETTER GET CONTROL OF YOUR OWN MEDIA INPUT OR IT WILL GET CONTROL OF YOU. OF ALL PEOPLE, MARKETERS AND GRAPHIC DESIGNERS SHOULD UNDERSTAND THIS PRINCIPLE.

Be Less Derivative

Unless you live in a very rural environment, being less derivative may be a challenge. It's a two-step process. First, turn down the amount of man-made media you receive. Second, seek more pure, immediate, natural sources of input and inspiration. How long should you keep this up? As long as it continues to benefit your output (or until you go crazy). Every city has its own semi-natural enclave and some sort of natural setting outside it. Take advantage of these resources.

Turn Down Man-Made Media

Cartoonist and marketing consultant Hugh Macleod suggests, "Don't try to stand out from the crowd. Avoid crowds altogether." Graphic design can be a trendy, ephemeral, fickle profession. Graphic designers feel they need to keep up with latest trends in the industry or they may find themselves out-of-date and irrelevant. A host of design magazines, publishing companies, and Web sites thrive on this fear of being out of the loop. But if you spend all your time immersed in graphic design journals, you may be tracking the scene so closely that you can't see the forest for the trees. Stop keeping up with the Joneses (or Frere-Joneses) and drop out of the race for a while.

It's like this story: A pilgrim visits a guru hermit living on a remote mountain. The pilgrim asks, "Doesn't it bother you living out here all by yourself and not knowing what's going on in the world?" The guru answers,

"I'm not missing out. I know there are wars, earthquakes, floods, political corruption, greed, and intrigue." And of course he's right. Dig up a three-year-old issue of *Print*, *I.D.*, *HOW*, *Communication Arts*, or *Eye* and see if the articles are really that much different from last month's. Granted, ten-year-old issues will be different. But do we really need to track contemporary graphic design as closely as we do? Stop reading graphic design magazines for a few months. Your design may actually improve.

Go one step further and remove as much man-made media from your life as possible. Turn off the television and leave it off for weeks. Stop reading newspapers. Turn off all audio. Stop renting movies. Get offline and stay offline for a while. Get out of the city.

Media theorist Marshall McLuhan observed that media fundamentally shift our sense ratios. Prior to the invention of the printing press, humans experienced the world in a deeply different way than we do living in the television age. We can't alter the sense ratios of our entire culture. There is no way we can turn back the clock and return to a world prior to television or the Internet. But we can at least turn off these media in our personal lives for a season and experience a fundamental (albeit temporary) shift in the way our senses balance input. Such a shift in our sense ratios is bound to affect the design we output.

Turn Up Nature

Don't just turn down derivative influences; simultaneously turn up natural influences. Surround yourself with natural objects (shells, leaves, flowers) and sketch them daily. Beyond this, get outside and walk around in the woods.

It should go without saying, but don't bring your cell phone or your MP3 player with you. If you can help it, don't even bring your watch. If you're the "I came, I saw, I conquered" type, don't bring your camera. You're not on a reconnaissance mission to collect piecemeal data samples from nature and bring them back to the design lab. The idea is to immerse yourself in nature and let it change you in a more holistic way.

CHEW THE CUD

One of the advantages of getting outside is that it forces you to stop working and contemplate. If I'm in my office and I have an idea, I can implement it immediately. But ideas often improve when they are allowed to stew for a while. We augment our limited human memory with memory media—sketchbooks and computers. These memory extensions are useful but sometimes counterproductive. Leaving an idea in your mind for a while instead of immediately dumping it forces you to turn the idea over, like a cow chewing cud. The idea improves as you

STOP READING GRAPHIC DESIGN MAGAZINES FOR A FEW MONTHS.

YOUR DESIGN MAY ACTUALLY IMPROVE.

digest it. Go on a walk or a run without your pocket notebook or PDA and chew the mental cud for a while.

Running, in particular, helps me think. My body is engaged and occupied, leaving my mind free and alert. Engineers Robert McKim and James Adams call this state "relaxed attention." I put a problem in my mind prior to my run, and when I come back 30 minutes later, I understand it better. I don't propose to solve the problem, but usually about halfway through the run, clarity and insight begin to dawn.

View from the Hangover in Slickrock Wilderness outside of Robbinsville, North Carolina, with storm coming on. Where I go to get the big picture.

GET THE BIG PICTURE

Painter Paul Klee said, "An artist cannot do without his dialogue with nature, for he is a man, himself of nature, a piece of nature and within the space of nature." At least twice every summer, I go into the woods by myself for a week at a time. It usually takes two or three days for my own internal voices to quiet down. The rest of the time I spend absorbing a proper, realistic perspective of just how big the world is and just how small I am. For me, a pervasive awareness of the creator God is unavoidable.

However long you are able to spend in the woods and whatever else you come away with, always leave yourself open to get the big picture. Effective communication (visual or otherwise) begins with knowing where you are in relation to your audience. If all you bring back with you is a refreshed perspective of your place in the universe, your design work will be more humane and empathetic as a result.

CONSIDER SCALE

Design is based on human scale. Typefaces are based on the writing motion of the human hand. Balance and proportion are based on the symmetry and scale of the human body. Any real understanding of scale necessarily begins from the starting point of the human body. An intuitive sense of scale and proportion are hard to come by in virtual computer space. Sitting in an ergonomically engineered chair in front of a computer monitor all day doesn't really help. Driving in a car and riding a subway are also poor substitutes for human-powered walking and running.

Exercise gets you in touch with the scale of your body in relation to itself and the world. Exercising in nature increases your intuitive sense of scale. You're not comparing your own frame to derivative, man-made architecture. You're comparing your own frame to trees and hills and roots and sky in a natural environment.

While in nature, keep your eyes open for macro-/microconnections. For instance, you might notice that certain leaves are shaped like the trees on which they grow. The connections you make don't have to be scientifically verifiable. They can be subjective and intuitive.

Hang out with your kids (or your brother's kids, or your friend's kids). Take them on a hike or to the park and let them set the pace. Children are great windows into the microcosmic. Get down on your knees and look at what they see. Every leaf and rock has its own unique character and individual worth. Nothing is taken for granted. Throwing rocks and leaves

EXERCISE GETS YOU IN TOUCH WITH THE SCALE OF YOUR BODY IN RELATION TO ITSELF AND THE WORLD. EXERCISING IN NATURE INCREASES YOUR INTUITIVE SENSE OF SCALE.

into the creek with my four-year-old son can turn into a four-hour outing. Touch stuff. Smell stuff. Heck, eat stuff if you're sure it's edible. Connect with the natural world in an immediate, visceral, unmediated way. Get a sense of how your body fits into the world in terms of scale.

REGAIN WONDER

Environmental sculptor Andy Goldsworthy works outdoors with found natural materials such as stone, wood, leaves, and ice to make ephemeral structures of amazing delicacy and balance. He describes the difference between working in the cubicles at his art college and working outside on the beach: "What struck me was that sense of energy when you were outside of the art college. It was very secure in the art college. As soon as you made something outside, there was this almost breathlessness and uncertainty."

Exposure to nature can restore a lost sense of wonder. The physical world in which we live is truly wonderful. That we have senses that allow us to experience the world is wonderful. That we have consciousness that allows us to reflect on our experience is wonderful. That we even exist at all is profoundly wonderful.

Children are right to be amazed at every turn. British author G. K. Chesterton observed, "When we are very young children we do not need fairy tales: we only need tales. Mere life is interesting enough. A child of seven is excited by being told that Tommy opened a door and saw a dragon. But a child of three is excited by being told that Tommy opened a door... [Fairy] tales say that apples were golden only to refresh the forgotten moment when we found that they were green. They make rivers run with wine only to make us remember, for one wild moment, that they run with water."

Amazement isn't just for children and artists. Albert Einstein himself was a great disciple of wonder. He said, "The most beautiful experience we can have is the mysterious. It is the fundamental emotion that stands at the cradle of true art and true science. Whoever does not know it can no longer wonder, no longer marvel, is as good as dead, and his eyes are dimmed." As designers, it's easy to get jaded and lose our ability to wonder and be amazed, but we wouldn't have gotten into graphic design were there not some spark of wonder, amazement, and desire resident in us. Nature can rekindle that spark because it is not subject to our man-made design. Despite our best efforts to tame it, nature still remains wonderfully beyond us.

Be Hyper-Derivative

But what about poison ivy and giant spiders? What if you absolutely hate the woods? Never fear. There is another tactic to intentionally disrupt your input patterns. Instead of turning off the man-made media input, turn it up and kick it into overdrive. Become hyper-derivative. If you live in rural areas, this may be a challenge, but even the most remote areas usually have access to myriad forms of mind-numbing, man-made media. Still, for the full experience, you may want to brave your nearest big city.

First, inundate yourself with graphic design influences. Surf the heck out of graphic design sites. Look at every link to every newly designed site. Check out design books from the library. Go to your local newsstand and read every magazine about visual culture you can find. Heck, read magazines about rock music, hip-hop, skateboarding, and professional wrestling as well.

Rent and watch at least two movies per night—from underground cult classics to Hollywood blockbusters. See movies at the theater. Crank up the audio 24/7. In your car, while you work, in your sleep—never be without music (except when you are watching television, which you should do as much as possible). MTV—yes, of course—but also the Style Network, HGTV, Animal Planet, and large quantities of the Home Shopping Network.

Play video games as much as possible. Regularly eat at the mall. And so you don't deny yourself the finer things in life, make sure you visit three art galleries or museums per week. In the evenings, go to clubs and listen to live music (preferably with multimedia light shows).

Carry a camera with you at all times—a small one that fits easily into your pocket. Don't sweat the resolution or the image quality. Snap pictures like Dustin Hoffman's character, Raymond Babbitt, in *Rainman*. Don't even frame or focus. You are striving for an anti–big picture, anti–direct experience approach. Use the mediating technology of your camera to intentionally inject an extra layer of derivation between you and your immediate environment. Walk around looking for pictures and textures of anything. Hunt and gather.

The more you inundate yourself with man-made media, the more you begin to notice the seams and cracks in the surface of the city. Posters peel away, building facades crumble, local newscasters stutter, pipes rust. Derive inspiration not just from the sanctioned public face of the city but from its dark underbelly. Don't just read the official narrative of PR people and politicians; bone up on the subtext that the city writes about itself.

If I've just described your average week, then you really should unplug and get away for a while. Otherwise, go for it. You can't live in this hyper-derivative state forever. Just do what it takes to disrupt your regular input in order to tweak your creative output. While you are glutting yourself on all this media, keep your eyes open for patterns and connections that emerge. Look for influences that you can use in your design. Carry a notebook with you and write down absolutely everything. You can sort it out later when you come up for air.

From media professor Marshall Soules's *Urban Wallpaper* project. The accidental story that the city tells about itself is often more inspirational than the official story from the tourist guidebook.

(Hypothetical) Frequently Asked Questions

How can you advise me to be simultaneously more derivative and less derivative?

I'm not advising you to be both at the same time. I'm advising you to occasionally alternate between these two extremes, while mostly living life as you normally do. Occasional disruption of your media input is the goal because the same old stuff *in* can lead to the same old stuff *out*.

Why don't you suggest which woods to visit or which television shows to watch or which music to listen to?

Because it's not the specific content of the input that's important; it's the *kind* of input—natural or man-made—and the amount (a lot).

Why not alter other areas of life like sleep, diet, or exercise?

Because designers output media, and altering media input seems most directly related to altering media output. But feel free to get plenty of sleep, exercise regularly, and eat a balanced diet. Or not.

Isn't it a bit extreme to alter your entire life just to improve your design?

Not at all. A master designer does whatever it takes to improve her craft. If temporarily modifying certain aspects of your life makes you more creative, and you are in a creative profession, then what's to consider? An athlete will modify her diet and exercise to prepare for a competition. An actor will modify his entire appearance to play a role. It's what professionals do.

Aren't we all victims of our contemporary culture? Can anyone really control her our own media input?

Billy Joel sings, "I got remote control and a color TV / I don't change channels so they must change me." You'd better get control of your own media input or it will get control of you. Of all people, marketers and graphic designers should understand this principle.

So if you're feeling creatively stagnant, or you just want to maintain your creative edge, try varying degrees of derivation. It may take some getting used to—if you ever get used to it. But the results will be worth it.

■ ■ ■

YOU CAN'T GET WHAT
YOU WANT

TILL YOU KNOW WHAT
YOU WANT

—SONGWRITER JOE JACKSON

6 | HOW I STOPPED WORRYING AND LEARNED TO LOVE THE EDIT

In the movie *Dirty Rotten Scoundrels*, elegant con man Lawrence Jamieson (played by Michael Caine) describes how he got into the business of swindling rich, corruptible women out of their money: "As a younger man, I was a sculptor, a painter, and a musician. There was just one problem: I wasn't very good…. I finally came to the frustrating conclusion that I had taste and style but not talent…. Fortunately I discovered that taste and style were commodities that people desired." Mr. Jamieson might also have made a successful interior designer or, dare I say it, a fine art director.

I'm not saying that graphic designers lack talent or don't need it. I'm saying that much of graphic design is simply having "good taste." Knowing when something works and when it doesn't is half the battle. This is why art directors who know what they want but don't do a lot of hands-on design work still make more money than junior designers who spend all day doing hands-on design work but don't really know what they want.

This situation used to bother me because I thought there was something inherently noble about making work from scratch and something inherently ignoble about editing, remixing, focusing, directing, channeling, collaging, and otherwise assembling elements you didn't make from scratch. It didn't seem right that a designer could take stock photography, stock typefaces, a grid template, and someone else's preselected pantone color scheme, assemble them in a certain way, and still be credited with having created something. Then I had the revelation that there is no "scratch," and it changed my whole approach to design.

I USED TO THINK THERE WAS SOMETHING INHERENTLY NOBLE ABOUT MAKING WORK FROM SCRATCH. THEN I HAD THE REVELATION THAT THERE IS NO "SCRATCH," AND IT CHANGED MY WHOLE APPROACH TO DESIGN.

Debunking the Myth of "Scratch"

The truth is, no human ever created anything from scratch. "In the beginning, God created the heavens and the earth," Genesis tells us—and we've been remixing His work ever since. As an undergraduate, I took a class in "painting materials and techniques." It was actually a lot like cooking. We mixed our own paints from beautifully colored pigmentary powders, but we didn't actually "make" the powders. Mounds of these colorful powders were already waiting for us in the studio at the beginning of the semester. They looked like they must have come from roots, or berries, or clay, or some extremely primal source. I imagined our professor trekking across the globe collecting rare berries, grinding them up, and making all these brightly colored powders. Of course, he just ordered them from an art supply catalog.

Now this begs the question: Were our paintings that semester more "creative" because we mixed our own paints? Would our paintings have been even more "creative" had we found the berries and crushed them ourselves?

However close to or removed from "scratch" an artist chooses to work is entirely a matter of personal preference. A painter paints with brushes. A Web designer paints with Photoshop and Flash. A conceptual artist "paints" with interns and apprentices. An art director may "paint" with junior designers. Note that making one's own paintbrush does not necessarily make one a good painter, any more than hiring a third-party construction company to implement one's architectural blueprints makes one a bad architect.

The trick is to find a balance that leads to the creation of interesting work. Work too close to scratch and you'll spend all your time crushing berries (or programming in binary code). Work too far removed from scratch and you'll never be intimate enough with your medium to know what it's good for.

It is a great luxury to be able to shoot your own photography, design your own custom typefaces, draw your own illustrations, devise your own grids, mill your own paper, and manufacture your own packaging at your own custom-designed factory. But how far do you want to take this? Will you hand-chisel your own quarry stones and build the walls of your factory, brick by brick? There is a limit to what any single person can do well. At a point, it becomes sensible to subcontract some of this work out to other craftsmen more skilled than you in their particular areas of expertise.

More than painting or sculpture, graphic design has always been an inherently collaborative effort. Even a purist who owns his own printing press, designs his own typefaces, and casts his own metal type still winds up printing texts written by someone else.

In 1965 designer Armin Hofmann observed, "Today it is a practical impossibility to acquire a mastery of every separate technical and artistic aspect of the creation of pictures and lettering. There has been a change in the functions of the graphic designer. Today he must know, on the one hand, precisely what can be offered him by the highly specialized branches into which the originally simple and readily understood printing trade has split and, on the other hand, he must develop and realign his artistic perception accordingly. Only then will he be able to find creative solutions to the problems presented by a confrontation of opposites." Decades prior to the widespread use of digital design tools, Hofmann foretold the paradigm of "designer as editor."

WERE OUR PAINTINGS THAT SEMESTER MORE "CREATIVE" BECAUSE WE MIXED

OUR OWN PAINTS? WOULD OUR PAINTINGS HAVE BEEN EVEN MORE "CREATIVE"

HAD WE FOUND THE BERRIES AND CRUSHED THEM OURSELVES?

Designer as Editor

Since the creative human makes nothing "from scratch," it can be argued that every artist is merely remixing preexistent materials—paints, clay, code, words, whatever. Most house and hip-hop DJs spin records that they themselves didn't record, so what makes one DJ different from another? Most of it has to do with editing—which songs are chosen, the order of the songs, the transitions between songs. There is a modicum of physical dexterity involved, but most of the "art" of DJ mixing is simply good editing—the DJ, or "artist," as editor.

What exactly does an editor do? It depends on the industry. A film editor establishes pace and drama by cutting and splicing footage. The editor of a novel keeps the overall story in mind, making sure that all the little vignettes along the way add up to a consistent whole. This may mean cutting, adding, revising, rewording. It may simply mean recognizing where the author took a wrong turn in the narrative and sending him back to that place to start over.

A photographer can be seen as a kind of editor. She tweaks a camera's parameters and frames her picture. She selects which images to print from a roll of negatives. In the darkroom she crops, accentuates, mutes, burns, dodges. All these actions are primarily editorial.

As a rule, the more "assertive" an artist's tools of production, the more that artist is acting as editor. Turntables and auto-generative design software are assertive tools, but a rigorously defined formal process (like a grid system) can also be an assertive tool. (We'll talk more about tools and systems in Chapter 7.)

All creative humans are editors to some degree, particularly graphic designers. This is why people who don't have strong opinions make poor designers. The designer who believes that all paths are equally valid is going to wind up indiscriminately shepherding his design up some pretty banal paths.

I'm not advocating the abandonment of craft. The great Italian Renaissance painter Raphael employed a small army of artisans on his murals, and it didn't bother him (or his employers) that these artisans did much of the actual painting. It certainly wasn't that Raphael lacked the skill to do the painting himself. It's just that Raphael thought it was more efficient to spend his creative energies on the master design and hire assistants to help with the execution.

The closer to scratch you have worked, the better designer you'll be. The graphic designer with no knowledge of HTML will probably design a worse Web page mock-up than the graphic designer of equal skill with a working knowledge of HTML. The architect who also works as a construction foreman will have a

ALL CREATIVE HUMANS ARE EDITORS TO SOME DEGREE, PARTICULARLY GRAPHIC DESIGNERS.

THIS IS WHY PEOPLE WHO DON'T HAVE STRONG OPINIONS MAKE POOR DESIGNERS.

Brainstorming:
Expand and Contract

more intimate understanding of cost, materials, and production than an architect who has not. The print designer who works at a quality paper mill will better understand material substrates than the print designer who does not.

While such well-grounded experience can contribute greatly to their work, however, creativity is often exercised at the more abstract, conceptual level. The architect may quit his job as a construction foreman and still be a fine architect. And the print designer who continues to work night shifts at a paper mill in order to remain in intimate contact with his materials probably needs psychiatric help.

Of course, you have to have source material before you're able to combine it, and you have to have a series of possible options before you're able to edit them. Brainstorming is one way to generate a lot of possible options. Exploratory sketching, as discussed in Chapter 3, is a form of visual brainstorming. But brainstorming need not be so specific or rigorous. Brainstorming as a general approach can be applied throughout the entire creative process.

Psychologist J. P. Guilford says there are two types of production: convergent and divergent. Convergent production begins with the problem and follows deductive reasoning toward what seems to be the best single solution. Divergent production begins with the problem and generates a bunch of different solutions; then it selects the best solution from among them. Of the two, I find divergent production better suited to graphic design because there is no single "right answer" to a given design problem. One of the most popular manifestations of "divergent production" is brainstorming.

The term "brainstorming" was actually coined by advertising agent Alex Osborn in the mid-1900s. It is interesting and telling that although brainstorming has been practiced in nearly every academic and professional field, it originated in the field of graphic design. It turns out the stereotype of a bunch of ad agents sitting around a table reeling off one ridiculous idea after another actually has some historical precedent.

"Dilbert" cartoonist Scott Adams has said, "Creativity is allowing yourself to make mistakes. Art is knowing which ones to keep." Adams indirectly describes the two steps of brainstorming: expanding your ideas and then contracting them. It is crucial to take these two steps in order—expand first, then contract. Let yourself go during expansion; don't try to reel yourself in or keep yourself in check during this step. Such contractions will happen later. Instead, freely explore, play, let one idea lead to the next, get on out there, expand.

Expand

Philosopher Emile Chartier observed, "Nothing is more dangerous than an idea when it is the only one we have." I concur. The best way to come up with a good idea is to come up with a bunch of ideas—good, bad, mediocre. You can weed through them later. In the expansion step of brainstorming, go for quantity regardless of quality.

There are some advantages to expanding collaboratively as a group. The more minds, the more ideas. With a group, you can designate a recorder/moderator whose sole role is to record all the ideas and keep the group from contracting (getting critical) too soon.

Ideas lead to other ideas. The more people contributing ideas, the more possible connections to be made. Former Disney imagineer C. McNair Wilson suggests what he calls the "yes and..." strategy. Whenever an idea is thrown out, no matter how ridiculous, the next person follows up by saying, "yes and...," then proposing another idea. When Wilson was in charge of brainstorming at Disney, he placed a large bowl in the middle of the group.

Whenever someone said "no" or "but," that person had to put a dollar in the bowl. The "yes and..." strategy encourages continued idea expansion while discouraging premature idea contraction.

Let your expansion session continue even after all the easy and obvious ideas are used up. The pace of the session may slow down, but if you hang in there, the best ideas will often surface toward the end of the session.

Contract

Most people identify brainstorming with the initial expansion step. But the artist as editor is most involved in the contraction step.

While there are advantages to expanding ideas as a group, it may be more advantageous to contract ideas as an individual. This way you can approach all the brainstormed ideas from a single editorial perspective, and you are less likely to get bogged down in argument and debate.

Edward de Bono's famous "thinking hats" are good tools to use when contracting ideas.

COMMERCIAL DESIGN ISN'T LIKE A BOXING MATCH, IN WHICH TWO OPPONENTS OF EQUAL WEIGHT FIGHT AND THE BEST ONE WINS. IN COMMERCIAL DESIGN, EVERYONE IS IN THE HEAVYWEIGHT CLASS, AND IF YOU HAVE A HANDICAP, YOU'D BETTER FIGURE OUT HOW TO OVERCOME IT.

De Bono lists six colored hats, or critical perspectives, for analyzing a design problem:

1. White hat (symbolized by a blank sheet): Look at the objective facts.

2 Red hat (symbolized by fire): Involve your subjective opinions.

3. Yellow hat (symbolized by the sun): Be affirming; look at the positive aspects.

4. Black hat (symbolized by a judge's robe): be critical; look at the negative aspects.

5. Green hat (symbolized by a plant): Ask, "What if?" Speculate; use your intuition.

6. Blue hat (symbolized by the sky): Get the big picture.

Switch back and forth between these different critical perspectives while "contracting" your expanded ideas and then synthesize your conclusions.

The Proof Is in the Product

Commercial design isn't like a boxing match, in which two opponents of equal weight fight and the best one wins. In commercial design, everyone is in the heavyweight class, and if you have a handicap, you'd better figure out how to overcome it. If you are a weak photographer, subcontract your photography. If you are a weak coder, subcontract your programming. In the end, your client has hired you for your ability to pull all the elements together and create a winning design. Your main skill is understanding the nature of the design problem and translating it into the best possible design solution, on time, within budget. Heroic as it may seem to roam through the forest gathering roots and berries to grind into pigment to mix into paint to hand-paint your original design comp, don't waste your time doing it unless your particular design problem requires such a solution. Work as close to scratch as benefits the project, always keeping in mind that there is no scratch. So much of contemporary design is editing— knowing what works and how to achieve it. Once you embrace this truth, you'll spend less time being a purist for purity's sake and more time coming up with good design solutions.

■ ■ ■

IF EVERY TOOL IS A HAMMER,
EVERY PROBLEM LOOKS LIKE
A NAIL.

—PSYCHOLOGIST ABRAHAM MASLOW

7 | SOFTWARE AND SYSTEMS

Since designers don't really make any-thing from scratch, tools and systems play a critical role in their process. The computer is a powerful design tool and the grid is a powerful design sys-tem. We'll look at some ways to get the most out of both in this chapter. Both computer and grid limit the possibili-ties of design, and in doing so give the designer the freedom to work creatively within a bounded range of possible solu-tions instead of having to work "from scratch" with every possible solution in the known universe. Total unbounded "freedom" can actually be crippling and counterproductive to the creative process.

Software and the typographic grid effectively automate some of the more rote aspects of design, freeing the designer to work at a more intuitive, intelligent, conceptual level. In his book *A Whole New Mind*, author and business consultant Daniel Pink proposes that we are transitioning from the information age to the "conceptual age." In the past we transitioned from the mechanical age to the information age, and the factory worker gave way to the knowledge worker. According to Pink, three forces—abundance, Asia, and automation—are currently displacing the knowledge worker. In time, mere software skills will become increasingly less valuable than the conceptual ability to recognize what works and what doesn't.

Designers often feel threatened by systems and software, but the truly creative designer need not fear. Increased automation is actually good for the design industry. As the software that designers use becomes increasingly automated, they will be forced to excel at those aspects of design that are uniquely human—namely, generating smart visual concepts and implementing those concepts in a way appropriate to the goals of a given project.

Machines never steal human jobs; they just shift them. The machine age promised less work, but in reality it generated more work. In the legal field, mimeograph machines replaced the time-consuming process of hand copying,

but rather than relax with the time saved, lawyers simply sped up the pace of their lawyering. Overnight delivery services made it possible for people to ship things at the last minute, so people began working all the way up to the last minute. The Internet promised less use of paper, but increases in digital communication actually generated more use of paper. So don't fear the loss of your job unless you're relying on nothing but your Photoshop skills to keep your job.

Experimental designer and educator Katherine McCoy puts it this way: "Designers must deliver conceptual innovations and new insights, the things that computers cannot do. This challenge will lift design beyond a service trade into the role of interpreter for culture."

Ultimately, good design is technology-agnostic. Technology will never automatically make you a good designer, but uncritical acceptance and application of technology can make you a bad designer. In 1965 master designer and educator Armin Hofmann warned, "The instruments and aids that are placed in our hands nowadays are far too tricky for us to use them unquestioningly. The more cunningly devised they are, the greater the knowledge that is required before they can be put to wise and responsible use."

Graphic design and computers have had a notoriously delicate, often tempestuous relationship. Staunch advocates of digital

DESIGNERS OFTEN FEEL THREATENED BY SYSTEMS AND SOFTWARE, BUT THE TRULY CREATIVE DESIGNER NEED NOT FEAR. INCREASED AUTOMATION IS ACTUALLY GOOD FOR THE DESIGN INDUSTRY.

design tools such as Illustrator, Photoshop, and QuarkXPress see them as great equalizers, empowering anyone to become a designer. Staunch critics of such tools see them as a necessary evil at best and blame them for removing much of the hand-skill and craft from graphic design. I think the truth lies somewhere between the two extremes. Ultimately, design software is just a tool, and skilled designers make use of it as they will.

Nevertheless, I'll let the critics have their say. Designer and author Willi Kunz says, "Electronic equipment has replaced the traditional tools of design expression: pencil, crayon, pen, blade, and brush. The tactile qualities of materials such as trace and colored papers, boards, and overlay film that often inspired ideas are no longer viable. For the designer who enjoys the sensuality of working with actual materials, the absence of touch, smell, and even sound is disarming, as if part of the nervous system has been deactivated."

Designer Paula Scher echoes: "The computer made me feel like my hands were cut off because you don't type a design—that seems dumb.... And it doesn't smell right. It doesn't smell like an art supply. It smells like a car."

One of my design students asked, "If traditional print designers criticize what we consider to be commonplace digital tools, what will we criticize?" The answer may well be generative software.

Generative Software

A few contemporary designers are using what has been termed *generative software* to automate an increasingly large portion of the creative process. Automation has always been part of graphic design: Gutenberg automated hand calligraphy, the Linotype machine automated hand typesetting, page-layout software automates the "paste-up" layout process. But generative software takes automation a step further—automating layout, composition, scale, typography, and even color scheme based on designer-specified parameters.

In one sense, the use of generative design tools represents a radical shift in the design process. Generative tools don't simply afford a new way to produce a single work. They represent an entirely new process that alters the production of all work. Yet in another sense generative tools are less a clean break from the standard design process than simply the next step toward a more "editorial" design process.

Chance is a part of any design process, digital or otherwise. In the process of using tools to make ideas real, "happy accidents" often occur. Of course, *unhappy* accidents also occur. (These are otherwise known as plain old accidents.) One of the goals of generative software is to mine happy accidents. By automating certain functions, generative software allows the designer to explore a wide range of possible outputs quickly. The software takes its best guess at what the designer wants, and then the designer as editor decides which guesses work best. Only the designer can decide because only he knows the conceptual goals of the project.

The trick is to find a fruitful balance between control and chance. If the software allows you total control and there is no element of chance, it's not generative software. If the software is totally random and you can't control it, then it's merely an interesting exercise in artistic programming.

There are two basic kinds of generative software: off-the-shelf and custom made. Off-the-shelf software allows you to tweak your output based on the given parameters of a predefined interface. Some off-the-shelf generative software affords the designer lots of control; other packages offer almost no control. Designers who build custom-made generative software have nearly unlimited control of their output because they are able to "retool" the entire software product to suit their particular desires.

Off-the-Shelf Generative Software

We'll begin with off-the-shelf software that affords little control and then proceed to software that is more customizable.

Adrian Ward is a software artist who makes conceptual software art at www.signwave.co.uk modeled after standard graphic design software art. Ward began with Autoshop (a modification of Adobe Photoshop) and then moved on to his masterpiece, Auto-Illustrator (a modification of Adobe Illustrator). Auto-Illustrator's tool palette and interface appear similar to Adobe Illustrator's, but once you click on a tool, you have no control over what it does. Periodically the software itself will even close your working window without saving, if it "decides" that your design is no good. Auto-Illustrator is less a practical design tool and more a conceptual critique of the ways in which digital design tools can color the aesthetic of our output if we fail to use them critically. Still, commercial designers occasionally use the tool to create individual elements that they then incorporate into a more controlled overall layout.

Büro Destruct Designer, available free at www.burodestruct.net/bd/bddesigner, is generative logo software by the Swiss design firm Büro Destruct, which makes playful, colorful, '60s-era bubble logos. Users have a modicum of control over the forms and colors, or they can simply click a Randomize button that automatically generates a random logo. The software even allows you to save your final designs as EPS files. Multiple-grid overlays of small, medium, and large circles generate the shapes. The colors are chosen from a limited, predetermined palette. The software itself is more of a novelty, but it

ONE OF THE GOALS OF GENERATIVE SOFTWARE IS TO MINE HAPPY ACCIDENTS.

BY AUTOMATING CERTAIN FUNCTIONS, GENERATIVE SOFTWARE ALLOWS THE

DESIGNER TO EXPLORE A WIDE RANGE OF POSSIBLE OUTPUTS QUICKLY.

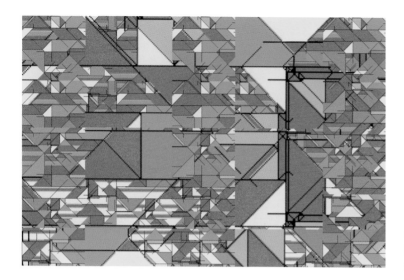

Three experimental designs I made incorporating the same source pattern created in Autoshop.

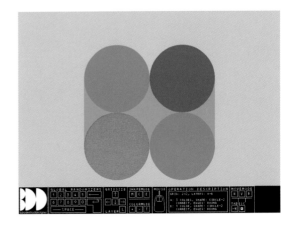

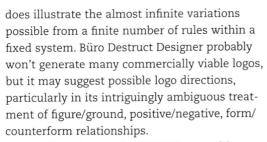

Three "logos" randomly generated by Büro Destruct
Designer software. The software's interface allows you
to control any design by selecting various parameters
(number of colors, grid size, shape, transparency), but there
is always a random element involved in the final output.

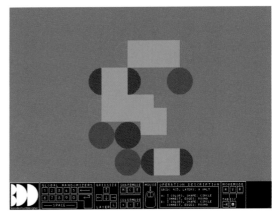

does illustrate the almost infinite variations
possible from a finite number of rules within a
fixed system. Büro Destruct Designer probably
won't generate many commercially viable logos,
but it may suggest possible logo directions,
particularly in its intriguingly ambiguous treatment of figure/ground, positive/negative, form/
counterform relationships.

At robmeek.com, the MEEK Typographic
Synthesizer by programmer Rob Meek is a
wonderfully funky piece of generative design
software. Its interface looks and acts like the
interface of a Moog synthesizer, except instead
of tweaking an analog audio tone, you are
tweaking a font set. You are given several different parameters to modify (everything from
glyph rotation modulation to x-skew sine wave
phase shift), but the parameters are so abstract
and the faux-analog knob interface so inexact,
chance is bound to enter into the process. Once
you've modified the letter A to your satisfaction,

the software then applies your settings to a
complete character set (capitals, miniscules,
numerals, and punctuation). You can then save
the whole typeface as a TrueType font.

William Caslon is probably turning in his
grave at this kind of modular, prefabricated
approach to "drawing" type, but the design firm
Designershock has used software based on the
MEEK Typographic Synthesizer to create some
legitimately interesting, technoesque display
faces at designershock.com.

One of the most intriguing pieces of
off-the-shelf generative design software is
the n-Gen Design System by n-Generate, at

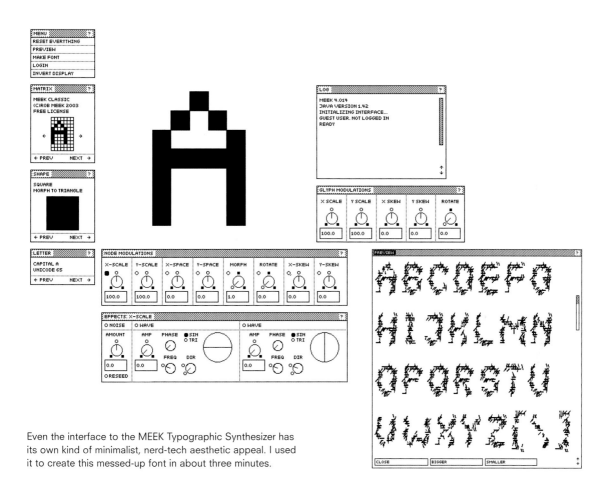

Even the interface to the MEEK Typographic Synthesizer has its own kind of minimalist, nerd-tech aesthetic appeal. I used it to create this messed-up font in about three minutes.

www.n-generate.com. San Francisco firm Move Design originally created it as a research prototype known as the n-Gen Design Machine. To use the Design Machine, you chose between five prefabricated design modules (California Noir, die Modernist, Future Tool, Spacefarm, and Urbivore), entered your copy, and clicked the n-generate button. Every time you clicked, an entirely new design was created in your chosen style.

The software parodied several popular visual styles—from Bauhaus modern to Raygun grunge—as a way of critiquing the cut-and-paste, trend-following contemporary design culture. The critique runs something like this: If software can generate trendy designs at the click of a button, perhaps your trendy design "skills" are not so valuable after all. Of course, not every iteration was a winner, but many looked quite competent. And no wonder—the software was created by graphic designers who knew their stuff. Each design module drew from a library of stock photography and typefaces suitable to its genre. Even the rules for type sizing, grid structure, and layering were tailor-made to create the signature look of that particular style.

Potential book covers automatically generated by the n-Gen Design Machine. I simply entered the book's title, byline, and a quote by Tibor Kalman. Each row is "designed" in a different style. This page top: die Modernist; bottom: California Noir. Opposite page, top to bottom: Urbivore, Spacefarm, and Future Tool.

n-Gen achieved its initial purpose by pissing off a bunch of trendy designers. It also raised the question of what constitutes good human design. The initial prototype wasn't very customizable. But what if its automatically generated layouts could be saved as layered PSD files for further hand tweaking in Photoshop? What if users could define their own style modules and populate them with their own source images and typefaces? Then it would indeed be a useful, idea-generating, head-start tool.

The n-Gen prototype has evolved into commercial brand management software. Corporate brand managers can use it to define brand rules and assets as they would in a corporate identity brand book. Then others in the corporation use it to create layouts in various formats that adhere to the rules of the brand. The n-Gen Design System doesn't create the brand rules; it just helps ensure that they are uniformly followed.

Custom Generative Software

It's one thing to use someone else's automated machine; it's another thing to build your own. Most designers initially balk at off-the-shelf generative design software, and understandably so. You probably already have a creative system that works for you, so why adopt someone else's kooky tool? Their tool wasn't created to fit your specific hand, much less to solve your specific problem.

According to design educator Thomas Fischer and architect Christiane M. Herr, "Due to the uniqueness of every design problem, a generative design tool developed in one design context is not very likely to make equal sense in other design contexts.... Designers who develop generative design tools do this quite enthusiastically but designers who are offered the use of other designers' generative tools often respond with refusal."

But what if you were able to create your own generative design tools and customize them per project to suit your own particular goals and aesthetics? Designer, artist, and technologist Joshua Davis does just that.

MOST DESIGNERS INITIALLY BALK AT OFF-THE-SHELF GENERATIVE DESIGN SOFTWARE. BUT

WHAT IF YOU WERE ABLE TO CREATE YOUR OWN GENERATIVE DESIGN TOOLS AND CUSTOMIZE

THEM PER PROJECT TO SUIT YOUR OWN PARTICULAR GOALS AND AESTHETICS?

Interview: Joshua Davis

At joshuadavis.com, Josh Davis creates and modifies his own design engines using Macromedia Flash's ActionScript language. He hand-draws a series of source illustrations and saves them in the computer as vector shapes. Then his software arranges, resizes, makes transparent, colors, and animates them automatically based on strict rules that Davis himself defines. The software automatically generates layout after layout until Davis finds one he likes. He then opens that layout in Illustrator and proceeds to further refine its composition by hand. Davis's final static design is a combination of hand-illustration, custom programming, and editorial selection. I talked with Josh about his generative design process.

How much of your design is coding, how much is illustration, and how much is having an eye to see when the whole thing is finished?

I would love to say I spend more time in one place or another, but really I don't. My role splits into three—I get to be the programmer, I get to be the designer, and finally I get to be the critic and choose what lives and what dies. The longest process is probably the critic, weeding through the iterations trying to find that beautiful accident. Writing a program probably only takes me two days. Designing artwork may only take me four days. But I might spend three weeks changing the system, trying to find that perfect composition.

Do you just use one generative design program, or several?

A single program will usually mutate over the course of a year. I'll have one that does sine waves, then it will mutate to draw lines, then I'll start mapping artwork onto those lines. Once a program is written, it may mutate into 50 different miniprograms or variations of its initial base. It never really ends.

It's like saying, "I'm a painter, and for this painting I'm going to use cadmium red, and as soon as I'm done with this painting I can never paint with cadmium red again," which is ridiculous. I don't have to reinvent the wheel every time. Everything becomes a mutation off of an initial base idea. And I come up with four to eight base ideas a year.

Once you've modified the code and it's running the way you like, do you use the exact design it generates, or do you go behind it and clean the design up by hand?

When the software generates, it's random, and random isn't always pretty. So it generates the initial idea and then I'll spend a week cleaning up stuff, removing stuff, moving things around in Illustrator to find that harmony because that harmony might not always be executed from the random process. There is a ton of human intervention.

Joshua Davis designed this cover for *Zink Magazine* using a combination of his custom generative software and traditional digital illustration software.

Is the final design ever executed solely from the random process?

An artwork project I did for BMW was completely hands-off. I was working with three different colors schemes, and there were 500 unique prints in each color scheme. There's no way I could do human intervention on every single detail. But then that program took the longest to write. Over the course of two months, I had to set up all these checks and balances and rules and boundaries—I was programming Josh Davis's human intervention into the system because I knew I wasn't going to be able to use human intervention.

What are you exploring at your experimental site, once-upon-a-forest.com?

once-upon-a-forest is currently about starting graphic design and letting its color and form mutate over the course of a year. Right now I'm up to 22 plates of mutation. It's the same base program that's been mutating over the course of a year. You can see in the beginning the generative aspects of the code are very basic. And now it's gotten more robust because I keep cutting things away and adding new things on. It never ends; it never feels finished.

At one point, you talked about creating software that would parse through the output of your generative software and select the iterations that you were most likely to choose.

That's something [programmer] Branden Hall and I worked on called Genetic Aesthetic. It uses a neural network and genetic algorithms to create a "hot or not" situation. It says, "Rate this composition I generated on a scale from 1 to 10." If I give it a 1, it says, "This isn't beautiful. I should look at what kind of numbers were generated in this iteration and record those as unfavorable." You have to train the software. Because the process is based on variables and numbers, over a very short period of time it's able to learn what numbers are unsatisfactory and what numbers are satisfactory to that individual human critic. It changes per individual.

If you were unable to customize your own generative software, and you had to use off-the-shelf generative software, would you like it as much? Would your work be as good? Would you still consider the process interesting?

The whole prefab mentality reminds me of Kai's Power Tools plug-ins for Photoshop. Here was an extension of an application that allowed you to do things prefabbed, but it didn't have any longevity. Working that way doesn't make sense. I don't mind teaching workshops on how to program, but this idea of writing programs and giving them away for design is not a successful endeavor.

Three unique prints from a series of generative designs Joshua Davis did for a BMW promotional campaign. Davis hand-drew the forms from parts of the BMW car. He then programmed the software to control the visual composition of the posters. Each print is its own unique manifestation of the rules of the software engine.

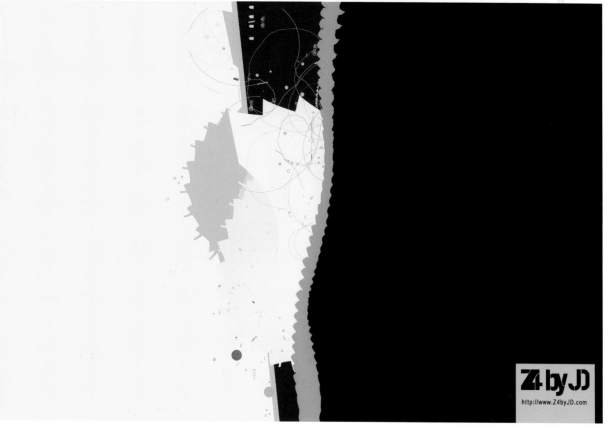

Iterations 4, 10, 16, and 22 of Joshua Davis's experimental Web site, www.once-upon-a-forest. com. As the generative software that creates these compositions mutates, so does the complexity of the compositions. Compositional continuity is still maintained from one iteration to the next because Davis himself draws the source illustrations and governs the mutation process.

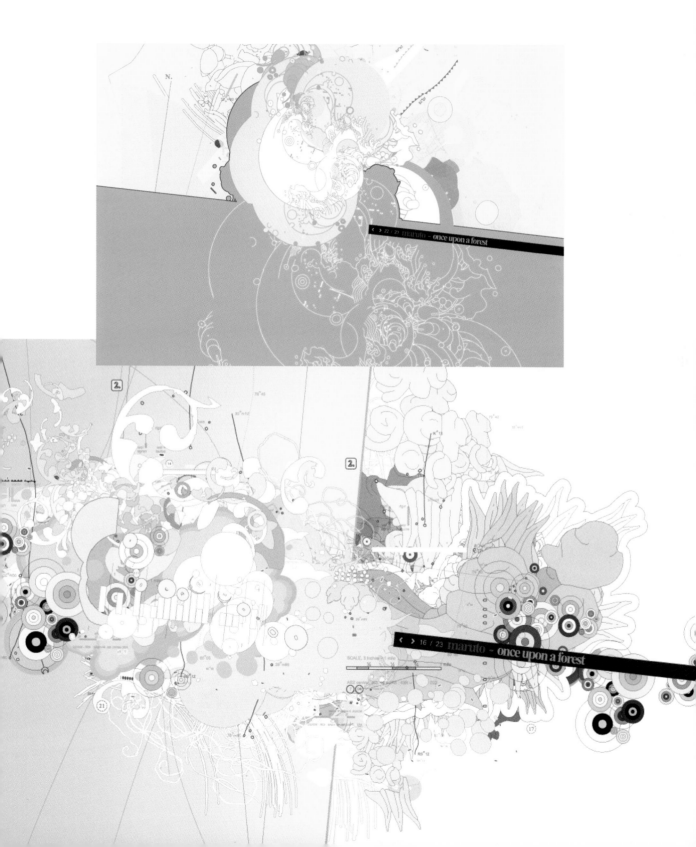

Why?

It just becomes like Kai's Power Tools. You're one button click away from being Josh Davis. But it doesn't work that way. That kind of software doesn't have longevity because it's not customizable. The good thing about knowing programming and being able to modify your ideas is that you're allowing this software organism that you created to live; you're extending its life by adding on to its base features. If you release something that's a closed environment like Kai's Power Tools, it only does a, b, c. It's cool for about five minutes, and then it doesn't have any sustainability or longevity in the industry because it's not extensible.

Having said that, do you feel limited by Flash?

Flash gets a bad rap because it was initially branded and marketed as an animation tool. But ideas are ideas, and Flash will help you execute your ideas. People think there are these magic applications that will help them execute creativity, but creativity rests on the shoulders of individuals. I hate when people ask me, "What's the future of Flash?" Who cares? Flash was magical back in Flash 4. If you had good ideas, you were able to do some amazing things. Focusing on new builds of software deters people from creating. People think at some point there will be the "auto kick ass" button and everyone will kick ass.

You used to give away your Flash source files for free, and you teach students how to make their own generative engines. Are you afraid of giving away the shop? If someone has the ability to make your tools, why won't they be as good a designer as you? What do you bring to the project in addition to your generative systems?

In the years I've taught workshops and given away code, I have yet to meet one individual who has taken my files and replicated exactly what I do. What I bring to these tools is my own creative artistic impression. I have certain forms that I like, certain movements that I like, a certain balance that I like, certain colors that I like; it's all about being an artist/designer. Rembrandt could give you his brushes and paints, but you wouldn't be able to paint like Rembrandt. Just because I give you my software doesn't mean you're going to be able to do what I do. You have to bring some sort of creativity to the table—shapes, colors, forms, balance, chaos, or simplicity. That's what it means to be a designer. So I'm not really worried about people having my code or sharing my code or teaching my code. If I give this stuff away to 50 people, you're just going to get 50 different impressions, based on each individual. It's really all about the individual and the creativity they bring to the tools they use.

■ ■ ■

Grid Systems

The potential impact of generative software on the standard creative process is fascinating to consider. Still, there is nothing magical about the digital computer. It is simply a tool that rapidly executes a given set of instructions based on certain conditions. You don't need a digital computer to execute a given set of instructions based on certain conditions. Prior to computer software, humans still managed to devise systems based on rules. The modernist grid is one such predigital, rules-based system.

The shape of any horizontal or vertical frame (book page, outdoor billboard, television screen) already suggests a grid structure. We rarely design for circular or triangular formats. Our formats are almost always rectangular, and rectangles beg to be subdivided into subordinate rectangular modules.

The grid has been around at least as long as humans have been making books—in the form of a simple manuscript grid (a content area surrounded by four margins). But leave it to the rational, everything-in-its-place modernists to take grid systems to new and gloriously subtle levels of complexity.

The seeds of the modernist grid were sown by architect JL Mathieu Lauweriks as early as 1904. The grid as a formal system was quintessentially codified by Swiss designer and educator Josef Müller-Brockmann in the early 1960s (the modernist grid is also know as the Swiss grid). Jedi grid master Massimo Vignelli has taken grid systems to thrilling extremes of elegance, function, robustness, and intricacy. And other designers, such as Wolfgang Weingart and Willi Kunz, have deconstructed the formal grid to achieve beautiful, intriguing, expressive results.

All grids have four margins and a content area. The most basic grid is the *manuscript grid*—simply a single rectangular content area in the middle of a page, surrounded by margins on four sides. The margins keep the text in the content area from running into the binding of the book or off the edges of the book. The proportion of the margins also adds an aesthetical quality to the overall composition of the page. Modernist designers always seek asymmetrical balance, so your modernist margins should never be the same size. According to Müller-Brockmann, "Lack of contrast is unpleasant and looks wishy-washy…. Margins of the same size can never result in an interesting page design; they always create an impression of indecision and dullness."

Ideally the left and right margins are in some "correct" mathematical relationship with each other. This relationship is sometimes based on the quasi-mystical proportions of the Golden Ratio (a.k.a. Golden Section, Golden Mean, Divine Proportion). To find it, take a line and divide it unequally into two sections so that the short section is to the long section as the long section is to the undivided line. If we call the long section a and the short section b, the ratio is expressed as a:b = (a + b):a. So for example, if the entire line is 8 units long (a + b = 8), to achieve the Golden Ratio, the long part of the line needs to be 5 (a = 5), making the short part 3 (b = 3). The short part divided by the long part (b/a) should equal about 0.6. The whole numbers that work neatly in this equation happen to be part of a Fibonacci sequence—a series of numbers in which each number is the sum of the two preceding numbers (1, 2, 3, 5, 8, 13, 21, and so on).

Who cares and what does this have to do with *your* margins? The simplest way to apply the Golden Ratio to your grid (and there are many more convoluted ways) is to apply it to your margin widths. If your left margin is 3

units, then according to the Golden Ratio, your right margin should be 5 units, since 3/5 = 0.6, and since 5 follows 3 in the Fibonacci sequence. If your left margin is 2 units, then your right margin should be 3.3 units, since 2/a = 0.6, making a = 3.3. Or just use an even 3 (the next number after 2 in the Fibonacci sequence).

Some people swear by the Golden Ratio and others dismiss it as complete garbage. I do think there is aesthetic value to asymmetrical balance, but that can be achieved with any ratio other than 1:1. For example, a left margin of 2 units and a right margin of 4 units (a 1:2 ratio) might work perfectly well. The Golden Ratio is groovy because it's not perfectly divisible (the

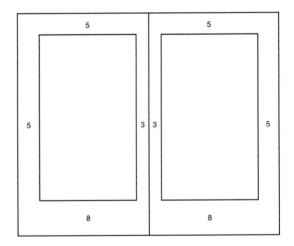

Facing pages of a manuscript grid layout with Golden Ratio proportions applied to opposite margins. The fact that the top (head) margin and the outer margin are the same width further harmonizes the composition.

true Golden Ratio is an irrational number closer to 0.618) and yet it still contains within itself a kind of subtle, organic symmetry. Does simply applying the Golden Ratio to some microcosmic aspect of your design automatically impart its groovy mathematical essence to your visual aesthetic? No.

Your margins have to harmonize with the typography of your content area. All compositional grid decisions are intimately related to your typography. (The modernist grid is also called the typographic grid.) Areas of continuous type have texture, tone, and rhythm. The forms and counter-forms of the typeface are related to the size of the type, which is related to its tracking, which is related to its line length, which is related to its leading. All of these aspects combine to give your typographic area a certain character (texture, tone, and rhythm). The margin proportions that best balance, accentuate, and harmonize the character of the type in your content area are the "correct"

Books on Grids

Of all the things I teach my freshman design students, the one that most improves their work is the grid. Unfortunately I'm only able to scratch the surface of grids in this section. My favorite books on the grid are Josef Müller-Brockmann's classic *Grid Systems in Graphic Design: A Visual Communication Manual*; Willi Kunz's *Typography: Macro- and Microaesthetics*; and Timothy Samara's *Making and Breaking the Grid: A Graphic Design Layout Workshop*.

Start with the Müller-Brockmann. He cuts to the chase and breaks it all down very practically. As a bonus, *Grid Systems in Graphic Design* regularly evinces the author's earnest modernist optimism. For example, Müller-Brockmann writes, "The systematic presentation of facts... should, for social and educational reasons, be a constructive contribution to the cultural state of society and an expression of our sense of responsibility." And I love this gem of a statement: "A sensitive interplay between good type design, type size, regular spacing between letters and words and open leading can make the formal pattern of a poem into an artistic event." *Hear Hear!*

Willi Kunz's book is in the same vein as Müller-Brockmann's, but from a more deconstructive perspective. Like *Grid Systems in Graphic Design*, *Typography* is opinionated and written by a master who uses his own meticulous work as figure examples.

Samara's *Making and Breaking the Grid* serves to harmonize and integrate these other two texts. It contains a concise history of the modernist grid and a plethora of commercial examples of grid construction and deconstruction, complete with diagrams and commentary.

proportions. As such, correct margin widths can't be formulaically decided without careful consideration of your typography.

Furthermore your margin widths should be appropriate to the purpose of your publication. A novel will have wider margins than an office supply catalog. Generous margins look luxurious and impart to the text a certain import, but margins that are too large can seem like you're padding pages because you don't have enough content.

The manuscript grid is the simplest kind of grid, yet it illustrates well the subtleties inherent in grid systems. How can you successfully use the grid without a working knowledge of typography? More to the point, how can I impart to you a working knowledge of typography in a couple of paragraphs? I can't. Suffice to say that typography and grid systems are intricately related.

Slightly more complex than the manuscript grid, the *column grid* contains two or more columns in its content area. Vertical gutters separate the columns. Text goes into the columns, and photography can be sized and cropped to fit the width of a single column or to span multiple columns and gutters.

Even more complex is the *modular grid*, sexiest of all grid structures. In addition to vertical gutters, horizontal gutters are added, dividing the content area into discrete modules. Modules may then be grouped into content "fields" and used to house similar content. Ragged right text may span multiple modules as long as its left-justified edge aligns with the left edge of a module. Photography may span multiple modules as long as its rectangular edges align with the outer edges of the modules that contain it.

Font size and line leading (the space between lines of type) are particularly important in modular grid design. The height of any individual module plus its neighboring horizontal gutter should be evenly divisible by the font size plus its line leading. Often the horizontal gutter is sized to contain a single line of body copy type plus its line leading. This intentional mathematical relationship ensures that photographs and figure captions will align precisely with any adjacent lines of body text. Every element of the design is initially harmonized to the grid so that a continuity of design is maintained throughout the publication, regardless of the variety of its content.

There are all sorts of combinations and variations of these three basic grid structures, and each basic structure can be implemented in many different ways. For example, not all modules in a modular grid have to be a uniform size. Furthermore, modules may be subdivided and regrouped for different purposes per spread.

What kind of grid should you use? It depends on the nature of your content. Building your grid system is a back-and-forth, trial-and-error dance between content and prototyping. First get your hands on as much of your content as possible. Next begin looking for extremes. What is the longest header? What is the shortest figure caption? How tightly can I crop these images before they cease to be recognizable?

Next build a best-guess prototype grid system based on your observations and populate

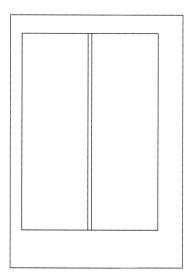

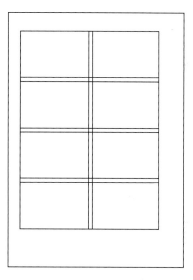

Single page of a simple two-column grid layout. Incidentally, the opposite margins are based on a 1:2 ratio, and they look just fine.

Single page of a basic modular grid layout. I simply added three horizontal gutters to the two-column grid layout to create eight modules of equal size.

it with some real content. Sit back and ask yourself, "Does it look good? Is it too cluttered? Is it too monotonous? Is it too chaotic? Is it robust enough to accommodate the extremes of my content?" If you see problems (and you will), go back and modify your prototype grid system to address those problems, repopulate it with content, and make new observations. Page layout software is your new best friend in this laborious process.

Once you've customized your grid system to your satisfaction, the next step is to fully populate it with your content. Even in this, you have to be creative. You want to vary the rhythm of

your page compositions so that the pace of your publication is lively and compelling. If you've designed your grid system well, it will automatically give your publication a kind of subconscious continuity. Your job as a compositor is to make sure that this continuity doesn't turn into monotony.

A word on complexity: A fine-meshed grid with 64 modules is harder to control than a course-meshed grid with only 9 modules. Grids are meant to simplify, not complicate. Only make your grid system as complicated as your content requires. Don't use a modular grid system when a column grid system will do.

A word on structural visibility: Just because your layout is based on a grid doesn't mean that the structure of your grid will be automatically apparent once you hide your guidelines. Your grid's structure is only made visible by the content you align to it. The more sparsely and irregularly you populate your grid with content, the less visible your underlying grid structure will be. A good compositor capitalizes on this principle to vary the pace of her layout. Some spreads should be dense and regularly populated with content, reinforcing the underlying structure of the grid. Other spreads should be populated with content sparsely and irregularly, downplaying the underlying grid structure and opening up the layout.

A word on media: The grid is most advantageously applied to books, magazines, corporate identity systems, a series of publications, a series of posters for an organization—any project in which multiple pages of content need to have a unified look. What about a one-off poster or CD cover that's not part of a larger series? You can still use the grid to achieve compositional balance or an intentionally allusive modernist style.

Grids are particularly applicable to Web design because a Web site is really just a single project with a series of digital pages that need to have a unified look. For Web design, author and designer Timothy Samara suggests using a *hierarchical grid*, a looser grid made up of fields containing different functional content—header field, main menu field, submenu field, body copy field, featured product field, or other.

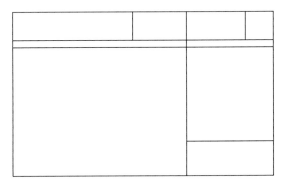

A hierarchical grid layout for a Web site. The fields are positioned and sized based on the nature of the content they contain rather than on strict mathematical proportions.

These fields are arranged in a meaningful, hierarchical relationship to each other.

Strict multicolumn grid layouts don't really work on the Web. You don't want to split up your body copy into two columns or your reader will have to scroll back to the top of the window to finish your story. It's fine to have multiple columns in your hierarchical Web grid, but each column should have its own discrete type of content—for example, main body copy in one column and sidebar copy in a second column.

Strict modular grids don't really work for Web design because they are based on a fixed module height size that is mathematically related to a strictly controlled font size. But HTML and CSS fonts are displayed at slightly different sizes depending on the user's operating system, and the user can always choose to drastically resize your fonts at the click of a browser button. Web design calls for a looser, less-rigid grid structure: the hierarchical grid.

A word on breaking the grid: You don't have to religiously adhere to grid systems in order to benefit from them. If you dare, you can break the grid. I'm not talking about intuitive free-form spatial layout. That's more like ignoring the grid altogether. Instead start with a grid structure and intentionally depart from it in some interesting visual way or for some larger conceptual purpose. Let the formal, semiotic, or conceptual nature of your content push the standard modernist grid beyond its limits until you arrive at a deconstructed, post-grid layout.

Foundational free verse poets such as Walt Whitman, Ezra Pound, and T. S. Eliot began with an intimate knowledge of metered verse. Likewise, all good deconstructed grid design begins with an intimate knowledge of the grid. It's probably harder to write good free verse than good metered verse. Likewise it's probably harder to break the grid well than to make the grid well. Proceed with caution.

In truth, you don't have to deconstruct the grid architectonically in order to break it. Because modernist designers were so square and bombastic, they took it upon themselves to banish all superfluous ornamentation from the practice of graphic design. Consequently the modernist grid was meant to incorporate typography, photography, geometric lines, and little else. By simply including some organic, nongeometric ornamentation and allowing it to lasciviously meander across the gutters from one grid module to another, you effectively "break" the grid.

Extreme grid enthusiasts hail grid systems as the next best thing to sliced bacon. Extreme grid critics blame grid systems for all that is mindless, mechanical, and boring in the world of design. Like generative software, grids are neither magical nor evil. They are simply one more tool in the designer's toolbox. Müller-Brockmann rightly observes, "The grid system places in the hands of the designer no more and no less than a serviceable instrument, which makes it possible to create interesting, contrasting, and dynamic arrangements of pictures and text but which is in itself no guarantee of success." Like the creative process itself, grid systems work, but you've got to work them.

Nonstandard [Ab]Use
of Standard Software

Designer Bruce Mau observes, "The problem with software is that everyone has it." The easier Photoshop makes it to bevel, chrome, drop-shadow, and lens-flair typography, the more unrestrained bling proliferates through the lower ranks of hobbyist design. Still, you don't need to program your own generative software in order to use "standard" design software experimentally. Just understand that the built-in special effects that software manufacturers tout as "experimental" are the very ones you want to avoid.

Simple layers are one of the most fundamental but amazing features of Photoshop and Illustrator. Try designing in Photoshop using just one layer, and you'll quickly appreciate their power. When I was in high school (in the mid-1980s), I spent hours making abstract art with my mom's Xerox machine. The primary techniques were layering, reversing, scaling, tiling, cutting out transparent areas, and varying printer tone. I would rerun the same poor sheet of paper through the machine, submitting it to all sorts of abusive permutations, until it finally ripped. Then I would make a fresh copy of it

WITH EVERYONE RUSHING FROM ANALOG
TO DIGITAL, TRY PILOTING YOUR PROCESS
IN THE OPPOSITE DIRECTION. EITHER
THAT OR USE DIGITAL TOOLS TO DO
THINGS THEY WEREN'T MEANT TO DO.

and continue the process. It was an old-school form of machine-aided collage.

Photoshop allows you to do much more robust layer experimentation without having to abuse your local copying machine. Several analog drawing exercises incorporate tracing paper. Turn the opacity down on a Photoshop layer and you've got digital tracing paper. Silhouette, scale, and rotate two formally disparate but symbolically related subjects on separate, semitransparent Photoshop layers. Superimpose one on top of the other, looking for positive/negative patterns and relationships.

Scale the same object to a number of different sizes; place each scaled instance on a separate, semitransparent layer; and rearrange their location, looking for interesting visual relationships. Revisit and modify each layer's transparency and see what new patterns emerge.

Another way to capitalize on the power of layers is by dividing your overall composition into discrete sets (foreground, middle ground, and background, for example). Rather than trying to balance 15 individual design elements, break your elements up into three sets of five, balance five elements at a time, and then balance the three sets with each other. Since each set is harmonized with the same grid, all three should ultimately synchronize. Use a different layer group in Photoshop for each set. Work with one layer group at a time, turning off the visibility of the other two. According to Willi Kunz, "In an optimum solution, each visual layer should be effective on its own." Then turn on the visibility of all three. You will still have to fine-tune your final composition, but this is a

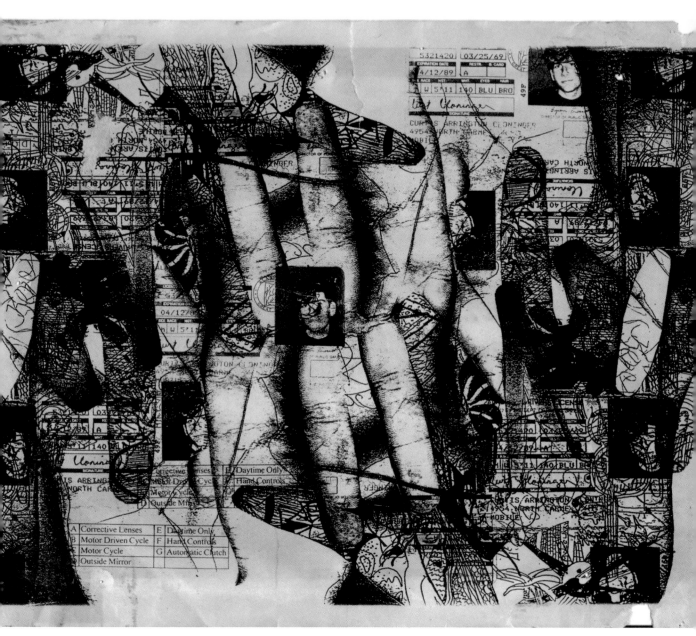

Xerox art self-portrait of the author, age 16. If Xerox machines were the tricycle of automated, multilayered collage, then Photoshop is the Rolls Royce.

clever way to keep from getting compositionally overwhelmed.

Another happy feature of Photoshop is tiling. Select what you want to tile and then choose Edit > Define Pattern from the menu. Then fill your canvas with your selected pattern. Celtic and Arabic scribes spent laborious days hand-drawing the same repeating ornamental patterns. Today we are able to fill any background with tiling ornamentation in an instant. I like to tile stuff—entire photographs, closely cropped sections of photographs, full illustrations, extreme details of illustrations, typographic forms, abstract lines, anything. Tiling can create fascinating patterns from even the most banal source material. Observe the patterns that emerge, trace over them, and create your own abstract ornamental forms.

I know I said to avoid Photoshop filters, but here is a technique that attempts to put them to good experimental use. Apply Photoshop filters to your source images and print the results. Then try to copy the prints from scratch using analog media (pencils, pens, paints). Unless you are a perfectly meticulous painter, your final results will be different, more human, and preferable to the digital "originals." Director Michel Gondry's nondigital special effects inspired this technique. In an era when every other Hollywood blockbuster is awash with digital effects, Gondry's old-school effects (*Eternal Sunshine of the Spotless Mind*) have a peculiar visual immediacy that makes them immediately distinguishable. With everyone rushing from analog to digital, try piloting your process in the opposite direction.

Either that or use digital tools to do things they weren't meant to do. The godfather of grunge design, David Carson, uses digital software to create distorted planar forms. Bézier curve spline handles are a standard design software interface element that allows the manipulation of vector shapes. But once the shapes have been manipulated and saved, the spline handles disappear in the final rendered output. Carson includes his spline handles in his final design by taking screenshots of his software interface window. This technique conceptually deconstructs the creative process by revealing its hidden details in the final product.

All these experimental approaches can be applied to nondigital tools as well. Computers don't ensure experimentation, but they certainly don't preclude it. The more things that can go wrong with a process, the more things you can tweak to your experimental advantage. And a lot of things can go wrong with graphic design software.

The Art of Design

Discussion of software and systems always leads back to this question: Wherein lies the "art" of design? If your design skills are too closely allied with and dependent on a specific technology, beware. Manuscript calligraphy, Gutenberg's letterpress, Linotype machines, phototypesetting, desktop publishing, Flash vector animation, After Effects motion graphics—all these things shall pass, making way for whatever design technology is next. What endures is the designer's eye, hand, mind, and soul.

Tools are just tools. They work for you, not vice versa. Don't be afraid to exploit any and all technologies in the service of your conceptual and aesthetic goals.

Likewise don't be afraid to adopt and exploit systems, even if they are based on premises with which you disagree. You don't have to buy into modernist ethics to benefit from the modernist grid. So much of design is about limiting your options, which are initially infinite. It helps to start with some angle, aesthetic, foundation, theory, or system. If for no other reason, grids are useful because they give you something to deconstruct. An imperfect theory can still give rise to an excellent visual solution, just as a perfect theory can still lead to a safe, pedantic solution. So much depends on the interplay between the theory, the designer, and the design problem. Don't hesitate to retool grid systems for your own peculiar aesthetic purposes. As we say in the South, "Drive it like you stole it."

■ ■ ■

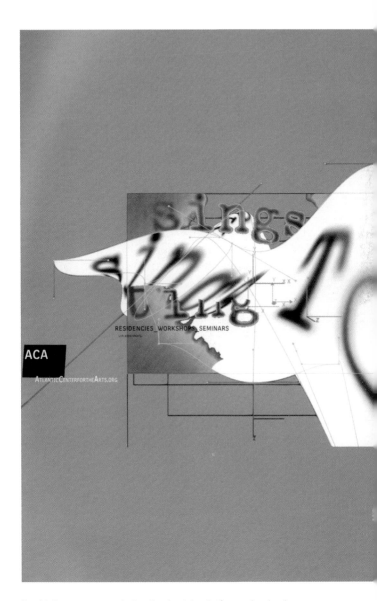

David Carson poster design for the Atlantic Center for the Arts. Carson warps planes into 3D space and leaves his Bézier curve spline handles showing, intentionally revealing his sleight of hand.

THERE'S A WORLD WHERE I CAN GO
AND TELL MY SECRETS TO
IN MY ROOM, IN MY ROOM
IN THIS WORLD I LOCK OUT ALL MY
WORRIES AND MY FEARS
IN MY ROOM, IN MY ROOM

DO MY DREAMING AND MY SCHEMING
LIE AWAKE AND PRAY
DO MY CRYING AND MY SIGHING
LAUGH AT YESTERDAY

NOW IT'S DARK AND I'M ALONE
BUT I WON'T BE AFRAID
IN MY ROOM, IN MY ROOM

— THE BEACH BOYS

8 | MAINTAINING A PERSONAL DESIGN PLAYGROUND

One of my mantras has always been: "Everybody needs a place to fail." One day I will get around to making the bumper sticker. I'm not advocating failure in and of itself. I'm talking about having a pressure-free environment that encourages free play and daring experimentation without fear of failure. In country music songwriting, there is a fine line between the sublime and the sappy. The trick is to get as close to that line as you can without crossing over. You have to risk sappiness to achieve sublimity. The same may be said of great design. You have to risk failure to achieve success.

When I say, "fail," I don't mean that you should sabotage yourself intentionally every time you design (although that might be an interesting experiment). I simply mean you should *blatantly risk failure*, which will inevitably mean some actual failure. Now obviously you don't want to fail on a client project. Everybody needs a place to fail, but that's not it. One way to keep commercial failure at bay is by allowing yourself ongoing room to fail in a less risky context.

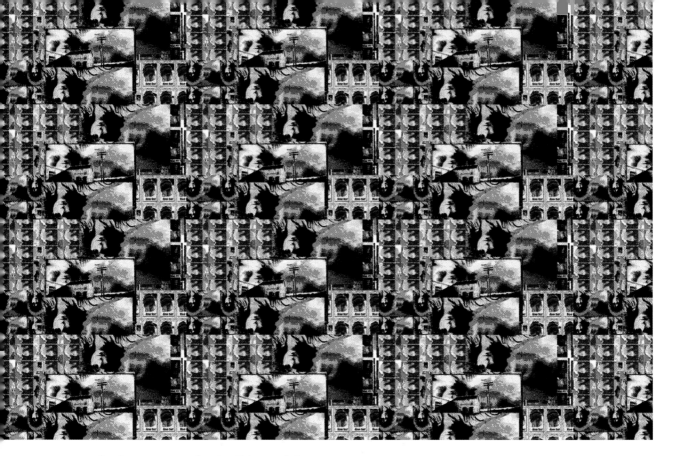

Playdamage.org experiments with low-resolution animation and subjective narrative. Everybody needs a place to fail, and this is mine.

Randy Nelson, head of Pixar University, approaches creativity at the animation studio's internal training program as "a team sport" by having Pixar's animators go through sketching and brainstorming exercises in groups to overcome their fear of public failure. He says, "You have to honor failure, because failure is the negative space around success." Think about it this way: Failure is the "rough"—or the minefield—in which the "diamond" of successful design hides. If you're unwilling to venture into that field, you will settle for passable, safe, mediocre design. You may never flub it, but you'll never nail it either.

FAILING PUBLICLY WILL GIVE YOUR EXPERIMENTAL PROCESS AN ELEMENT OF EXCITEMENT AND ACCOUNTABILITY THAT MORE ACCURATELY MIRRORS "REAL WORLD" DESIGN, BUT WITHOUT THE PRESSURE OF DEADLINES AND CLIENTS.

Playground Rules

Or think about it like this: Ideas are like cafeteria plates stacked up in one of those spring-loaded dispensers. When you take the top plate, the next one rises up. One of the plates in that pile is your best visual idea, but it may be buried 20 plates down. The only way to get it to surface is to "use up" the 19 plates above it. A personal design playground is the perfect place to use up those top 19 plates.

Your playground should probably be a Web site, whether or not you do new media work professionally. For instance, if you do print work, it's logistically easier to save your files as high-resolution GIFs or JPEGs and post them online than it is to print out posters and put them up around town weekly. Video work becomes a bit more troublesome online due to bandwidth restrictions, but it's still possible at short lengths and low resolutions.

Since 2000, playdamage.org has been my personal place to fail. I began it as a way to experiment with unorthodox DHTML tricks, and I still keep adding to it years later because there are creative things I want to explore that simply can't be explored in any other forum.

Now that you understand what I mean by "failure," you may want to follow some of these suggestions for how to get the most out of your personal design playground:

Fail publicly. It's not enough to merely fail in a charcoal sketchbook hidden in your bottom drawer. You need to fail in your actual professional medium—Web, print, video, whatever—and you need to fail publicly. There is a freeing, confidence-building, inhibition-destroying strength that only public risk taking can produce.

Failing publicly will give your experimental process an element of excitement and accountability that more accurately mirrors "real world" design, but without the pressure of deadlines and clients.

Fail at the medium in which you hope to improve. If you want to improve your Adobe Photoshop skills, work in Photoshop and export your finished experiments as image files. If you want to improve your Macromedia Flash skills, work in Flash and export your experiments as SWF files. By all means, feel free to keep a personal sketchbook in addition to your playground. Regular sketching keeps your hand and eye in practice, and even if you're not an illustrator by trade, sketching can't help but improve your design work. But a playground is something beyond a sketchbook, something more polished and closer to finished. Take each playground piece to full completion, or at least make it complete enough to upload for someone to see. Going beyond the thumbnail/sketchbook phase of design on a regular basis in an

The Yancey Tire Chapel in Sawyerville, Alabama is a quintessential example of low-budget, experimental architecture. Student architects Steven Durden, Thomas Tretheway, and Ruard Veltman of Auburn University's Rural Studio constructed this striking chapel out of recycled tires, salvaged beams, tin, and rocks from a nearby river.

experimental way makes you that much more confident to risk greatness on your next commercial mock-ups.

Even architects can risk failure in their actual 3D medium without having to acquire a large commercial building contract. In Alabama, visionary architect Sam Mockbee pioneered a program at Auburn University's Rural Studio that allows students to design and construct ingeniously efficient, low-cost structures that meet the practical needs of the surrounding rural community. Architect David Baird regularly takes his Louisiana State University architecture students to a squatter settlement in the border town of Renosa, Mexico, to build improved housing out of concrete, tin cans, and found materials. These projects are more than just mere design playgrounds. They are providing real solutions to challenging social problems. Still, if nothing else, architects can build tree houses, doghouses, or even (appropriately enough) actual playgrounds. As long as the experimentation extends beyond mere blueprints and into 3D space.

Fail anonymously. Remember, this is not your online portfolio. There shouldn't even be a link from your online portfolio. If you can afford to, choose a completely different URL for your playground. If you're extremely paranoid—or just for fun—register your domain name under a pseudonym. Design technologist Joshua Davis maintains www.once-upon-a-forest.com in the persona of a mysterious artist named Maruto. He's not paranoid; it's just for fun, to explore experimental design work he wouldn't otherwise explore in his everyday persona. You don't have to create an alter ego in order to maintain a design playground, but keeping your playground separate from your commercial portfolio will encourage you to risk more and fear less.

Fail early. Don't wait until your skills are more polished before you start or you'll never

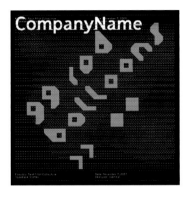

In these testpilotcollective.com splash pages from November 4 to13, 2003, the same basic layout is explored using a variety of typefaces, type sizes, textures, layout directions, and color schemes. The goal is not the production of a masterpiece but the growth of the designers.

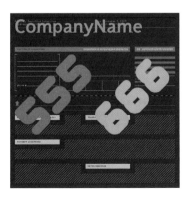

EXPLORING WHAT DOESN'T WORK CAN BRING YOU ONE STEP CLOSER TO WHAT DOES WORK.

BESIDES ALL THAT, SOMETIMES IT'S SIMPLY FUN AND CATHARTIC TO DO THINGS "THE WRONG WAY."

start. There's an old hymn that says, "If you tarry 'till you're better / you will never come at all." Come as you are and start there. Your playground isn't the opening night of a ballet; it's more like rehearsal.

Fail often. Update your playground as regularly as opportunity allows. For more than five years, the three designers at testpilotcollective.com put up a new splash page for their digital typography Web site every day. That's over 1,825 separate designs. Don't wait until you come up with work that blows people away. This is not a polished portfolio; it's an ongoing experimental design laboratory. Former Disney imagineer and brainstorming guru C. McNair Wilson says the best way to have one good idea is to have 300 ideas. Self-censoring and editing can come later. Create first, and create a lot.

Fail compulsively. Now is the time to explore specific design avenues exhaustively. Is there any way to make Times New Roman look fresh and sexy? Are you any good at hand illustration? How about vector illustration? How about animation? Get on a particular design track and run it into the ground. Graphic designer S. Bradley Askew is infamous for exhaustive experimentation with the same color schemes and typefaces at www.hellmedia.com. After the twentieth screen of yellow and baby blue, I'm personally ready to move on. But it's not about me as the visitor. It's about the designer's personal explorations.

If a certain design approach keeps yielding fruit, you know you're onto something. Keep tweaking it. If another design approach fizzles out and dead-ends, that's one less path you'll have to head down only to discover that it doesn't work. Later, in a commercial setting with a tight deadline, knowing what *not* to try can be half the battle.

Fail with fun content. Don't try to simulate commercial projects or commercial constraints. Work with content that interests you personally. It's a *playground*, not a work camp. Some designers might even be tempted to think of their playground as "art." It may well be art (depending on how you define art), but art comes with its own sets of expectations and pressures. It might be safer not to call it much of anything at all. "Media experimentation locale" will do in a pinch.

Fail ephemerally. Don't feel obliged to archive your playground work. When Mike Cina began www.trueistrue.com, he completely replaced each piece with a new one. As a visitor, if you didn't want to miss a piece, you had to visit regularly because there was no index of previous works. Of course, Cina was archiving all these pieces on his hard drive and they were later released on a CD-ROM. The point is, it's the process that's most important, not any single finished piece of work.

An alternative method is to work series by series. Each new series marks a new exploration. Leave your work online until you have finished with that series and then remove it to begin a new series. Or you can leave all your work online and archive it according to series.

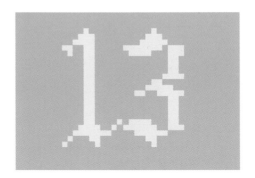

Designs that compulsively explore a Day-Glo dead-end from S. Bradley Askew's playground, www.hellmedia.com.
If Askew can make this color scheme work, imagine what he could pull off in a nice burgundy and teal.

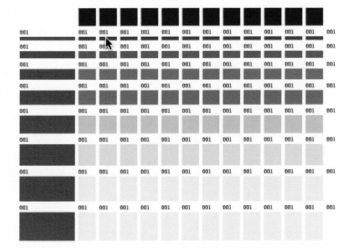 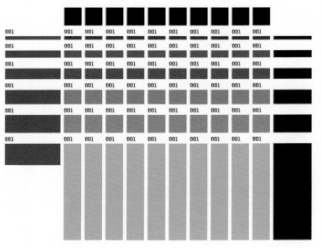

Mike Cina's www.trueistrue.com circa 2002 is an elegant example
of an unapologetically cryptic interface. Clicking on a color swatch
triggers a unique animation that overwrites the entire grid. There are
over 14,000 possible combinations, all of them counterintuitive.

Fail cryptically. Your playground is not obliged to make sense. Some interactive designers use their playgrounds to experiment with antinavigation, intentionally attempting to disorient their visitors. Exploring what doesn't work can bring you one step closer to what does work. Besides all that, sometimes it's simply fun and cathartic to do things "the wrong way." Your playground is a place to get such horseplay out of—or into—your system.

Fail unobligatedly. Don't let your playground become a burden or a drain. That takes the "play" out of it and defeats the whole purpose. If it gets old, take a break from it. Avoid imposing regular update schedules on yourself unless regular experimentation is one of your self-improvement goals. Set your online playground up so that it's easy to update. Many online design playgrounds are simply a series of image files linked one to another in reverse chronological order. Simply put up the new image and link it to the last one. Don't kill yourself worrying about usability or accessibility. Remember: This is not commercial work; it's more like personal design therapy.

Archive success. If any experiments happen to succeed, feel free to save those pieces and link to them from your commercial portfolio. You might want to create a special section for them called "personal experiments." This can be a way to attract new commercial work that is more experimental and may be more "up your alley" than other work in your commercial portfolio. Just don't let your playground become a portfolio-building tool, or you'll defeat its purpose. Any successes should be seen as happy accidents. And if no smashing successes ever materialize, no worries. It's a playground. Keep playing.

ONGOING PLAYGROUND EXPERIMENTATION KEEPS YOUR DESIGN WORK FROM BECOMING TOO STILTED AND FORMULAIC. IT INJECTS YOUR PERSONALITY AND PERSPECTIVE INTO YOUR DESIGN STYLE.

Playground Advantages

With commercial deadlines constantly looming, why waste time on experimental graphic design that doesn't pay the bills? Because it's not a waste of time. Think of your design playground as a professional development laboratory, which will eventually result in your ability to pay even more bills! Here are several good reasons to maintain a personal design playground:

Playgrounds instill boldness. Olympic gymnasts practice their routines hundreds of times before performing them in competition. This doesn't guarantee their competition performances will be flawless, but it does give them the confidence to attack their routines boldly, without fear of falling. It's true that overconfidence can lead to bad design, but timidity inevitably leads to horrid design.

Playgrounds allow you to amass a catalog of successful design approaches. None of your playground work will be perfectly suitable for commercial design in and of itself, but some of the techniques you've explored will be readily adaptable to various commercial projects. And they will be *your* techniques, not someone else's. You will *own* them. You will be comfortable implementing them on commercial projects because you will have already explored them compulsively in the safety of your own playground.

Playgrounds allow you to develop and advance your own design style. It takes a combination of experimental lab work (playground tweaking) and actual field experience (commercial work) to develop as a great designer. Ongoing playground experimentation keeps your design work from becoming too stilted and formulaic. It injects your personality and perspective into your design style. This is as it should be.

Playgrounds also allow you to track your growth as a designer. Flipping back through your playground work over the years is a helpful means of self-assessment. If you observe yourself falling back on the same obvious solutions, you can challenge yourself to explore new directions.

Playgrounds allow you to receive critical feedback from the online design community. Once you've put up a decent amount of work at your playground, submit its URL to an online design community site. (Several sites are listed in the back of this book.) Then somewhere on your playground, include an e-mail link so visitors can send you feedback. The feedback may

DESIGNER MILTON GLASER SAID, "PROFESSIONALISM AS A LIFETIME ASPIRATION IS A LIMITED GOAL." DESIGN PLAYGROUNDS ARE VEHICLES TO HELP YOU MOVE BEYOND MERE PROFESSIONAL COMPETENCE AND ON TO SOMETHING GREATER.

be encouraging, discouraging, banal, instructive, or just plain ridiculous. The point is that you're getting free feedback from people other than your coworkers and clients, and they're commenting on experimental work that you may never show to your coworkers or clients. Of course, take it all with a grain of salt; not everyone with an Internet connection is a competent design critic. Take what you can use and leave the rest.

Playgrounds can lead to interesting commercial work. The London-based design firm Hi-Res began its new media career with an online playground called soulbath.com. That experimental playground site landed Hi-Res a gig to design the even more experimental movie promotion site www.requiemforadream.com, and it's been a successful commercial ride ever since. Hi-Res designers started off doing the kind of experimental work they enjoyed, and that attracted the kind of commercial work they enjoyed. Of course, Hi-Res also happens to be a group of absolutely brilliant new media designers, and not every playground leads to a gig with Artisan Entertainment, but it could happen.

Playgrounds keep you passionate about design. Some people are reading this thinking, "I work all day in Illustrator; the last thing I want to do when I get off work is come home and open up Illustrator." But playground design is an entirely different animal because you're in complete control. It can inspire you to remember why you got into design in the first place,

which can inspire you to push your commercial projects beyond merely competent because you can't wait to get back to work and try out the new design approach you just discovered over the weekend. Ultimately, the reclamation of your professional passion and purpose is worth the extra time.

In a 2001 talk at an AIGA conference in London, designer Milton Glaser made this bold statement: "What is required in our field, more than anything else, is the continuous transgression. Professionalism does not allow for that because transgression has to encompass the possibility of failure and if you are professional your instinct is not to fail, it is to repeat success. So professionalism as a lifetime aspiration is a limited goal." Design playgrounds are vehicles to help you move beyond mere professional competence and on to something greater.

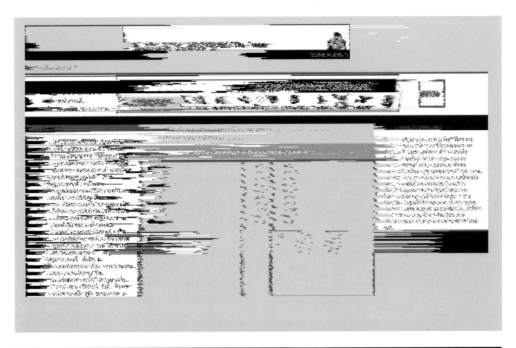

Hi-Res built an experimental playground at www.soulbath.com, which eventually led to commercial work designing www.requiemforadream.com. Both sites employ intentionally disorienting Flash interfaces to compelling narrative effect.

Dustin Hostetler's upsod.com is a playground of experimental illustration in which faces, hands, and skulls figure prominently. The face and hands are his. I'm not sure about the skull.

Playground Interview:
Dustin Hostetler of upsod.com

Dustin Hostetler is an illustrator and graphic designer who has maintained a personal design playground at upsod.com since 2000. *Upsod* stands for United Planets Space Organization Diary (in case that wasn't immediately apparent). www.Upsod.com is arranged in batches of 50 illustrations. When Hostetler

reaches 50 illustrations, he archives those 50 and begins a new batch. The illustrations range from figurative to abstract, with an inordinate emphasis on hands, faces, and skulls. I asked him about his playground and the influence it has on his commercial work.

UPSOD HISTORY AND PRACTICE

Why did you start upsod.com?

Sometime during 2000 I realized I needed a Web site. I had just been to Flashforward [a Macromedia-sponsored Web design conference] and was totally blown away by all these really dynamic personal Web sites. It was a scene I immediately wanted to be a part of, but since I had zero Web experience, I needed to make something that was easy for me.

At first the site was housed at a secret address only my friends knew about. I was the first person any of my friends knew who had a Web site, so every day I would make a small group of people (including my mom) new things to look at.

I updated it quite frequently, and if I didn't keep up with it people would e-mail me and ask, "What's up?" Even though these people were just my close buddies, it really motivated me to keep updating. My audience was small but dedicated, and it got me excited about producing work on the computer. I had only gone into design because art school was uninspiring, but realizing I could make art on the computer was a real life-changing moment.

Currently, who is your intended audience?

I don't really have an intended audience. I put up a lot of work that I'm not very proud of or happy with. Then I get motivated to put up something better so that a first-time viewer won't see a shitty image on the front page. In that way, I am my own audience because if I'm not happy with what I have up, I make more work.

A lot of the pages have become inspiration for other projects, like my band's CD covers. In that way, my friends are also my audience because they can visit my archives and say, "Can we make our poster or cover look like this page?"

Does upsod.com have a regular production schedule?

Initially I told myself I would update it daily. Of course anyone who tries something like this knows it's very difficult to keep up with. As the versions have progressed, I've deemphasized the frequency of updates and focused on the concepts.

As far as breaks between versions of 50, initially I looked forward to the end of each version because I could immediately start thinking about the next. Now I take up to a month off between versions, so I can reapproach each version with a clear head.

How much time do you spend executing each screen?

One hour max.

How do you know when a screen is finished?

When I'm sick of looking at it.

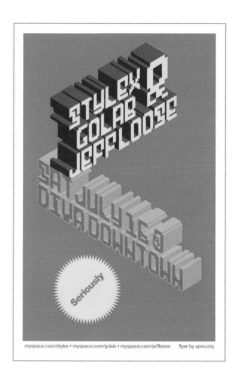

What kind of things do you explore on upsod.com that you can't explore in a physical sketchbook?

I currently have five notebooks on my desk, filled with to-do lists, doodles, and random phrases. It's really important to me to put things down "on paper" so I don't forget any potentially great ideas. But upsod provides me with a vehicle to make immediately archived work. In general, working on the computer allows me to realize my ideas much more quickly than I could in my days of paint and pens.

Do you get ideas for upsod.com beforehand, or is it all exploration from the time you begin working on the computer?

I may scribble a phrase down in my notebook and then come back to it later, but a lot of the work is still created all at once. I plop in front of my computer and just start playing around.

How intentionally thematic is each series of 50 illustrations? Do you set out to pursue certain themes and recurring images?

Sometimes I go into a series with an idea, like all black and white. But I get bored really quickly, and I tire of my own work quickly as well. So even if there is a theme, it seems to fall apart fast. Upsod.com is generally whatever I've been exploring at the moment, sort of documented in diary form.

What are some recurring themes throughout the whole site?

The main theme that continues throughout the whole site is me. It really is my diary. Sometimes the images obscurely document serious emotions I'm having, and sometimes not so obscurely. People often tease me for using hands so much, but the thing is, the hands I use are my own. So it is a way for me to bring myself into my work.

UPSOD INFLUENCE ON COMMERCIAL WORK

What is your day job? Do you consider yourself mainly an illustrator, a designer, an artist, or what?

My day job is creating illustrations for magazines and doing different design projects with my wife, Jemma Hostetler. I consider myself a professional graphic artist. I don't usually call myself an illustrator because I am self-taught, and I don't think it is fair to assume I have the talent of someone who has dedicated his life to this profession. I also don't usually call myself an artist because even though I am trying more and more to get my work into galleries and out of the computer, for the most part I make my living by creating graphics in an artsy sort of way.

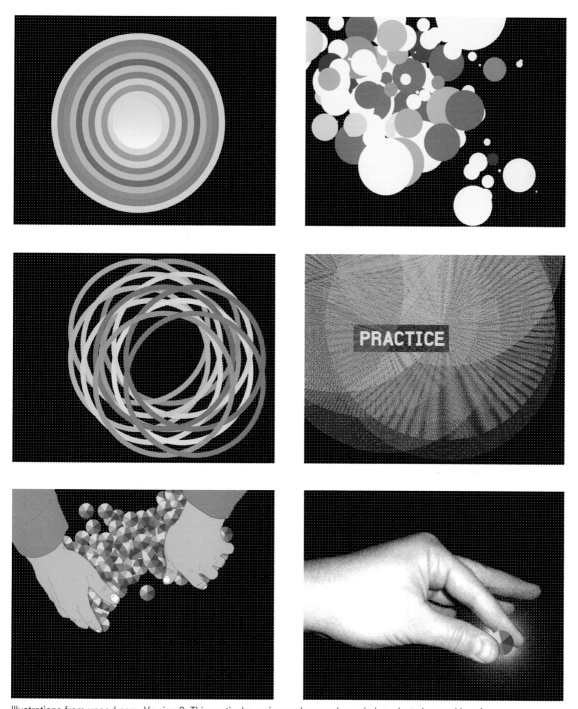

Illustrations from upsod.com, Version 9. This particular series explores colors, circles, clustering, and layering.

Has any commercial work come directly from clients seeing upsod?

I don't think so. I'd like to think at some point I will put something on upsod that will inspire an art director to call me, but I haven't seen any direct evidence of that happening yet. I tend to steer people toward my online portfolio at upso.org for my "professional" client work, and if they like what they see enough to dig around for more work, upsod isn't hard to find.

How has doing upsod improved your commercial work? What have you learned about design and illustration from doing it?

Without upsod, I wouldn't be doing what I do today for a living. Upsod encouraged me to pursue illustration as more than a hobby. It allowed me to create a body of work (as far as style and assets are concerned), and gave me the confidence to create an illustration portfolio site. Upsod has also given me a chance to fail enough times that I tend to fail less for clients. It encourages me to try new things publicly, which has kept me on my toes.

Do you use upsod as a sketchbook for ideas that later turn up in your commercial work?

Yes, I do. When I went to Flashforward in 2000, one of the big things I took away was a comment Joshua Davis made about his site pray-station.com. He was publicly giving away code at the time and showcasing a lot of different experiments. He said it wasn't wasted effort on his part because if a client approached him to work on a project, he may have already created what they needed, and he could basically just sample himself. That really stuck with me.

Will you ever stop doing upsod.com?

I often think about retiring it, but I know I can't. That site is the reason I am able to do what I do today for a living, and I owe it to the domain to keep it alive and active for as long as I am alive and active.

Bpm Magazine cover by Dustin Hostetler. Hostetler has developed a signature illustration style at his playground that is colorful, playful, and particularly suitable to entertainment industry magazines.

Playground Gallery

What does design playground experimentation actually look like? It varies widely from designer to designer, depending on personal interests, visual style, and chosen medium. Some designers experiment almost exclusively with typography. Others experiment with illustration. Others experiment with audio, animation, and programming.

What follows is selected work from four of my favorite playgrounds. I chose these particular pieces not because they are the "best" work ever done by these designers, but because they represent the kind of experimentation that each playground affords.

Mike Cina of trueistrue.com

At www.trueistrue.com, Mike Cina (of the design partnership We Work For Them) has experimented with everything from Flash interaction to homemade book deconstruction, but his specialty is typography. Any phrase at all affords Cina an excuse to get at the heart of the typeface he is exploring. These minimalist studies are beautiful in their restraint and in the asymmetrical balance they achieve using type as pure form.

CINA

VIVA EL
TYPE DESIGN

Jemma Hostetler of prate.com

Jemma Hostetler uses prate.com to explore combinations of texture, layout, typography, and photography in search of original, expressive design styles. Her abstraction of world maps has produced work more akin to conceptual art than to commercial design.

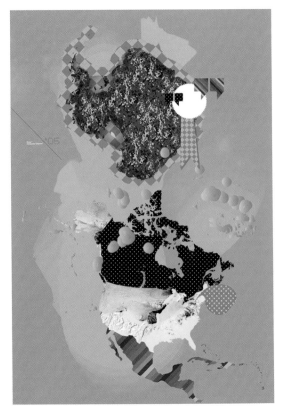

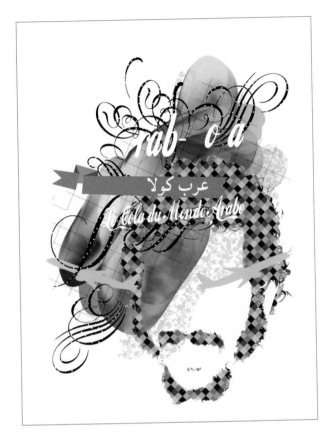

Being Quiet.
Small Mistakes.
Charm Spent.

Talk Lost.
Queer Grace.
Occur Sans.

Queer Lost.
Grace Sans.
Talk Occur.

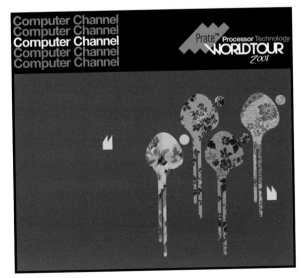

Computer Channel
Computer Channel
Computer Channel
Computer Channel
Computer Channel

Prate™ Processor Technology
WORLDTOUR
2001

Curt Cloninger of
playdamage.org

Playdamage.org experiments with low-resolution animation and short audio loops. Visit the site to see each of these stills in motion with an accompanying mini-soundtrack. The house rules are that no screen can be fatter than 200K. The challenge for me is to generate as much sensory narrative as possible within these limitations.

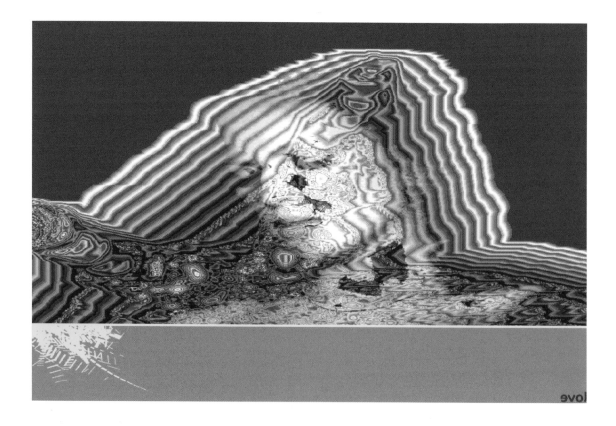

Geoff Lillemon of oculart.com

Geoff Lillemon combines a background in painting with a disturbingly unorthodox Flash animation style to perpetrate the gorgeous hallucination known as oculart.com. If you think these images are haunting in print, visit the site to see them flicker and sway. Oculart feels like a night out with Toulouse-Lautrec on absinthe-soaked mushrooms.

Willful Superfluity

In *Civilisation*, art historian Kenneth Clark wrote of northern Italian courts of the late fifteenth century: "It's only in a court that a man may do something extravagant for its own sake, because he wants to, because it seems worth doing... and it is sometimes through such willful, superfluous actions that men discover their powers." For better or worse, most of us don't have the finances to provide ourselves with such full-time, courtly leisure. But none of us are so poor that we can't devote a few occasional hours to practice our own "willful, superfluous actions."

Personal design playgrounds are safe places of play and experimentation, free from outside censure and nagging self-doubt. Kublai Kahn had his Xanadu, Alice had her Wonderland, Willy Wonka had his chocolate factory, and now you, too, can have your very own playground.org. Because, as Willy Wonka so acutely observed, "We are the music makers, and we are the dreamers of the dreams." Oscar Hammerstein further elaborated, "You got to have a dream, if you don't have a dream, how you gonna have a dream come true?"

■ ■ ■

TRY LOOKING AT IT ANOTHER WAY.

—JAMES'S FATHER, *JAMES AND THE GIANT PEACH*

9 | THE FIVE REALMS OF DESIGN

Most of us wear several different hats on any given day. I am simultaneously husband, father, son, teacher, friend, writer, artist, designer, musician, and so on. Many of these roles overlap, and sometimes they compete with one another. Likewise, designers perform multiple roles. We are media tamers, audience advocates, client liaisons, ethical professionals, and aesthetic watchdogs of our projects. Each of these roles operates in its own "realm" of design.

I propose that there are five design realms. Each realm overlaps the others, and sometimes they conflict with one another. The designer must be aware of these realms in order to successfully balance the demands of a project.

The five realms are

- **Media constraints:** Does the design work in the medium?
- **Audience needs:** Does the design meet the needs of the audience?
- **Client needs:** Does the design meet the needs of the client?
- **Professional ethics:** Is the design ethical?
- **Aesthetics:** Does the design look good?

The Realm of Media Constraints

First and foremost, a design must work within its medium. A Web site that takes forever to load fails because no one will wait around to see it. Animated typography that moves too fast in a movie title sequence fails because no one will be able to read it. Lots of tiny text on a highway billboard fails because no one racing past will be able to read it.

New media designer Hillman Curtis discovered this when he pioneered Flash animation narrative strategies in the days when Internet bandwidth was low. He found that simply porting a high-resolution video advertisement to the Net used too much bandwidth. He had to tell an entirely different kind of animated story. Every movement was precious and had to be carefully considered. How much meaning and visceral impact could he convey at eight frames per second? In essence, Curtis had to invent an entirely different kind of motion graphics vocabulary, defined largely by the constraints of the medium. He developed this new vocabulary through experimentation and refinement. What was true for Hillman Curtis and Flash animation is true for any designer in any medium: The first step to mastering the language of a medium is to work in that medium *a lot*.

Know Your Medium Experientially

Roll your sleeves up, get in there, and test the limits of your medium. If its constraints are to inform your design approach, you have to push the medium enough to discover its boundaries. There is an unquantifiable aspect of creativity that can't be taught theoretically or conceptually. It is only discovered by experientially pushing actual media around. It is dangerous to conceptualize design solutions without a working knowledge of your medium because the best concepts don't arise from the void; they arise from an ongoing dialogue with the medium.

Design is a bit like the parable of the blind men feeling the elephant. One man feels the body and thinks the elephant is like a wall. Another feels the leg and thinks the elephant is like a tree. Another feels the trunk and thinks the elephant is like a snake. Another feels the tail and thinks the elephant is like a rope. There are so many different types of design (industrial design, packaging design, interactive design, motion graphics, poster design, book design, logo design, corporate identity systems, and so on), and everybody thinks that their type is design. Yet each design discipline requires different emphases throughout the creative

SENSIBLY BALANCING THE FIVE REALMS OF DESIGN IS ONE WAY TO SUSTAIN THE

CONSISTENT PRODUCTION OF QUALITY WORK THAT YOU'LL WANT TO KEEP DOING.

process, and many even require different processes, outlooks, and approaches. An intimate working knowledge of your design medium will greatly improve the way you approach your creative process.

A word on multimedia: Mastering the discrete components of multimedia (audio, video, animation, and interaction) doesn't automatically translate into a mastery of multimedia. Once these components combine, they take on a life of their own. For example, the groundbreaking movie titles created by designer Kyle Cooper—*Se7en*, *Mission: Impossible*, *Spider-Man*—have something in common with print typography and something in common with digital animation. But Cooper's work is really its own genre—animated type. Hybrid media are always more than the mere sum of their constituent parts.

And hybrid media don't necessarily have to be "digital media" or "new media." Any graphic designer who combines text and images is creating hybrid media. Designers need to realize they are speaking not just a compound language but also a hybrid language. Comics guru Scott McCloud says that if a prize-winning novelist and a prize-winning painter collaborated on a comic, the result would be less than prize

winning. The novelist crafts her words to stand on their own; the painter crafts her images to stand on their own. In the context of a hybrid-media comic, these independent words and images would both wind up shouting too loudly, competing for limited sensory attention. The words and images of comics should ideally meet somewhere in the middle, each yielding to and aware of the other. The same is true of graphic design. Which explains why great poets don't automatically make great marketing copywriters.

Even within the prescribed genre of graphic design, different media deliverables require different design approaches. In 1930 experimental design pioneer Kurt Schwitters devised a chart called "New Design in Typography." In it, Schwitters rated media deliverables from postcards to billboards based on how much each should rely on orientation versus advertising. By orientation, he meant something very akin to what we might call usability. By advertising, he meant eye-catching graphic design. According to Schwitters, posters should rely almost entirely on advertising. Invoices should rely entirely on orientation. It's not really important whether Schwitters's percentages are universally correct (although they do seem like

MASTERING THE DISCRETE COMPONENTS OF MULTIMEDIA DOESN'T AUTOMATICALLY TRANSLATE INTO A MASTERY OF MULTIMEDIA. ONCE THESE COMPONENTS COMBINE, THEY TAKE ON A LIFE OF THEIR OWN.

	principle of ORIENTATION	principle of ADVERTISING
letterhead		
envelope		
invoice		
form		
prospectus		
postcard		
poster		
brochure		
book		
advertisement		
program		
catalog		
ticket		
packaging		
announcement		
billboard		

An English translation of Kurt Schwitters' 1930 "New Design in Typography" chart. Each deliverable is rated on a sliding scale, from 100 percent orientation (usability) to 100 percent advertising (eye-catching design).

useful points of departure). What's important is the awareness that each specific deliverable requires its own unique design approach.

Usability fascists and experimental-design extremists still get in ridiculously heated arguments over whether a Web site should be all orientation or all advertising. Of course, it depends on the purpose of the site. An online bookstore should rely more on orientation. A movie promotional site should rely more on advertising. For every design project you

undertake, apply Schwitters's orientation-versus-advertising criteria prior to the design phase. It will clarify your thinking and help you determine the appropriate design approach to take.

Yield to Media Constraints

One way to react to media constraints is to yield to them, letting them guide your design. The reed that bends with the wind doesn't break, or so the saying goes. Bauhaus-era designers of the early twentieth century inherited the letterpress printing process, which enforced a kind of rigid rectangularity. The frame of the letterpress, the leading, the figure blocks, the designer's horizontal and vertical rules, and even the individual metal type were all rectangular. Rather than fight these constraints, Bauhaus designers yielded to them, letting the limitations of letterpress printing suggest a geometric, minimalist visual approach comprised of right angles and bold rules.

Some contemporary Web designers have yielded to the limitations of the Web and have arrived at similarly clever design solutions. In designing the online community site k10k.net, the design firm Cuban Council yielded to the limited bandwidth of the Web by using tiny pixelated avatars and non-anti-aliasing, bitmapped typography. Their site loads quickly, yet still retains a playful, nonutilitarian charm. This pixelated design approach has its roots in old-school, eight-bit computer graphics.

The design of k10k.net is partially influenced by the bandwidth limitations of the Internet. By adapting an old-school video game aesthetic to the Web, its designers achieve a lot of visual charm and functionality out of a few thin-loading GIFs.

TUESDAY EDITION
Writer Darin Painter takes a look at CP
for this article in Print Solutions.

COUDAL PARTNERS
About This Site

A CP CONTEST

Captain Beefheart of Darkness

The winners are posted. Thanks to everyone who entered our quick contest called Booking Bands.

LATER TODAY FIELD-TESTED BOOKS

Pack Carefully Books Are Heavy

We're deep into production on the 2006 version of Field-Tested Books, our summer reading feature, and have lined up dozens of people like George Saunders, Jonathan Eig, James Lileks, Maud Newton and Amy Krouse Rosenthal to write short reviews for us. We're also happy to report that Mike and Dan of Aesthetic Apparatus are doing this year's limited-edition poster. Sign up here for infrequent news on this and other stuff.

[Subscribe]

A CP FILM COPY GOES HERE

If You Only See One Short Film Made By a Chicago Design Studio This Year...

Please take a few minutes (eleven actually) to check it out our short feature film, Copy Goes here.

Thanks to everyone who has hooked it up, sent us feedback or even nice enough to buy the DVD or the tee shirt (now just $15). The reviews have been really nice except for the humorless and bitter ones, but those are pretty funny too. Oh, in case you missed it, here's

FRESH SIGNALS

For Flash animation fans: See Flashdestroyed from within. bb-today

Studio804 completes Modular3 in Kansas City's Strawberry Hill neighborhood. dw-today

There's been a lot of buzz about numbers stations all over the web this week because of a strange posting on Craigslist. The Conet Project is an archive of creepy recordings of numbers stations through the years. jw-today

An interesting, personal account: 10 years since Timothy Leary's death. sd-today

"You are the most cuddled generation in history. I belong to the last generation that did not have to be in a car seat. You had to be in car seats. I did not have to wear a helmet when I rode my bike. You do. You have to wear helmets when you go swimming, right? In case you bump your head against the side of the pool. Oh, by the way, I should have said, my speech today may contain some peanut products." ms-today

Kubrick A to Z at Visual Memory, which also houses the holiest of relics, the original cinema program for 2001 from 1968. Via Morning News. jc-today

FOVICKS, Friends Of Vast Industrial Concrete Kafkaesque Structures. Via GaB. jc-today

From the GDC event in Vancouver last week, check JC with lots of type projected on his face. cp-today

We're remodeling the studio. Here's what it looks like so far. Thanks to TSR. jc-today

A Conversation with Brian Ulrich at Conscientious. Brian is a Chicago photographer who

Cover
Page Two + Archives
About CP
Guest Editors
Museum of Online Museums
Copy Goes Here
Depth of Field
Reading + Writing
Reference Library
Photoshop Tennis
Verse By Voice
Western State

AD VIA THE DECK

Dreamweaver 8: CSS Best Practice case studies, seminars, tutorials and more.

15 MINUTES

Curtis, Adrian, and Little Debbie [?]

A THING WE MADE: JEWELBOXING

We hated the options available for custom packaging DVDs and CDs so we created a brand that gives creative professionals and hobbyists the tools to make great stuff. Here's a bit from the latest Jewelboxing weblog entry:

"Then it dawned on us that we have these terrific cases Susan painstakingly built in Photoshop that allow us to really easily drop in cover images and essentially build a virtual case. It's how we make all the sample case images we use here on the site. So why not just share those?" Read the entire post.

coudal.com looks elegant enough to be a classy print magazine, with its intelligent use of typography and generous negative space. But its designers actually use CSS-controlled, browser-generated HTML typography, working within the limitations of the medium to achieve surprising results.

GREAT DESIGNERS ALWAYS SEEM TO COME UP WITH GREAT DESIGN SOLUTIONS

REGARDLESS OF—OR EVEN BECAUSE OF—THE CONSTRAINTS OF THEIR MEDIUM.

For coudal.com, the design firm Coudal Partners used the limitations of Web typography to their advantage. Rather than rely on Photoshop-generated, anti-aliased GIF typography for their headers and subheaders, the firm achieved typographic elegance via CSS-controlled, browser-generated HTML typography. There are a number of visually engaging contrasts between header and subhead type. Header type is large, serif, one color, and negatively tracked (using the CSS *letter-spacing* property). Subhead type is small, sans serif, two colors, and positively tracked. These are the same approaches to typographic contrast that print designers have been using for years, but they are implemented at coudal.com within the constraints of the online medium. Even the Coudal Partners logotype is in HTML.

Late-modernist designer Willi Kunz purposefully limits himself to just one typeface (Univers). In his book *Typography: Macro- and Microaesthetics*, he eloquently advocates yielding to constraints: "What initially appear to be constraints can also lead to unexpected solutions…. When problems are too open-ended, the dazzling array of possibilities often leads to confused or chaotic results. A program such as a grid system, a series of carefully selected type sizes and weights, or self-imposed technical or economic limitations help channel the design process into a more productive and interesting course." Hillman Curtis points out another related advantage of constraints. They "purify" design by removing the extraneous: "Limitations can be seen as liberating frameworks that force you to streamline your work,

thus making it accessible to the most people possible, both technologically and aesthetically."

Mediocre designers complain about how their design would have been better if such and such a constraint hadn't limited their pure, original vision. Great designers always seem to come up with great design solutions regardless of—or even because of—the constraints of their medium.

Fight Media Constraints

You don't have to give in to media constraints in order to take advantage of them. Fighting constraints can also lead to creative design results. I'm not suggesting blindly running roughshod over obvious constraints. Don't design a project in full-color CMYK that will only wind up being printed in grayscale. Don't stream DVD quality video over a dial-up modem. That's not fighting constraints; it's blatantly ignoring them. I'm suggesting here that once you become aware of your media constraints, try to find a way to overcome them.

At the same time Bauhaus designers were yielding to the rectangular limitations of the letterpress frame, Dada designers were fighting to overcome it. For example, in order to set his type at an angle, John Heartfield simply poured plaster around his angled type and let the plaster harden into a rectangular block. He was then able to fit the plaster block into the rectangular grid of the letterpress and print his angled letters as if they were a woodblock image.

Designer/illustrator Karen Ingram and U.K. design firm Monkey Clan designed this engaging Web site for the U.K. band South. They overcame the rectangular confines of the medium by blurring the boundary lines between content sections—hand-drawing illustrations that overlap sections and collaging their photographic elements.

The U.K. design firm Hi-Res designed this baroque site for the pop band Ilya. Hi-Res overcame the rectangular limitations of the Web by using Flash animation to draw flowing, art nouveau lines into an unbounded, floating area of negative space. It looks less like a Web site and more like a Toulouse-Lautrec lithograph.

Look for ways to do what everyone says can't be done. Set aside your knowledge of media constraints and simply envision what you would like to accomplish. Then push your media constraints to accomplish your vision. I've basically just described the development of Hollywood special effects, from Ray Harryhausen's stop-motion claymation through George Lucas's early computer-assisted camera movement to Peter Jackson's generative digital crowd animation.

Web designers face some of the same problems that letterpress print designers faced. A Web image has to be square and type can only be "set" in horizontal rows. To overcome these limitations, a number of contemporary Web designers use hand-drawn illustrations, ornamentation, and typography in conjunction with Flash animation to design more organic, less grid-based layouts.

Whether you choose to fight or yield to the constraints of your medium depends on the nature of the project, the nature of the constraints, and your own personality as a designer. Whichever approach you choose, you can't do either without a working knowledge of the specific boundaries of the medium.

The Realm of Audience Needs

Ultimately your design is for an audience. Does the design serve them? Does it effectively communicate to them? Does it meet their needs?

This is the most important realm of design and often the most overlooked. Theoretically your client should understand the needs of her audience, but she may not understand how to best reach her audience via visual communication. That's why you've been hired. In the end, if you put your client's audience first, then you put your client first, because the audience ultimately pays your client's bills. In this sense, you really work for the audience. I teach at a state university, and my paycheck comes from the state. The university vice-chancellor signs my check. But my collective "boss" is really my students. None of them can fire me, but without them, there would be no reason for me to be there. The same is true of your client's customers. No customers mean no client means no graphic design job.

Edward de Bono says, "A design is judged to be satisfactory when it is judged to be satisfactory by those who are to use it." So although your client actually pays your bills, and although there are four other realms of design to consider, your design ultimately succeeds or fails based not on how good it looks to you or how happy your client is with it, but on how well it serves those who are to use it.

SET ASIDE YOUR KNOWLEDGE OF MEDIA CONSTRAINTS AND SIMPLY ENVISION WHAT YOU WOULD LIKE TO ACCOMPLISH. THEN PUSH YOUR MEDIA CONSTRAINTS TO ACCOMPLISH YOUR VISION.

IN THE END, IF YOU PUT YOUR CLIENT'S AUDIENCE FIRST, THEN YOU PUT YOUR

CLIENT FIRST, BECAUSE THE AUDIENCE ULTIMATELY PAYS YOUR CLIENT'S BILLS.

Most Advanced Yet Acceptable

Industrial designer Raymond Loewy coined the maxim of Most Advanced Yet Acceptable (MAYA). The MAYA principle basically says this: Make your design as advanced as you can but not so advanced that manufacturers and consumers won't accept it. For example, the "car of the future" may look so futuristic that it fails to sell today. You want your design to be on the leading edge without going over that edge. It's the *yet acceptable* part that considers the needs and tastes of the audience and that distinguishes graphic design from art. An artist ostensibly need not worry about whether his art is acceptable (although most still do). But if a commercial graphic designer fails to worry about whether her design is acceptable, she should probably start worrying about a new career.

By definition, how can MAYA *not* be a good idea? You are ahead of the competition but still attractive to your market. The problem is that MAYA is an elusive goal because there are no hard-and-fast rules for discovering the most advanced yet acceptable design for a given project. Market researchers are forever trying to "read" contemporary culture in order to discover where the MAYA line lies, but whenever the whims of human taste are involved, science falls short. Sometimes an experienced designer's intuition is worth more than thousands of pages of demographic case studies and market testing. A wise client will rely on a combination of experienced intuition and market analysis.

Who Is the Audience?

We know we need to consider the audience. We know it is our primary concern. But do we know who our audience is? It's very tricky to get a big-picture understanding of an aggregate group of people. It's tricky enough trying to understand a single individual. Heck, it's tricky enough just trying to understand yourself.

In this sense, marketing is also a bit like the parable of the blind men feeling the elephant. It's difficult to make sweeping proclamations across all markets about what kind of designs do and don't work because each market is different. And with the rise of the Internet and the targeted micromarketing it facilitates, markets are becoming increasingly fragmented and specialized.

In his essay "Quantum Cats and Mosquito Hunting," Belgian musician and online marketer Gerry De Mol adds yet another wrinkle: The individual audience member you are trying to reach may actually transition from demographic to demographic throughout the day. Our activities (and identities) are becoming increasingly fragmented as our media devices are becoming increasingly mobile, intelligent, customizable, and interconnected. The target demographic you are aiming to hit may morph into another demographic while your message is still in transit. De Mol writes, "When you call me I'm not where you think I am, and I may not be who you think I am, and I probably am completely uninterested in what you think I want. I want what I want when I want it and you can't predict it: I'll decide when to tell you."

The Internet has altered the standard relationship between marketer and consumer. Television and magazines are one-to-many broadcast media. But the Internet is a many-to-many medium. Your audience is no longer sitting around waiting to be sent content—they are publishing their own content. In 1999 an engineer, a consultant, a publisher, and a marketer realized this and teamed up to write the now-famous *Cluetrain Manifesto: The End of Business as Usual.* The manifesto proposes that markets are now more like conversations. This means marketers can no longer simply broadcast; they now have to dialogue. And 50 percent of dialogue involves listening.

This new paradigm can be good news. You no longer have to simply guess what kind of design your audience *might* like based on feedback from premarket focus groups. Now you can beta-test your design on your actual audience and get real-time feedback on the fly. Depending on how you have been marketing, the bad news may be that now your *actual* audience has a say in your design and you have to develop an entirely new strategy of on-the-fly design.

Some Internet software design firms have modified their creative process to incorporate an ongoing iterative cycle of improvements based on real-time customer feedback—such as Chicago's 37 Signals' merging of their development and implementation phases. To succeed with this approach, you must have some faith in your audience, you have to be honest about your mistakes, and you have to have a serious commitment to real-time customer support. What firms like 37 Signals are discovering is that this approach also builds brand loyalty and customer investment. Your audience is no longer merely a target to hit; they are now helping you improve the product they are using. What you lose in control (control that wasn't really doing you much good anyway) you gain in customer buy-in.

Another result of the Internet's many-to-many nature is that companies can be held more accountable. If a product is good, consumers will spread the word. If a product is bad, they will spread the word even faster. It's no longer sufficient to advertise, "We're great!" Now you actually have to be great. The *Cluetrain Manifesto* warns: "Corporations do not speak in the same voice as [the] new networked conversations. To their intended online audiences, companies sound hollow, flat, literally inhuman. In just a few more years, the current homogenized 'voice' of business—the sound of mission statements and brochures—will seem as contrived and artificial as the language of the 18th century French court. Already companies

THE INTERNET IS A MANY-TO-MANY MEDIUM. YOUR AUDIENCE IS NO LONGER SITTING AROUND WAITING TO BE SENT CONTENT—THEY ARE PUBLISHING THEIR OWN CONTENT.

that speak in the language of the pitch, the dog-and-pony show, are no longer speaking to anyone." This is a good thing for consumers and a bad thing for marketers relying on the same old marketing tricks.

Maybe you don't consider yourself a marketer, and you're wondering what all this has to do with graphic design. The design approach you choose is influenced not only by the audience to whom you are speaking but also by the nature of the marketplace in which you are speaking. Perhaps your client has already targeted his demographic for you in explicit detail. It's still your job to understand the way design dialogues in the contemporary marketplace. Mastering your medium involves more than just knowing about card stock weights, PANTONE chips, lighting techniques, standards compliance, and other technical constraints. It means being able to tailor your message so that it speaks the language of your medium *and* your market. Like it or not, the best designers are also marketers.

The Realm of Client Needs

If audience needs are the most overlooked realm, then client needs are the most overemphasized. It's not that client needs aren't important. It's just that they shouldn't be considered to the exclusion of every other realm of design. When I ask my design students why client needs are the most emphasized design realm, the ones who haven't done commercial work shrug their shoulders. The ones who have done commercial work immediately answer: "Money."

The client signs your paycheck, so you'd better give him what he wants. The problem is, he doesn't specifically know what he wants. That's why he hired you. He knows he wants to meet the needs of his audience, but his understanding of how to meet these needs through design is unclear. Or maybe he has some very specific graphic design ideas that aren't going to work as is, and part of your job is to help him understand why. This can get awkward. Someone is paying you to tell him something that he initially might not want to hear, and yet if you simply tell him what he wants to hear, you aren't doing your job. No wonder dealing with clients is so notoriously sticky.

Some designers adopt this attitude: "I'd love design if it weren't for the clients." If this is your attitude, you will have an unpleasant and difficult time succeeding in commercial design. Designers who see clients as a hindrance to solving what they consider to be the *real* design challenges have an overly narrow perspective. Designers who see client relationships as one of the *real* design challenges get the big picture.

Staying on the same conceptual page with your client is not a distraction from real design work; it's at the heart of real design work.

Veteran designer Paula Scher says, "It's the human factor—combustible client-designer relationships coupled with marketplace accidents—that inevitably lead to the visual gestalt of an era." From this perspective, even "bad" client relationships can act as a creative catalyst. For better or worse, client relationships are part and parcel of commercial design.

By definition, there is no "real" commercial design work without a client. You can be an amateur artist without an agent or a gallery, but you can't be an amateur commercial designer without a client. There is a name for a commercial designer without a client: unemployed.

Furthermore, even though the audience realm is ultimately the most important realm of design, you'll never get your user-friendly design out the door if you are unwilling or unable to address the realm of client needs. If only for the sake of your audience, it's important to establish a productive working relationship with your client.

Designer Steven Tolleson makes this remarkable statement about the overall success of a design project: "A really successful project has nothing to do with the way something looks. A successful project is one where everybody involved feels good about the process. We are almost never happy with the final product because there are always so many 'if onlys.' But a successful project means that both the client and the designer feel equal ownership of the result. They both have made significant contributions that influenced the final product. That it was a joint effort, a beneficial relationship, and an enjoyable process."

From a client's perspective, that's the kind of designer she wants to hire. Clients certainly don't want to hire a dictatorial designer who ignores their input. Some clients may think they want to hire a spineless designer who is nothing more than a glorified cake decorator, but they don't *really* want that. Wise clients want to hire a designer who is a working partner.

Client Relationships 101

This book is not about how to win friends and influence people. Still, a large part of successful client relationships is based on people skills, verbal communication skills, and business sense. I can't impart these things in a few paragraphs, but I can share three basic practices that facilitate better client relationships.

DEAL DIRECTLY WITH "THE BOSS"

If you do design work for Microsoft, it's probably not possible or even expedient for you to meet with Bill Gates on a regular basis. But if you were able to, your design would probably be better. Figure out who has the ultimate authority to sign off on the project within the corporation and then attempt to deal directly with that person. If you're designing for a sole proprietor, problem solved. If you are an in-house designer, you should have a working understanding of who is in charge. It's not always the person directly above you in the official organization chart. If your client is a larger corporation, make sure your contact person—creative director, art director, marketing manager—is authorized to sign off on design decisions. If not, try to deal with the person who is. If at all possible, avoid dealing with a committee. If you must deal with a committee, determine which person on the committee has the real authority.

If the liaison person assigned to you is not the boss of the project, it's no good pretending she is. Eventually her decision could be overturned by the real boss. Better to deal directly with the real boss. The real boss has authority to initiate and approve new avenues of exploration without having to ask permission from a higher authority. This makes the design process run much more smoothly. The real boss is personally invested in the corporation. This makes her input insightful and valuable. As a general rule, the more authority your contact person has within the organization, the better your design solution will be.

DON'T REPRESENT IDEAS OVER-SPECIFICALLY

If you are sharing rough conceptual ideas with your client, don't show her a full-color, high-resolution Photoshop mock-up. Simply explain your rough conceptual ideas with words or a simple sketch. When it comes time to show your client a proposed layout, show her one in black and white that focuses her attention on the layout alone. If you represent your ideas over-specifically, the client will invariably focus her attention on some tangential detail (usually having to do with color) that has nothing to do with the idea you are trying to convey.

Throughout the creative process, whenever you return to the client for feedback, always represent your ideas no more specifically than you mean them to be evaluated. The further along you are in the creative process, the more detailed your mock-ups should be.

JUSTIFY IDEAS IN TERMS OF OVERALL GOALS RATHER THAN AESTHETICS

Don't justify your design decisions to the client in terms of aesthetics. Your client doesn't care about your nuanced interpretation of Josef Albers's color theory, nor does she want to be lectured on it. Justify your design decisions in terms of the overall project goals that you and the client agreed upon in the creative brief.

MOK SAYS THAT INSTEAD OF PRESENTING DESIGN AS A VERB, WE PRESENT IT

AS A NOUN. WE DESCRIBE OURSELVES NOT IN TERMS OF WHAT WE DO, BUT

IN TERMS OF WHAT WE MAKE. OTHER PROFESSIONALS ARE SMARTER.

These agreed-upon goals are the common language of the project. If you can't justify your design decisions based on the goals of the brief, then your decisions are fair game for criticism and revision.

This doesn't mean that you can't operatively rely on intuition and your own personal aesthetics as guiding principles throughout the creative process. It just means that you can't use those aesthetics to justify your decisions to the client. As Willi Kunz observes, "The argument for any design should be based on communication goals rather than aesthetics—which of course does not mean that aesthetics are unimportant." It's just that aesthetics are a subjective language—slippery ground to stand on when you're trying to communicate the objective value of your work to someone who is paying you real money to achieve objective results.

Marketing the Value of Design

In 2003 designer Clement Mok, then president of AIGA, wrote an article in *Communication Arts* called "Designers: Time for Change." In it he challenged contemporary designers to reexamine the way we represent ourselves. Mok said we should be selling solutions and services ("I communicate corporate value to online markets"), but instead we're selling deliverable goods ("I make Web sites"). Instead of presenting design as a verb, we present it as a noun. We describe ourselves not in terms of what we do, but in terms of what we make. Other professionals are smarter. A surgeon doesn't say, "I make cuts in people." An attorney doesn't say, "I make paperwork." But we say, "I make Web sites."

By describing ourselves as simple artisans, makers of deliverable goods, we have effectively abdicated our seat at the predesign big boy table. No investor would dream of breaking ground on a new construction site without having had numerous preliminary meetings with the architect of the building. Yet clients frequently call in graphic designers at the last minute to implement predetermined design strategies.

Interview: Clement Mok

I talked to Clement Mok about how designers wound up underselling our role and what we can do to change it.

When you describe your occupation to people, how do you describe yourself?

It depends on who asks me that question. Here are three different ways:

1. I am a design consultant with experiences in design planning.

2. I am a designer with a background in dealing with emerging technologies in business or social applications.

3. I help companies amplify messages in the marketplace.

Notice that I never define who I am by what I make or deliver. I define myself by my activities.

You've written, "Designers give form to ideas, bring clarity to information, and imagine what's possible." Do you still stand by that definition?

Yes. That's the most functional definition.

Given a specific application like print design, do those fundamental functions still apply?

There are guiding principles of design, regardless of its applications and specializations. As an analogy, there are different kinds of doctors that specialize in different fields, but at some level every doctor should have a basic understanding of human anatomy. Likewise all design disciplines are about a set of best practices/methodologies that gives form to an idea. Yet we paint each design discipline as being so special that it becomes very difficult for anyone to grasp the core fundamentals of design. The challenge is to raise the level of discourse beyond just focusing on domain competency. A graphic designer, an architect, or an industrial designer should all be able to converse to their clients regarding "design thinking." Design practitioners, regardless of their vocation, should be able to explain and advocate design as "the art of possibilities." That's our lingua franca.

Do these subdivisions (product design, graphic design, interactive design, and so on) help the way our clients perceive the overall design profession?

The problem with separating various design professions by discipline is that it forces the client to self-select a solution. For example, a client (for whatever reason) deduces that she has a brand problem and decides that a graphic designer is the most appropriate person to solve it. But her problem could very well be a product-engineering problem, or some other problem.

Is it essential that every single designer at a design firm get the big picture and be able to intelligently interact with clients?

You're not going to force someone who's not particularly good at client interaction to do it. But even someone who just specializes in kerning type should still understand how they bring value to the overall cycle. She shouldn't think, "Kerning is the most important thing and you're idiotic to not understand how much value this brings to the table," when in fact lots of things bring value to the table.

Why have visual designers been dismissed by much of the corporate community as mere cake decorators, called in at the final hour once the fundamental decisions have already been made?

We earned that reputation over the years. We've been lazy as a profession. Designers by training don't have the rigor, the necessary vocabulary, and the confidence to converse in the "rules-based" world of business—a world grounded in the immutable realities of reliability. We need to get better at conversing in the language of business.

You talk about the difference between selling solutions and selling media deliverables. Can you elaborate on that?

Selling solutions is a way of thinking about or framing a problem; it's not dependent on the medium in which the solution is executed. Selling media deliverables is saying you are good at doing logos, posters, corporate identity, Web sites. You come out of the gate competing at a commodity level without the chance of solving the business problem. If you engage at the execution level, you will almost always be the cake decorator.

Why are designers so mysterious about the value they add to a project? Why is it so difficult for designers to explain the value of design to corporate clients?

Design operates in the world of possibilities. We designers are best at articulating what *might* happen. The world of business is most comfortable with what *will* happen. The language of these two worlds is very different. Rather than

learning a new language, designers—and I am saying this with a very broad stroke—prefer to operate in their comfort zone and play the role of the lone genius.

You've written that designers are sometimes granted a kind of "hipster" status in corporate culture. Should designers play into this role or is it disadvantageous to our profession in the long run?

In the long run, it's better to be viewed as the smart one than the trendy one.

It seems like the kind of design approach you're advocating is nothing more than negotiation and people skills.

No, I am just advocating the need to communicate effectively with the people we design with and for. If we talk in our own little language, our ability to make the kind of impact we want will be limited. Negotiation and people skills are now requirements in order to play.

From the perspective of someone who has worked on both sides of the corporate fence, what are some of the differences between in-house designing and freelance consulting?

In-house designing has its advantages and its disadvantages. If you're in-house, you actually see and understand the causes and effects of a particular problem, whereas an outsider won't notice these nuances. You are able to understand why a corporate culture resists a particular idea. You know how to navigate the politics around that resistance to sell the idea within the corporation. You understand which things are the economic drivers. A consultant might not understand these nuances enough. She might very well push the wrong buttons or focus on the wrong problems. A great in-house design team knows the nuances and can design a better solution.

On the other hand, an outside consultant is advantageous because she's got a fresh and unbiased view, so she will actually project a little further, push the boundaries a little further. But her solutions are much harder to sell through the organization. Very often clients simply hire an outside firm to get that outside thinking, and then the client will reverse-engineer the consultant's solution so it will work within the corporation. The outside consultant who has not worked inside might think, "They're screwing up my idea"—when in fact, the client actually likes the idea; she just has to make it work within the constraints of her business.

Since you wrote "Designers: Time for Change" in 2003, has the design profession changed?

That article said things that needed to be said, which no one was willing to say. Since then I've gotten a lot of emails from people saying, "Thanks for writing it. What can we do?" There are a lot of questions.

I have the same questions. How specifically do we implement this change?

It happens in subtle ways. It happens in language, how we talk about what we do. It's those subtle cues that over time we will cause change. Clear examples of day-to-day practical change are happening here and there, but it's not a trend.

I do see a change happening right now, but designers aren't driving it. The business world is driving it. *Business Week Inc.* and *Fast Company*—all of these publications are actually saying, "We get it. We've been talking about innovation and new ways of doing things, and we need someone to connect the dots differently." "Design" has been a buzzword in the business world for the last two years on the front cover of these publications.

Almost despite the design community?

Exactly. There is a whole new category of design firms like Ideo that are different. They say to the client, "You're embracing change. Let us facilitate that discourse." I'm seeing design firms playing the role of consultant and facilitating the conversation, asking hard questions about how to take change to the next level. Procter & Gamble has a design council of various practitioners helping them ask different kinds of questions: "Have you considered this kind of design product? If you want to revive this particular brand, let's look at these particular market segments and design specifically for them." Is this marketing or design? You can take a narrow view and say, "That's marketing. It's not my role." But marketing is one aspect of design thinking: Here is the problem. What are the possibilities?

Are interactive designers more willing to change their minds about the role of design than print designers?

Yes.

Why do you think that is?

Designers are reticent to recognize this fact, but technology has democratized the practice of design. In so doing, many of the old-guard print design values are now commodity values. Anyone can do stunning layouts. Anyone can learn to use the tools. Interactive designers are able to say, "OK, that old value set is just one of many other value sets I've learned." They are able to discard a set of values and embrace new ways of doing things—new collaborations, new ownerships, new authorships, all of those things. Interactive designers are less entrenched in an old set of values regarding what is good, what is craftsmanship. Print designers have to overcome old biases whereas in the interactive world, these old biases are somewhat disposable.

Some people have accused interactive design of ruining the design profession by bringing in amateurs and lowering standards. But you're saying that interactive design is actually good for the profession because it puts our focus back on design with a capital "D"?

Yes. And fear, uncertainty, and doubt are good things to inject back into the profession.

Why?

Fear is good because it makes you think harder, work harder, and challenge the status quo. You think, *What am I not doing that causes the client to hire that other firm? How is that other firm thinking differently than I am?* The fatalist designer will say, "The client just doesn't get it. They're stupid." That's certainly one view.

But that's an easy excuse?

It's easy to make a client the enemy. I've been there. Then I found myself on the client side, and I realized that all this "us versus them" stuff doesn't make any sense. Two minutes ago I was part of "us" and now I'm "them."

The Realm of Professional Ethics

In his 1971 book, *Design for the Real World*, designer/educator Victor Papanek wrote this famously polemical statement: "There are professions more harmful than industrial design, but only a very few of them. And possibly only one profession is phonier. Advertising design, in persuading people to buy things they don't need, with money they don't have, in order to impress others that don't care, it is probably the phoniest field in existence today."

Ouch! Is ethical graphic design an inherent oxymoron? I don't think so, but being an ethical graphic designer does require an extra modicum of caution and intentionality.

AIGA's standards of professional practice go a long way toward defining a kind of Hippocratic Oath for designers. These standards say what you would expect: Pay for your fonts, bill your clients honestly, pay your employees fairly, support sustainable production methods that don't harm the environment, and so on. The AIGA standards also say that a professional designer should correct any client or employer who gives instructions that violate the designer's ethical standards, or the designer should refuse the assignment.

Of course this begs the question: What are a designer's ethical standards? Everybody's personal ethics are different, but I hope we can all agree on some rudimentary basics.

Don't Work for Clients Whose Ethics Violate Yours

Try to foresee the results of your work to its logical conclusion. If you do good design work for this client, will it result in an outcome with which you ethically disagree? For example, gambling is a form of addiction for a lot of people, and I'm not terribly fond of it. I had the opportunity to design a Web site for a casino. Were I to have pursued the job and designed a successful site, more people would have gone to the casino. I didn't want that to happen, so I didn't pursue the job.

On the other hand, when I was apprenticing as a video editor, one of my jobs was to edit a "How to Win at Craps" instructional gambling video. Had I not edited it, someone else would have. Plus, the video strongly cautioned *against* a get-rich-quick mind-set. It was teaching you how to play conservatively and gradually beat the house. I edited the video.

DOING WORK THAT YOU FEEL STRONGLY ABOUT WILL HAVE THE

ADDED BONUS OF MAKING YOUR WORK BETTER.

As Much as Possible, Work for Clients Whose Ethics Coincide with Yours

Doing work that you feel strongly about will have the added bonus of making your work better. It doesn't have to be pro bono work for a homeless shelter. It can be work for a mountain bike company, a ballet company, a candy company, even a politician! Those details depend on your personal ethics. The Dutch design firm Wild Plakken is known for *only* doing design work for clients whose ideologies match their own. Imagine that.

Apply Mr. Cloninger's Three-Question Rule

I'm not here to tell you what your ethics should be, but you should probably have some (other than to make as much money as possible). The Golden Rule is, of course, the classic. ("Do unto others as you would have them do unto you," in case you've forgotten.) I used to teach middle school children, aged 12 to 14, and one of my class rules seems applicable to graphic design. Before you say anything to anybody, ask yourself three questions:

- Is it true?

- Is it necessary?

- Is it beneficial?

If you can't answer "yes" to all three questions, don't say it. Likewise if you can't answer "yes" to all three questions, don't take the gig. If all graphic designers on the planet would apply my simple three-question rule to their professional design practices, there would be a lot less graphic design on the planet.

Change the World

Can graphic design change the world? Every client who has ever paid money for graphic design services believes it can. So how can you use graphic design to change the world?

The obvious, hippie way is to do pro bono work for causes you support and put up protest posters against causes you oppose. But there are other, more subversive ways. Several historians believe that the countrywide riots in France during May 1968 were indirectly instigated by a small group of tactical media agitators called the Situationist International.

FROM PAYING FOR YOUR SOFTWARE TO INTENTIONALLY DEFACING PRIVATE PROPERTY, THERE ARE A LOT OF WAYS TO EXERCISE YOUR PROFESSIONAL DESIGN ETHICS.

Without going into the subtle nuances of their ingenious agenda, I will just say that they were basically art anarchists. They used a method called *détournement* to disrupt what they called the "society of the spectacle." They took ordinary media and altered it subtly, just enough to disrupt the normal flow of a normal person's normal media intake. Changing the text in cartoon word bubbles was one of their favorite tactics. They weren't trying to forward any overt political agenda. They were just trying to awaken people from their daily stupors.

Contemporary "culture jamming" is the slightly more overt and politicized heir of *détournement*. To oppose big tobacco, a culture jammer wouldn't just make protest posters or vandalize tobacco billboards. She would design and distribute her own advertisement of an emaciated Joe Camel in a chemotherapy ward. Culture jammers hijack a brand's signal, critically modify it, and send it back down the media pipeline. Preserving the look of the original campaign ensures that the branded viewer will initially receive the ad uncritically. The resultant cognitive disconnect is the goal. Graphic designers were born to propagate just this sort of subversive cultural misdirection.

From paying for your software to intentionally defacing private property, there are a lot of ways to exercise your professional design ethics. People in all professions, from medicine to plumbing, have to deal with basic ethics. Graphic designers are no exception. From those to whom much has been given, much is expected. In a world that increasingly relies on visual communication, graphic designers wield an inordinate amount of influence as skilled visual communicators. Whatever your personal ethics, don't conveniently overlook the ethical realm of design.

The Realm of Aesthetics

Most graphic design schools largely focus on the realm of aesthetics. For most designers, the aesthetic realm comes under attack as soon as they graduate and begin doing entry-level commercial design. Teachers judging work in terms of compositional aesthetics are replaced by clients judging work based on bottom-line economic effectiveness. The other four realms of design begin to crowd out the realm of aesthetics. With deadlines looming and money to make, the desire to make your work aesthetically interesting can seem increasingly unimportant.

Some commercial designers would argue that this is a good thing. Design is not art, after all, and who needs a bunch of self-serving designer aesthetes stroking their own personal egos? But function and beauty are not mutually exclusive. Just as the designer is obliged to be an advocate of the client, he is also obliged to be an advocate of visual aesthetics.

Whose aesthetics? The designer's, of course. In our relativistic era, it's taboo to come right out and admit this. But honestly, when designers talk about aesthetics, they're talking about their own aesthetics—what looks good to them as designers, and what they think will look good to their peers. According to this definition, even modernists have a subjective design aesthetic. Their aesthetic may be based on "fundamental" principles that are supposed to be objectively true, but it is a visual aesthetic nonetheless.

I don't have a problem with the subjective nature of aesthetics. Frank Lloyd Wright designed houses in a certain style. When someone hired Frank Lloyd Wright, he got a house that fit his specifications according to the architectural aesthetic of Frank Lloyd Wright. As long as the realm of subjective aesthetics doesn't inordinately dominate the other four realms of design, don't worry about wanting to make it look good *to you*. (Just don't rely on this as a justification to your client.)

Being true to your own interpretation of "good" visual design also qualifies as a kind of ethical behavior. Just make sure that your interpretation of "good" effectively communicates your client's message. As Paula Scher observes, "An environmentally sensitive design that doesn't communicate is a real waste of paper—even unbleached, recycled paper with the proper amount of post-consumer waste."

Arts & Crafts pioneer William Morris was the grandfather of twentieth-century graphic design. In the late 1800s he sought to rescue manufacturing and advertising from shoddy craftsmanship. To Morris, craftsmanship and beauty were ennobling, humanizing forces. They were the designer's way of showing concern and love for his fellow humans.

JUST BECAUSE THERE IS NO UNIVERSALLY "CORRECT" DESIGN AESTHETIC, DON'T

LET THAT DISCOURAGE YOU FROM TRYING TO MAKE EXTRAORDINARY WORK.

Can design still perform such a service? Design historian Philip Meggs believed so. Echoing Morris's priorities, Meggs wrote in the 1983 edition of his classic *A History of Graphic Design*:

> There is a growing awareness of the need to restore human and aesthetic values to the man-made environment and mass communications. The design arts… offer one means for this restoration. Once more a society's shelter, artifacts, and communications might bind a people together. The endangered aesthetic and spiritual values might be restored. A wholeness of need and spirit, reunited through the process of design, can contribute in great measure to the quality and raison d'etre of life in urban societies.

Meggs isn't the only contemporary designer to think that aesthetics can have a revolutionary impact on culture. In 1989 design maverick Tibor Kalman said:

> We have to be brave and we have to be bad. If we're bad, we can be the aesthetic conscience of the business world. We can break the cycle of blandness. We can jam up the assembly line that spills out one dull, lookalike piece of crap after another. We can say, "Why not do something with artistic integrity and ideological courage?" We can say, "Why not do something that forces us to rewrite the definition of *good design*?" Most of all, bad is about recapturing the idea that

a designer is the representative—almost like a missionary—of art, within the world of business. We're not here to give them what's safe and expedient. We're not here to help clients eradicate everything of visual interest from the face of the earth. We're here to make them think about design that's dangerous and unpredictable. We're here to inject art into commerce. We're here to be bad.

William Morris would probably not approve of Tibor Kalman's particular aesthetics, but that's hardly the point. Both men were revolutionary designers who believed that design aesthetics play an important role in shaping human culture. Just because there is no universally "correct" design aesthetic, don't let that discourage you from trying to make extraordinary work.

Balancing the Five Realms

The designer's goal is to balance all five realms of design. Shift your emphasis from one realm to another throughout the design process, trying to keep them all in the back of your mind. The realms often compete with each other, and this tension can lead to more holistic, intentional, well-rounded design solutions.

Avoid the temptation to inordinately focus on the immediate realm of client needs simply because the client signs your check. Avoid the temptation to inordinately focus on aesthetics at the expense of audience needs. Avoid the temptation to ignore the realm of ethics altogether just because no one is actively monitoring you.

Focus on the realm of media constraints early in the design phase instead of later in the development phase. You can have all the other realms in perfect balance, but if you haven't sufficiently considered the constraints of your medium, none of that will matter.

The five realms of design are related to the notorious dilemma of the "value triangle": good, fast, and cheap. Theoretically you can provide your client with any two, but not all three. You simply can't do good work for free and have it done by yesterday. As a designer, never sacrifice "good." Nobody wants to spend his career doing bad design really fast for cheap. Sensibly balancing the five realms of design is one way to sustain the consistent production of quality work that you'll want to keep doing.

■ ■ ■

THE FORM OF AN OBJECT IS
A "DIAGRAM OF FORCES," IN
THIS SENSE, AT LEAST, THAT
FROM IT WE CAN JUDGE OF
OR DEDUCE THE FORCES THAT
ARE ACTING OR HAVE ACTED
UPON IT.

—BIOLOGIST D'ARCY THOMPSON

10 | BALANCE FORMS AND RECONCILE PARADIGMS

So far, we've looked at specific strategies, tools, and best practices for hot-wiring your creative process. In this chapter, we'll step back and take a broader, big-picture look at design in general. A very literal way to approach design is through the lens of form making—you concentrate on the formal elements of the design and learn how to orchestrate them on the page in a way that forwards your message. We'll look at some classic ways to balance formal elements in the first half of this chapter.

A less literal but no less useful way to approach design is through philosophical paradigms. Paradigms define your general understanding of what design means and what it's good for in the world. They also shape your personal design practice—how you grow and develop as a working designer. We'll look at some relevant design paradigms in the second half of this chapter.

Both form making and paradigms are important. The best designer understands formal compositional rules as well as the philosophy behind what she is doing.

Balance Formal Elements

The idea of universal formal elements arises from *formalism*, an approach to form making that breaks down graphic design into basic formal elements and then purposefully restructures them based on certain "universal" laws of composition. Design programs—from the Bauhaus in the 1920s to the Basel School of Design in the 1960s to Yale in the 1980s—taught a kind of formalism. They didn't call it "modernist formalism"; they simply called it the correct way to design. A formalist understanding of composition is still considered foundational to graphic design. Formalism is not the be-all and end-all of graphic design, but it's at least a useful beginning.

A Brief Catalog of Formal Elements

Painter and educator Wassily Kandinsky proposed three main formal elements: point, line, and plane. A point is not dimensionless; it's just really small. It could hardly even be called a circle. Painter and educator Paul Klee calls it "an infinitely tiny elemental plane." A line is a point in motion that leaves a trace behind it. And a plane is a line in motion sideways that leaves a trace behind it. (Imagine holding a charcoal stick flat and dragging it across the page.)

Klee built on these three elements and added a fourth: dimension. Take a solid flat plane and raise it up and out into a semblance of 3D space; the trace it leaves is dimensional.

Most formalists agree on three elemental shapes: square, circle, and triangle. Klee's explanation of how these shapes are made is instructive. Like the plane, a square is made by dragging a line sideways. A circle is made by rotating a line around a point in its middle (imagine holding a charcoal stick flat and rotating it in a circle). And a triangle is created by the tension between the point at its apex and the line at its base. According to Klee, "The triangle came into being when a point entered into a relation of tension with a line and, following the command of its Eros, discharged this tension."

Entire texts have been written on the inherent formal properties of these three shapes, but I'll just write a paragraph. The square—or rectangle—is stable. Its form usually mirrors the form of the overall compositional space, unless you are designing something round, such as a button. The triangle is less stable than the square, but more stable than the circle. Plus it's all sharp and pointy. A circle is a strong compositional focal point in any design because it is so perfectly symmetrical and so in contrast with the rectangular boundaries of the compositional space.

Paul Klee's formalism distinguishes line, tone, and color. Each of these elements builds

FORMALISM IS NOT THE BE-ALL AND END-ALL OF GRAPHIC

DESIGN, BUT IT'S AT LEAST A USEFUL BEGINNING.

on the one before it. Line simply has the factor of *measure*—long/short, obtuse/acute. Tone is the grayscale—all the varying, colorless degrees between black and white. Tone adds the factor of *weight*—the relative heaviness and density, or darkness, of an area. Any area large enough to have weight also has measure. Thus you can talk about a gray area in terms of weight and measure, whereas you can only talk about a line in terms of measure.

Finally, color adds the factor that Klee simply calls *quality*. Color has all three factors: quality, weight, and measure. In contemporary terms, *color* is analogous to hue. This is by no means the extent of Klee's ingenious and extensive idiosyncratic formalism, but those are the basics.

Graphic designer and educator Armin Hofmann's basic formal elements include point, line, and plane, and he adds another: typeface. Though they are not necessarily basic geometric shapes, letterforms comprise a set of predetermined formal elements that graphic designers may use.

Formal design elements are often described in terms of opposites: thick/thin, long/short, straight/curved, rectangle/circle/triangle, flat/ textured, figure/ground, big/small, much/little, negative/positive, light/heavy, falling/rising, stable/unstable, front/back, pointed/blunt, smooth/rough, hard/soft, opaque/transparent, overstated/subtle, simple/complex.

Once you've broken design down into its universal formal elements, how do you combine these elements effectively? I want to focus on the modernist principle of *asymmetrical*

balance. It is the foundational principle upon which so many other formalist principles depend. Asymmetrical balance involves contrast and integration of opposing elements.

Contrast Formal Elements (Asymmetry)

Armin Hofmann encouraged what he calls *confrontation* of formal elements. His four basic elemental categories—point, line, plane, and letterform—could be brought into confrontation with one another, and they could also confront themselves. For example, in composition studies involving only circles, Hofmann would contrast the following:

- Thick-lined versus thin-lined
- Large versus small
- Complete versus fragmented
- Photographic versus hand-drawn
- Solid versus hollow
- Grouped circles versus isolated circles
- Circles that continued off the edge of the design space versus circles contained within it
- Black circles on a white ground versus white circles on a black ground

Hofmann rarely used color, trying to get as much variation, texture, and contrast out of just grayscale elements.

Contrasts should be pushed toward their extremes so that they may be recognized as contrasting. A line that is slightly thicker than another line doesn't really read as *thick*. *Thick* and *thin* aren't recognizable until you markedly contrast them with each other. Every element is relative to every other element within the environment you establish. Pushing contrasts is the only real way to explore the full gamut of formal possibility. You can always dial back from the extremes later.

Integrate Formal Elements (Balance)

Once your formal elements are contrasted dramatically to create tension and visual interest, the challenge is to bring them back into integration and thus balance them. Paul Klee called such a balance *active harmony*. Painter Piet Mondrian called it *dynamic equilibrium*. If all you have is visual conflict, your composition has interest, life, and motion—but no resolution or rest. If all you have is perfect symmetry, your composition is restful and balanced—but at the same time static, unenergetic, and dull. Asymmetrical balance achieves the best of both worlds: a dynamic restfulness or a restful dynamism—however you choose to consider it.

In *Pause & Effect*, interactive designer Mark Stephen Meadows explains how interaction works—the cognitive steps leading to a user's engagement with interactive media. Elements of difference (asymmetry) combine with elements of repetition (balance) to create this experience:

1. Difference provides information. A row of elevator buttons that are exactly the same doesn't really tell a viewer anything. Real information is conveyed only when at least one of the buttons differs from the others.

2. Repetition creates redundancy. If every button in the row is different in its own unique way, no pattern is formed. This is no more helpful than all the buttons being the same. It's too chaotic.

3. Redundant information (difference within repetition) provides context. So now you have a row of elevator buttons that are all circular (repetition), yet each button has a different number on it (difference). Only when there is difference within repetition are we able to recognize patterns. These patterns provide us with an overall context.

4. Context allows prediction. Once we are able to discern a pattern, we can begin to predict how the pattern might proceed.

5. Prediction allows participation. Once we get the gist of things, we feel confident enough to join in. We reach out and press the elevator button labeled 7, assuming it will take us to the 7th floor.

6. Participation is the cornerstone of interaction.

The same principles hold true for graphic design. The viewer of a billboard is not pushing elevator buttons, but he still goes through this same process of pattern recognition and involvement.

Although asymmetrically balanced designs are not perfectly centered, you can still use them to impose a quite rigorous hierarchical design structure—you are still able to lead your viewer's eye from place to place within your composition. It is all the more easy to do this once you have a feel for the "gravitational pull" of different formal elements and the way they interact with each other when combined. You should still group items with similar meanings and align items so that they aren't floating around in space. Asymmetry simply provides the kinetic interest that keeps the viewer's eye moving from area to area. And balance provides a stable visual ground where the viewer can pause to explore without being overwhelmed by visual chaos.

Asymmetry makes sense in terms of a poster, a single-page advertisement, or a single Web page, but how do you apply it to multi-page media such as an entire magazine or Web site? In his "Ten Rules of Design," designer Roger Black suggests a way: "Get Lumpy! The trouble with most design is it has no surprise. If you want normal people to pay attention, you have to change pace in your presentation. Monotonous rhythms of picture, headline, picture, text, ad, headline, picture, ad, et cetera is

like a pudding without raisins. A stew without lumps." In the context of an entire magazine or book, asymmetry translates into varying the pace—lumpiness.

A Word on Color Balance

You can also apply asymmetrical balance to the overall color tone of your composition. You probably don't want your entire composition to be the same shade of gray—that would just be symmetrical balance. To balance your color tones asymmetrically, go to extremes with them. Make some tones dark and some light. Just be sure that they ultimately average out to an even, mid-toned gray to ensure that your overall composition is tonally balanced. Once you arrive at what you think is a satisfactory composition, save it as a grayscale image, squint at it, and note how your tones balance. They don't need to be mathematically balanced to a perfect mid-tone gray; they just need to subjectively balance to your satisfaction.

As Paul Klee observes, color hues—red, orange, yellow, green, blue, purple—are psychologically and physiologically very subjective, so how do you balance them? You can balance colors with their complements—red and green, yellow and purple, blue and orange—or with their split complements—such as red balanced with both bluish green and yellowish green. Or you can simply balance warm hues (red, orange,

AS PAUL KLEE OBSERVES, COLOR HUES—RED, ORANGE, YELLOW, GREEN, BLUE, PURPLE—ARE

PSYCHOLOGICALLY AND PHYSIOLOGICALLY VERY SUBJECTIVE, SO HOW DO YOU BALANCE THEM?

and yellow) with cool hues (green, blue, and purple).

If you want to get mathematical about your hues, you might adopt the color system of German polymath Johann Wolfgang von Goethe, who assigned each color a light value: red = 6, orange = 8, yellow = 9, green = 6, blue = 4, purple = 3. According to this system, a composition with yellow and purple has a 9:3 light ratio. Because 9:3 is the same as 3:1, in order for the composition to balance, there should be three times more yellow than purple.

Color theory is probably not so simplistically reductive, however. Even Johannes Itten, the father of Bauhaus color theory, admitted his inability to reduce the subjective workings of color to an objective system: "If it be imagined that this systematic classification of colors and contrasts banishes all difficulties, I should add that the kingdom of colors has within it multidimensional possibilities only partly to be reduced to simple order. Each individual color is a universe in itself. We must therefore content ourselves with an exposition of fundamentals."

Feel free to try asymmetrically balancing your colors, as long as you rely on your eye and intuition more than your calculator.

Advanced Formalism

There are several advanced kinds of formalism. To describe them all in detail is beyond the scope of this chapter. I mention a couple of them here to provide a sense of other kinds of formalism. If they seem interesting to you and potentially applicable to your work, you may want to research them further.

In his four-volume work ambitiously titled *The Nature of Order*, architect Christopher Alexander applies a kind of neo-formalist approach to architecture, city planning, design, and the universe in general. Although he is primarily concerned with architectural space, his observations have been applied to computer programming and game design, and they can certainly be applied fruitfully to the "space" of graphic design.

Alexander arrives at 15 elements of style—his Holy Grail of formalist reduction. His formal elements are not individual components such as shape, line, or color, but spatial relationships or patterns. They are as follows:

- Levels of scale
- Strong centers
- Boundaries
- Alternating repetition
- Positive space
- Good shape
- Local symmetries
- Deep interlock and ambiguity
- Contrast
- Gradients
- Roughness
- Echoes
- The void
- Simplicity and inner calm
- "Not-separateness"

Alexander explains each of these elements in great detail, and several of them are related to concepts we have already discussed. For example, levels of scale is related to what I call fractal design (Chapter 4) and to designer Willi Kunz's idea of macro- and microaesthetics (Chapter 7). Alexander's 15 elements are not relevant to asymmetrical balance, however, because his elements propose their own much more involved system of balance.

Another interesting version of advanced formalism comes from problem-solving pioneer Genrich Altshuller. Between the wars in the Soviet Union, Altshuller developed a rigorous, formulaic problem-solving method called TRIZ (the Russian acronym for "Theory of Inventive Problem Solving") that is still used by engineers and corporations worldwide. Altshuller maintained that at the heart of every problem, there are inherent contradictions. The truly creative designer doesn't resolve these contradictions by compromise, but instead seeks to dissolve the contradictions altogether.

If a client has ever told you to make a design simultaneously bolder and subtler, you have felt the real-world pain of Altshuller's inherent contradictions. According to him, the solution is not to compromise and split the difference between bold and subtle. This simply gives you a mediocre design that is neither bold nor subtle. The solution is to somehow dissolve the contradictions. For example, a client wants a delicate typeface and a bold color for her company's logo, but the color and face are ill matched. That's the contradiction. The standard solution might be to *resolve* the contradiction through compromise. You make the typeface a little less delicate and the color a little less bold. The TRIZ solution is to *dissolve* the conflict. You ditch the type altogether and go with a logo mark of a delicately illustrated apple that is bright red.

ALTSHULLER MAINTAINED THAT AT THE HEART OF EVERY PROBLEM, THERE ARE INHERENT CONTRADICTIONS. THE TRULY CREATIVE DESIGNER DOESN'T RESOLVE THESE CONTRADICTIONS BY COMPROMISE, BUT INSTEAD SEEKS TO DISSOLVE THE CONTRADICTIONS ALTOGETHER.

Reconcile Opposing Paradigms

In addition to purely formal considerations, design is driven by paradigms, or models of understanding. Is it more important for design to be contemporary or classic? Should form follow content, or are designers free to experiment with form in its own right? Should design always make things clear, or is there room for intentional levels of ambiguity? Is design meant to sell as many products as possible, or can it be used more intentionally to form and inform culture? These are the kinds of questions that paradigms address.

In a book about practical design, why talk about the more abstract, long-term, big-picture concepts? Because they are related to practical design, though they may have less to do with how you immediately approach your next project and more to do with what kinds of larger career decisions you make. What kind of companies do you want to work for? What kind of work do you want to do? What kind of impact do you want to have on the future of design? On the future of the world? These are all practical questions for the committed, long-term professional designer.

As you advance in your practice, you may begin to question the status quo of the profession. You may even be ambitious enough to change the direction of the industry, or at least the direction of your practice. To do this, you'll want to have some knowledge of contemporary design philosophies—an understanding of how they are in dialogue with one another and with past paradigms—in order to develop your own dialogue with them. Reconciling opposing design paradigms is a way to see beyond established dichotomies toward new approaches and practices. It's a way to hot-wire your entire creative practice.

Many of our operative design paradigms are posed as dichotomies, when in fact they are not. One such dichotomy is *theory versus practice*. Perhaps theory is more important. Perhaps practice is more important. Perhaps they are equally important. Whichever is the case, once we put *versus* between them, we set them up unnecessarily as opposites. In fact, theory and practice often occur simultaneously and almost interchangeably. Practice leads to theory, which leads to a modification of practice, which leads to a modification of theory, and so on. Designer/educator Ellen Lupton points out that theory itself is a kind of practice.

Because many opposing design paradigms are rarely as oppositional as they seem, it's valuable to reconcile their differences as much as possible, or at least consider how they might be reconciled. Don't misunderstand me. I'm not

RECONCILING OPPOSING DESIGN PARADIGMS IS A WAY TO SEE BEYOND

ESTABLISHED DICHOTOMIES TOWARD NEW APPROACHES AND PRACTICES.

IT'S A WAY TO HOT-WIRE YOUR ENTIRE CREATIVE PRACTICE.

a moral relativist. Some things just don't recon-cile. (It would be stupid to reconcile *stupid* with *ingenious*. And how does one reconcile *reconcili-ation* with the *irreconcilable?*) I'm not proposing reconciliation of all opposites as a moral princi-ple in and of itself—only insofar as it improves your understanding of design paradigms.

Borrowing from classical philosophy, we could call this a *dialectic*—a way to advance thought. A thesis (some proposition) is opposed to its antithesis (some seemingly opposite prop-osition), and their dialectic leads to a synthesis (some new proposition). This synthesis then becomes the new thesis, which is then opposed to a new antithesis, and so thought "evolves." Design history can be seen as an ongoing dia-lectic. In one sense, modernist design sought to end this dialectic by having the absolute last word on everything. But cultural conversations don't stop simply because someone writes a manifesto saying they are over.

For example, German typographer Jan Tschichold was perhaps the most outspoken evangelist for the new modernist typography in the 1920s. Yet 20 years later, he had recanted many of his views. He even returned to using *serif* typefaces! Why? A world war had inter-vened. In 1946 Tschichold wrote, "[The new typography's] impatient attitude conforms to the German bent for the absolute, and its mili-tary will to regulate and its claim to absolute power reflect those fearful components of the German character [that] set loose Hitler's power and the Second World War."

I'm not convinced that modernist design is inherently fascistic, but I *am* proposing your approach to graphic design not be dogmatic. In the words of experimental designer Karel Martens, "One has to find one's own rules and I realized that there is not a single truth or true rules. Common sense and curiosity—that's what we need." Culture is changing design, design is changing culture, and the relation-ship between culture and design is changing. The more open you are to new paradigms and ways of thinking about design, the more nimble you'll be at adapting and evolving your personal design practice to keep up with (and even influ-ence) these changes.

What follows is a list of quintessential design opposites that we'll seek to explore and reconcile.

(Form vs. Content) vs. Context

The separation of form and content is a major dichotomy of formalism. Theoretically, form is supposed to be derived from content. You examine the nature of the content you must present and then devise a form that best serves the inherent needs of that content. Modernism claims that the best design is invisible. Design is merely a transparent container that holds and presents the content within. Yet the form of your design actually affects the nature of its content. The truth is, content and form are inextricably intertwined—each affects the other.

This same dichotomy can be thought of in another way: style versus concept. Theoretically, according to formalism, style should follow concept. But design cuts both ways. You can stumble onto a concept while sketching stylistic forms. Design critic Lewis Blackwell writes, "The debate of 'style-over-concept' is a false one. It comes down to this: Style that works is a concept, and a concept that doesn't work has not been styled effectively."

There is an alternative paradigm to the form-versus-content dichotomy: context. A contextual design approach admits the inseparability of form and content, and analyzes the context in which the form/content relationship occurs. Contextual design takes a step back from language, graphic design, and human communion. It begins to ask questions about communication itself. What is the relationship between the words we speak and the ideas they represent? Do words merely convey meaning, or do they create meaning? What is the relationship between the spoken word and the written word, between the written word and the photograph? How much of the content's meaning does the design form convey, and how much is supplied by the audience?

I recognize two flavors of contextual design: semiotic and performative. Inspired by twentieth-century theories about the nature of language, *semiotic* design develops a new approach to visual communication that uses language to question itself. *Performative* design leaves the boundaries of the 2D picture plane. Its message is communicated not only through the design object, but also through the way in which the design object is delivered. Both of these contextual approaches are helpful to understand if you're wanting to move your design beyond the classic form-versus-content dichotomy.

Semiotic Design

The first thing to understand about semiotic design is that it's an approach, not a style. It doesn't look like any one thing. Semiotic design is a stance that critiques the relationship between form and content to arrive at a more nuanced understanding of communication. Thus, to associate semiotic design with a certain visual form is to miss its point.

To understand semiotic design, you have to know a bit about semiotics and the history of twentieth-century French philosophy. Stay with me. It should be relatively painless.

AN INSANELY BRIEF INTRODUCTION TO SEMIOTICS

Before the 1900s, words were generally thought to describe the ideas they represented. For

CONTEXTUAL DESIGN TAKES A STEP BACK FROM LANGUAGE, GRAPHIC DESIGN, AND HUMAN COMMUNION. IT BEGINS TO ASK QUESTIONS ABOUT COMMUNICATION ITSELF.

instance, the word *beauty* described the idea of beauty—an idea that existed beyond the word itself.

Then linguist Ferdinand de Saussure noted that there is no intrinsic relationship between words and the ideas they signify. For example, any group of letters can be used to signify the idea of beauty. The idea of beauty is described by 50 different words in 50 different languages, and none are any more intrinsically related to beauty than the others. Saussure called words (like beauty) *signifiers*, and the ideas they pointed to (like beauty itself) *signifieds*. A signifier plus its signified equals a complete *sign*. Saussure went on to say that a sign could only be understood in the context of an overall system of language.

If "meaning" is largely determined by language systems, then we can begin to dissect language systems into their elemental components, discover how they work, and thus understand meaning. Saussure was approaching language in the same way that modernist formalists were approaching graphic design. He broke language up into its fundamental elements and tried to discover a system of universal laws that governed these elements. Thus, semiotics was born. Enter philosopher Jacques Derrida, who had a serious problem with all this. Saussure observed that the word beauty didn't fully signify the idea of beauty, but he still believed that the idea of beauty existed. To Derrida, there were no ideas apart from language. Who could know if the idea of beauty (the signified) was even out there? (If you dis-

agree with him, try proving it without using language.)

To understand Derrida's position, an analogy might be helpful. Baseball umpire Bill Klem once took an inordinately long time to call a pitch. The impatient batter turned to him and asked, "Well, which is it, a ball or a strike?" Klem calmly replied, "Sonny, it ain't nothing till I call it." To Derrida, language didn't guess at balls and strikes; it created them. Derrida's agnostic nonposition is known as *deconstruction*. It's basically an advanced form of semiotics.

SEMIOTICS APPLIED TO DESIGN THINKING
Let's apply all this French philosophy to our style-versus-concept dichotomy. Style is like the signifier and concept is like the signified. Before Saussure, style would have been obliged to faithfully embody the concept. After Derrida, style was free to create the concept.

Semiotic design foregrounds the relationship between form and content. It seeks to show how they reciprocally affect each other. This is a postmodern kind of design thinking. Modernist design thinking says that content always drives style. Intuitive grunge design thinking says that style dominates and can do what it likes regardless of content. Semiotic design doesn't take sides. Instead, it inverts these relationships to show how they inform each other.

Semiotic design is self-aware and self-critical. It considers the accepted conventions of graphic design, and then seeks to expose these conventions as self-contradictory.

Designer Zak Kyes created these posters for the Architectural Association of London's School of Architecture using multiple layers of text to suggest multiple levels of meaning. He constructs a kind of typographic waterfall where a poetic cloud of data announces lectures, events, and exhibitions from contemporary avant-garde architectural designers and theorists. The A side of the poster contains the names, dates, and times (content), while the B side is an abstraction of keywords that is also overprinted onto the front of the poster.

SEMIOTICS APPLIED TO DESIGN PRACTICE

All this is well and good and very abstract, so how do you practically apply it to your design practice? As you might have guessed, there's no single, formalistic way to do that. Remember, semiotic design is a tactic rather than a visual style.

Given that, the following stylistic approaches have been employed with varying degrees of success by designers under the influence of semiotic thought. These tactics are by no means prescriptive. In many senses, the Holy Grail of semiotic design has yet to be discovered. Still, these strategies should get you started on your quest.

Layering

Semiotic design comments on the relationship between form and content, introducing a third "layer" of contextual commentary. The problem is, where do you position this third layer of commentary in the actual design space? Consider the "director's commentary" option on a DVD. The form (visuals and dialogue) and the content (plot) of the movie are imposed upon by a third layer of meta-commentary (the director's voice). Similarly, the most basic semiotic design technique is to superimpose your third layer of contextual commentary on top of your regular design, kind of like subtitles.

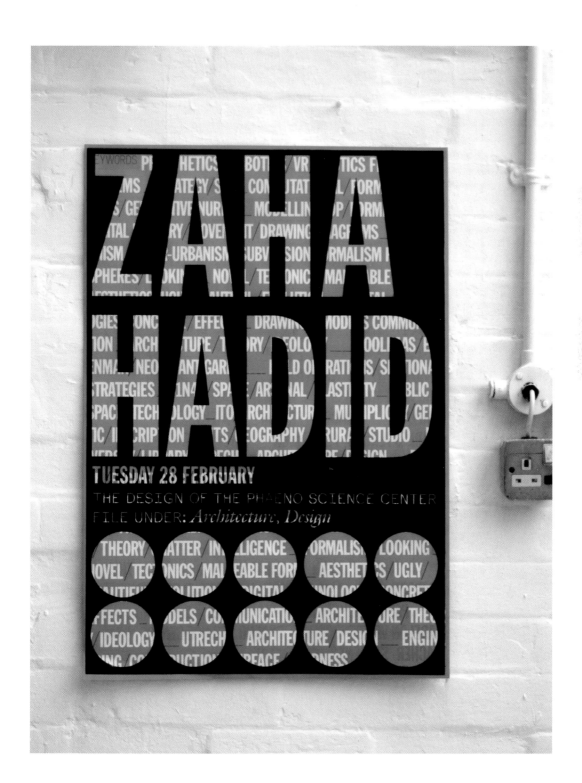

nOulipo:
A 2-day public meditation on the future of constraints in writing.
Organized by Matias Viegener & Christine Wertheim
Sponsored by The Annenberg Foundation and CalArts MFA Writing Program

October 28th & 29th, 2005

at REDCAT, The Roy and Edna Disney/CalArts Theater in downtown Los Angeles
On daytime panels and two evening readings, plus public workshops
More info: www.redcat.org, e-mail: noulipo@gmail.com

Participants
Caroline Bergvall, Christian Bök, Johanna Drucker, Paul Fournel, Tan Lin, Harry Mathews, Bernadette Mayer, Joe Milazzo, Harryette Mullen, Doug Nufer, Vanessa Place, Janet Sarbanes, Brian Kim Stefans, Juliana Spahr, Rodrigo Toscano

I'll s/nd you info on th/ noulipo conf/r/nc/ today (sorry I m/ant to do that y/st/rday). Oulipo is th/ Fr/nch /xp/rim/ntal writing group that has b/com/ r/nown/d for /xploring th/ us/ of constraint. Th/ir b/st-known m/mb/r is p/rhaps G/org/s P/r/c, who wrot/ *Lif/*, *A Us/r's Manual*, and th/ book that b/st illustrat/s th/ir prin- cipl/s is his disapp/aranc/ nov/l, *A Void*, which is a d/t/ctiv/ story tracing th/ lif/ of a disapp/ar/d writ/r, in which h/ n/v/r onc/ us/s any words with th/ l/tt/r "/." W/ put th/ n at th/ b/ginning of th/ titl/ to signify both n/w and th/ id/a of math or alg/bra, as in "l/t x = 1." (A lot of noulipo's /xp/rim/nts ar/ influ/nc/d by math. N+7 is a con- straint which substitut/s all th/ nouns in a t/xt with th/ 7th noun b/low it in th/ dictionary.) A constraint is a sort of limiting d/sign principl/ that a writ/r assigns hims/lf to guid/ him in cr/ating an /xp/rim/ntal t/xt, for /xampl/: to writ/ /v/ry word in a po/m in alphab/tical ord/r (as in "And B/caus/ Carla…")

I can't r/ally /xplain our logic for choosing th/ Ouchi Illusion* /xc/pt that Op Art s//ms lik/ a good match – Oulipians hav/ d/scrib/d th/m- s/lv/s as "rats who build th/ maz/ from which th/y plan to /scap/." (Th/ history of th/ Ouchi at HTTP://MATHWORLD.WOLFRAM.COM/OUCHIILLUSION.HTML).

Mor/ info: noulipo is th/ s/cond annual /xp/rim/ntal writing /v/nt to b/ h/ld at R/DCAT, th/ Roy /nd /dna Disn/y | CalArts Th/at/r in down- town Los Ang/l/s. It tak/s plac/ on th/ w//k/nd of Octob/r 28th and 29th, 2005. *n*oulipo puts n/w and /stablish/d writ/rs into dialogu/ about issu/s in cont/mporary writing and its r/lations to /v/ryday lif/.

This y/ar our focus is on th/ l/gacy of th/ Fr/nch lit/rary group Oulipo, inviting a conv/rsation b/tw//n th/ originators of this major /xp/rim/n- tal coll/ctiv/ and som/ of th/ir /nglish sp/aking count/rparts and h/irs. Our aim is to discuss curr/nts in cont/mporary writing that combin/ strat/gi/s d/v/lop/d by m/mb/rs of Oulipo with oth/r t/chniqu/s, to mov/ b/yond an oppositional id/a of form and d/v/lop n/w mod/s of wordwork that chall/ng/ structur/s of domination by s/riously play- ing with th/ wor(l)d.

A poster by Zak Kyes for nOulipo, a conference on the French experimental writing group Oulipo that was renowned for using systems of constraint. Its best-known member, Georges Perec, wrote an entire detective novel without ever using the letter *e*. Accordingly, Kyes inserts slashes to replace the letter *e* whenever it occurs, playfully inverting hierarchy and creating an apt tension between form and content.

This approach can range from simple and iconic, such as artist Barbara Kruger's bold Futura type directly superimposed on black- and-white photographs, to complex and involv- ing, like Katherine McCoy's Cranbrook poster in Chapter 4. Just make sure that your meta-layers are somehow in dialogue with the form and content of the rest of your design. Simply add- ing layer upon layer to achieve visual texture doesn't necessarily constitute semiotic design.

Inverted Hierarchies

Derrida was interested in the nuances of typog- raphy and the ways in which it could "say" things that speech could not. His book *Glas* uses experimental design as part of its overall vocabulary. Footnotes are enlarged and headers are shrunk. Arguments are arranged spatially rather than sequentially. Again, this disruption of conventional design hierarchy is not simply arbitrary. It is in conscious dialogue with the content of the text. The book is a deconstruc- tive critique of philosopher G. W. F. Hegel. As Derrida's writing subverts and disrupts Hegel, the book's designer, Richard Eckersley, subverts and disrupts the conventions of book design. Inverting standard design hierarchies can be a useful way of designing content that is itself subversive and unconventional.

The Slow Sell

Since we can't read one another's minds or do a Vulcan mind-meld, we have to communicate via other means. Graphic design is one. But there will always be a gap of understanding between the designer and her design, and then again between the design and the audience. Modernist design seeks to close that gap immediately by suggesting simple, easily digestible definitions. Semiotic design seeks to widen the gap. It refrains from suggesting specific definitions, forcing the viewer to more fully examine the entire design in context before coming to any definitive conclusions.

As book readers, we "defer" definitions all the time. For example, let's say you're reading *Hamlet* and you come across the word *fortune*. You have some idea of what fortune means, but you go ahead and read the rest of the section to see what it might mean in context. Perhaps you're still not exactly sure, so you finish the scene looking for more clues. By the time you've read the entire play, you have a much better understanding of what fortune means in *Hamlet* than you did when you first came across the word.

Likewise, semiotic design encourages you to defer your immediate interpretation until you have "read" more of the design. This approach is inconsistent with an old-school marketing desire to hurry up and close the deal. Semiotic design is by no means a hard sell or even a soft sell. (For Derrida, it would be a "no sell" because he's suspicious of arriving at any definitive conclusions.) But for our purposes, let's call it a *slow* sell. The viewer is empowered to make up his own mind, and this empowerment eventually leads to a personal buy-in—if the tactic works. If it doesn't work, the viewer takes one look, scratches his head, shrugs his shoulders, and moves on.

The craft of slow-sell design is to leave the interpretation open for a while but not so ambiguously that it completely baffles your audience. Teaser billboard campaigns that gradually reveal their meaning over time are examples of the slow sell. For three weeks, you drive by a billboard that merely poses an intriguing question; on the fourth week the billboard actually answers it. The "Got Milk?" slogan created by ad agency Goodby, Silverstein & Partners is a bit of a slow sell in that it poses a question that doesn't immediately reveal an answer. The answer is implied with visual connections to celebrities, cookies, and peanut butter sandwiches. A series of follow-up questions is even implied: "No? What's wrong with you? What are you waiting for?"

SEMIOTIC DESIGN ENCOURAGES YOU TO DEFER YOUR IMMEDIATE

INTERPRETATION UNTIL YOU HAVE "READ" MORE OF THE DESIGN.

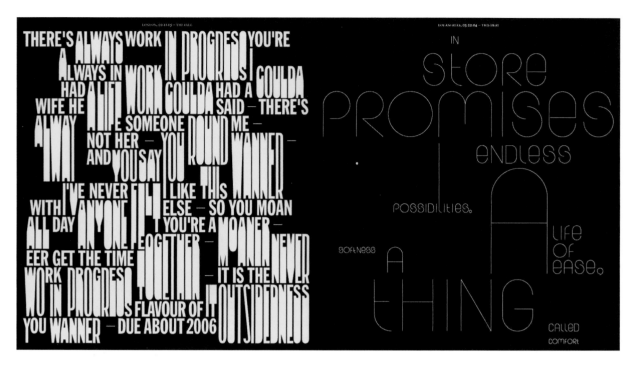

Zak Kyes designed this contribution to *Crossfields Magazine*. He emphasizes figure/ground ambiguity and dramatically contrasts thick and thin type to create visual involvement. The design doesn't reveal itself immediately, but instead unfolds slowly upon closer examination.

You could implement this tactic by grossly mismatching type choice with word content, creating a disconnect that causes the viewer to reflect on the relationship between form and content, involving them longer and more actively in the decoding process. You could incorporate figure/ground, positive/negative visual ambiguities into your design. Again, the goal is not simply to prolong viewer involvement by deferring closure. You also want to pose a dilemma that is directly related to the content of your design.

Interactivity

Semiotician Roland Barthes proposed that the best fiction intentionally opens itself up to multiple interpretations. The reader does not simply receive the text passively; she actively engages in the construction of its meaning. Barthes believed that fiction could better achieve this kind of open-endedness by losing its linear timeline. Interestingly, hypertext fiction engages in Barthes' kind of nonlinear storytelling. Furthermore, interactive media allows the reader to actively participate in the construction of the text's meaning in a very literal way.

While print designers in the '80s knocked themselves out trying to be semiotically interactive, Web designers in the 1990s achieved this by default. In many ways, interactive media is inherently semiotic. Good luck getting a passerby to spend several minutes decoding the layered meta-language of your semiotic poster, but even the most conservatively designed Web site, such as www.amazon.com, inherently invites hours of interactive user engagement. Amazon even has a feature called "the page you made." The way in which the surfer "reads" Amazon actually constructs a new page of text at amazon.com.

So is www.amazon.com semiotically designed? Perhaps functionally, but not visually. There's nothing about the visual design of Amazon that encourages you to think contextually about the relationship between its form and content. On the other hand, requiemforadream.com, by the design firm Hi-Res, is a much better example of intentionally semiotic Web design. Its interactive design is derived from the theme of *Requiem for a Dream*, a film about a mother and son who become cripplingly addicted to different drugs. The characters in the film are doomed by the addictive choices they make. All the while, however, they think they are making right choices. At the Web site, the user is also given a series of misleading choices that promise one thing but deliver the opposite. There are several paths through the site, but all end very badly. By clicking through the site, the user is allowed to identify complicitly with the characters of the film. If the user feels duped, so do the characters. In this instance, the third layer of "meta-commentary" is "located" in the interactive design itself.

Self-Deprecation Through Disclosure

Semiotic design calls attention to the fact that it's selling you something. This can act as a kind of goodwill gesture to gain audience credibility. Semiotic design says (either directly or indirectly), "Hey, why kid around? We both know I'm an advertisement. I'll just go ahead and make my pitch, and whatever you want to do after that is up to you." The more cynical your market, the more this approach is likely to work (until your market gets cynical about this approach).

A classic example of self-deprecation through disclosure was Dave Thomas's television advertisements for Wendy's. Thomas was just some guy who started a fast-food restaurant named after his daughter, and there he was on television talking plainly about the restaurant he started. My favorite example of self-deprecation is the Make 7-Up Yours campaign. The campaign is clever because it ridicules some fictitious marketer who didn't catch "up yours" in the slogan. He's on the street, enthusiastically selling 7-Up in an old-school, hard-sell way, using this implicitly offensive slogan. Someone yells, "Up yours!" back at him, and he's pleased because he thinks his branding is finally catching on. The campaign is especially brilliant because this wink then allows 7-Up to actually use "up yours" in their slogan.

Desire and Branding

Semiotician and psychoanalyst Jacques Lacan said that desire arises from a discrepancy between the real world and the world of language. We are born as real organisms of pure existence into a world of linguistic signs that don't exactly point to what we experientially know is real. We all desire the unnameable "real," and words always let us down.

Semiotic advertisements take advantage of this inherent desire by using vague, open-ended words that don't specify anything. "Coke is it." "Coke. It's the real thing." What exactly is *it*? What exactly is *the real thing*? We're left to fill in the blanks, and we always fill them in with the ideal, unnamable object of our desire. By not saying anything, semiotic advertisements can imply everything.

This approach works especially well for products such as Coke that aren't really anything to begin with. Coke is just carbonated sugar water. It's nothing apart from its brand. Since Coke isn't anything specific—like hemorrhoid cream or motor oil—we can imbue it with loads of unnamable desire.

A Word on Semitransparency

There is a misguided notion that because semiotics is confusing, any confusing design can be justified as semiotic. This is not the case. There is a difference between an authentic semiotic approach to design and bad design using the jargon of semiotics to defend itself.

Semiotic design works best when the message of its content is amplified, commented on, and made richer (although not necessarily more "true" or more "definite") by adding a third layer of contextual commentary. Semiotic design fails when this third layer of commentary completely obscures and covers up the content.

Your third commentary layer should be semitransparent but not opaque. I don't mean literally, as in "Photoshop layer transparency = 50%" (although that may be applicable if you're literally layering). I mean that your meta-commentary shouldn't completely obscure the meaning of the content.

If your third commentary layer is merely decorative, without any critical stance, then it obscures your content and thus becomes your new form. In which case, we're back to the intuitive, grunge, form-over-content approach. Such opaque design is fine, but it's not semiotic. It has less to do with Saussure and more to do with the Sex Pistols.

CRITIQUES OF SEMIOTIC DESIGN

It's easy to critique semiotic design, and many have. Here are some of the most common critiques:

"COKE IS IT." "COKE. IT'S THE REAL THING." WHAT EXACTLY IS *IT*? WHAT EXACTLY IS *THE REAL THING*? BY NOT SAYING ANYTHING, SEMIOTIC ADVERTISEMENTS CAN IMPLY EVERYTHING.

- **It's too critical.** Deconstruction is inherently critical. It seeks to undermine our confidence in communication. Furthermore, it is openly hostile toward capitalism and advertising. Why build a commercial design approach on such foundations?

- **It's too progressive.** What about industrial designer Raymond Loewy's Most Advanced Yet Acceptable (MAYA) rule (discussed in Chapter 9)—that design should be as innovative as possible without being too advanced? If your audience has already accepted the language of modernism, why seek to speak a new language? Can a commercial designer afford to fight this revolutionary cultural battle? Eventually, audiences may come to accept the language of semiotic design. Until then, you are communicating to no one.

- **It's too noncommercial.** There's only one thing more pretentious than lecturing your clients on subjective aesthetics, and that's lecturing them on twentieth-century French philosophy. Furthermore, how many clients are going to let you use the language of graphic design to deconstruct itself on their dime? Firestone wants to sell tires. They don't want to sell signified ideas that will never be fully reconcilable with the arbitrary signifier known as "tires." Such messages don't exactly build consumer confidence.

- **It's too esoteric.** None of these philosophies tell you how to design anything. They are philosophies of analysis, not philosophies of production. Graphic design is not literary criticism or culture theory. It can certainly be evaluated through those lenses, but ultimately it must work as graphic design. If these philosophies don't practically improve design, they are an esoteric distraction.

Of all those critiques, the last one is the most troubling and difficult to answer. How do you translate these abstract philosophies into a working design practice? The good news is: You don't have to be a philosophy major to make interesting semiotic design. A student who has barely read Barthes can still do strong semiotic design work. A professor steeped in the subtleties of Derrida can still do crappy semiotic design work. Furthermore, you don't have to fully buy into these philosophies in order to get something out of them tactically.

HOW DO YOU TRANSLATE THESE ABSTRACT PHILOSOPHIES INTO A WORKING

DESIGN PRACTICE? THE GOOD NEWS IS: YOU DON'T HAVE TO BE A

PHILOSOPHY MAJOR TO MAKE INTERESTING SEMIOTIC DESIGN.

Interview: Zak Kyes

Zak Kyes is a designer working in the semiotic tradition whose work also happens to look great. Samples of his work in this chapter illustrate semiotic design. I asked Zak about his approach.

How is your personal approach to design different than the culture jamming approach?

My approach has little to do with activism. I actually have a problem with the style of activism that tells an extremely simplified story and leaves out the complexity, almost becoming the kind of propaganda it critiques—for example, a design that says, "Corporations lie." The reality is that corporations are now the major cultural producers, a much more complicated story. Once purely cultural entities such as museums and even high-profile artists now more closely resemble corporations.

This is not to say there is no chance to change values; not at all. In a recent exhibition at the Serpentine, the artist Rirkrit Tiravanija re-created his apartment in the gallery—complete with kitchen, books, beds, and music to play. Within the social and behavioral confines of a white cube, he took a strategic position and created a livable world where you could eat, relax, and relate to other people. His world proposed a different set of values for an arts institution but yet existed within its framework. This relationship of symbols, organization of information, and self-imposed constraints could be compared to the design of a book—or the graphic

designer's role in contemporary culture. Warhol had it right. He didn't want the boutique; he wanted the supermarket.

Marshall McLuhan says, "All advertising advertises advertising." Advertising and marketing (and graphic design, in their service) have become intrinsically related to the corporate system of selling stuff. How can graphic design critique the very language it speaks? Is there a tactical way around this paradox?

Where the designer stands in relation to the cycle of production or "language" is an interesting starting point. The idea that the designer as a cultural producer is outside (but occasionally contributes to) this cycle and is therefore an impartial voice is impossible. In reality the designer is equally consumer and producer of culture. Design can take a strategic view that attempts to create an amalgamation, where the content/facts/information/production are no longer separated from the form/thrill/pleasure/consumption. For example, work being produced at CalArts in the early '90s developed an approach that focused on the designer's subjective role in creating design's message. The pages of *Emigre* magazine offer a visual history of this evolution, where the designer's unique interpretation is central. In the generation just preceding mine, some very informed designers worked in an almost classical typographic manner, not in opposition to the past but as a way to shift the frame toward other concerns, like

Zak Kyes and Tahli Fisher designed this invitation for the 2005 CalArts MFA Thesis exhibition *Shipping & Receiving*. The invitation is designed into the envelope itself. These envelopes were mailed empty. By integrating the message (content) into the container itself (form), the designers create a tension that acts as a semiotic critique of communication in general.

the use of language. Both are attempts to rejoin facts and form to create a new approach. I think the "design-frame" shifts when the traditional forms of organizing information start to break down. That's certainly visible now and you can also see it in the way people dress.

For me it's important that design is informed by the world around it and has an edge that is avant-garde—that it experiments with ways to make information remarkable and exciting.

Why do you design instead of just making art?

I like Brian Eno's suggestion of an "art experience." He proposes that we think of our relationship with objects as an experience located on a continuum (art/design or art/non-art). In some moments, you have more of an "art experience" and in others, more of a "design experience."

The work I create is for an imaginary person whose frame of experience is not relegated to either end of this spectrum, and who is comfortable with a little bit of ambiguity, of being between, and looking beyond.

Having worked on art-world projects with etoy [an experimental conceptual art "corporation"], or finding myself naturally more attracted to the work of some artists at CalArts, I somehow had a vision that this overlap was interesting but still wanted my work to be viewed as communications, so I never went too far toward art.

What are your criteria for selecting clients to work for?

To be prosaic, it's not always my choice whom I work for. I have to design what is given to me. Luckily the projects often come from commissioners who do not have a fixed position on what the final product will be and are attracted to the experimentation and thinking of my previous work.

The ideal of many graphic designers is to become a figure who is able to work with any type of client, with any content, under the guise of solving any problem. I don't know what the point of this is. If you do not already share a similar world with the people you work for, it's probably for a good reason. This connection is something I look for, so I mostly work for people that make things—writers, fashion designers, architects, and artists.

"THE IDEAL OF MANY GRAPHIC DESIGNERS IS TO BECOME A FIGURE WHO IS ABLE TO WORK WITH ANY TYPE OF CLIENT, WITH ANY CONTENT, UNDER THE GUISE OF SOLVING ANY PROBLEM. I DON'T KNOW WHAT THE POINT OF THIS IS."

En El Borde:
El Feminicidio en Ciudad Juárez

On The Edge:
The Femicide in Ciudad Juárez

Alma Mireya Chavarría Favila Angélica Luna Villalobos Jessica Lizalde de León Luz Ivonne de la O García Yolanda Álvarez Esquihua Elizabeth Ramos Verónica Huitrón Quezada Guadalupe I. Estrada Gabriela No Identificada Domínguez Aguilar María T. Contreras Hernández María Esther López de Ruiz Marcela Santos Vargas Mireya Hernández Méndez María de J. Barrón Rodríguez Tomasa Salas Calderón Esmeralda Leyva Rodríguez Rebeca E. Escobedo Sosa No Identificada Yolanda Tapia Vega Esmeralda Urías Sáenz Guillermina Hernández Chavez Ana María Gil Bravo María Quezada Amador Esmeralda Andrade Gutiérrez Graciela García Primero Leticia Reyes No Identificada Benítez Emilia García Hernández Carla M. Contreras López María del Rocío Cordero Esquivel Rosa V. de Hernández Cano Patricia Alba Ríos Alejandra Bisecas Castro Lorenza I. González Alamillo Gladys Janeth Fierro Vargas María Osuna Aguirre Rosario Aguayo No Identificada Donna Maurine Strippling Boggs Fabiola Zamudio María Agustina Hernández María Enfield de Martínez Karina Daniel Gutiérrez No Identificada Rosa María Lerma Hernández Patricia la Burra Hilda Fierro Elías Antonia Ramírez Calderón Silvia E. Rivera Morales Elizabeth Martínez Rodríguez Viridiana Torres Moreno Rosalba Ortega Saucedo Araceli Esmeralda Montañés No Identificada Graciela Bueno de Hernández Liliana Frayre Bustillos Érika García Moreno Francisca Lucero Gallardo Teodora de la Rosa Martínez Olivia G. Morales de Ríos Patricia Cortez Garza Cecilia Covarrubias Aguilar Silvia Alcántar Enríquez Olga Alicia Carrillo Pérez Claudia Escamilla Alcántar No Identificada Elizabeth Castro García María Máynez Sustaita Francisca Lucero Gallardo Ignacia Rosales Soto Gloria Elena Escobedo Piña No Identificada Rosa Ivonne Páez Márquez Rosa Isela Tena Laura Ana Irene Elizabeth Robles Gómez María de los Ángeles Deras María Moreno Galaviz No Identificada Norma Mayela Palacios López Rosa Isela Corona Santos Martha Arguijo Castañeda Francisca Epigmenia Hernández Adriana Martínez Martínez Adriana Torres Márquez Estefanía Corral Martínez Silvia Valdez Martínez Silvia Ocón López Luz Martínez Reyes Rita Parker Hopkins Victoria Parker Hopkins Hilda Sosa Jiménez Guadalupe Castro Pando Luz M. Jiménez María Marisol Franco de García No Identificada Claudia Ramos López María Domitila Torres Nava Antonia Hernández Pérez Leticia de la Cruz Bañuelos Rosario de Fátima Martínez Araceli Gallardo Rodríguez Leticia García Rosales No Identificada María S. Luján Mendoza Silvia Rivera Salas Brenda Lizeth Nájera Flores María Navarrete Reyes Susana Flores Flores No Identificada Sandra Luz Juárez Vázquez Rocío Agüero Miranda Gloria Moreno Avilés

Illegal Art / IA901

DVD cover design by Zak Kyes for *On The Edge: The Femicide In Ciudad Juarez,* a film by Steev Hise. The cover lists the names of the female murder victims from Ciudad Juarez. Kyes uses text to draw an abstract picture of these murders that is more holistic and chilling than any single photographic image could be.

Zak Kyes designed this cover for issue 15 of *Specialten Magazine*. He creates visual tension by combining overprinted typography with a photograph of physical objects printed with the same typeface. Further tension is created in the photograph by figure ground ambiguity and overlapping planes of type. The miniature broom and filing boxes disrupt our sense of scale. A final layer of irony is added by using a color photograph to represent a scene that is largely black and white.

I love the aesthetic of your work. How is the look of your work related to your tactical approach?

The aesthetic is sometimes a byproduct of content-based decisions but is also "front-loaded," based on research and directions I want to explore. This unguided, unrelated research often takes the form of a secondary "counter-voice" to the content. There is room for the unconventional, awkward, strange, and uncertain. There is also a general attraction to twisting and warping images to create a distorted secondary meaning. This secondary meaning tries to address more abstract topics like noise or change or complexity—which eventually form the message of the work, once you look beyond the facts.

Performative Design

Semiotic design is one kind of contextual design that usually happens within the 2D picture plane. Another approach to contextual design is what I call performative design. Rather than trying to fit the third layer of contextual commentary into the dimensions of the design space (printed page, video screen, computer monitor), performative design puts the third layer of content entirely outside the frame of the design space and into 3D physical space. The performative designer functions like a sculptor in some instances and a performance artist in others. Of course, we can't use those terms because design is not art. For *sculptor*, substitute *expert in experimental materials*. For *performance artist*, substitute *expert in experimental marketing strategies*.

Performative designs reference, incorporate, and recontextualize the environments in which they appear. Sandwich boards are an example of performative design. A person is hired to wear the 2D design on himself and walk around town as a mobile, sculptural, performative advertisement. People who wear T-shirts that say Tommy Hilfiger, Old Navy, or Abercrombie & Fitch are in effect walking sandwich boards for those brands, except that instead of getting paid to spread brand awareness, they pay these companies for the privilege. Kooky.

Performative design is a great strategy for setting yourself apart from the pack. It's literally thinking outside the box of the 2D page. It involves a concern for marketing, materials, and delivery mechanisms, but this concern can actually improve the interest of your overall design concept.

MOVE BEYOND THE FRAME

In the world of painting, frames provide a kind of context that separates the painting from the wall. Derrida says that when the frame is doing its job properly, we don't even notice it. It's not part of the wall, and it's not part of the picture. Graphic design has its own frame—the edge of the 2D design space. Performative designers intentionally move beyond the boundary of this frame, and in so doing, make the frame visible. They do this in a way that intrinsically relates to the content of their design.

In theater, the "fourth wall" is the imaginary boundary between the actors and the audience. This boundary ensures that an actor won't come out of character mid-performance and ask the gentleman in the front row for a cigarette. There is a kind of fourth wall between graphic design and its audience. Magazine advertisements don't pop out of the magazine and into dimensional space. Billboards don't walk up to you and ask for a cigarette.

PERFORMATIVE DESIGN PUTS THE THIRD LAYER OF CONTENT ENTIRELY OUTSIDE THE FRAME OF THE DESIGN SPACE AND INTO 3D PHYSICAL SPACE.

One of the goals of performance art is to break down the fourth wall of theater. A performance artist might start a dialogue with his audience, throw things at them, or invite them up on stage. Likewise, performative design seeks to break down the fourth wall of advertising. The results are initially startling to the audience, but this surprise soon turns to delight if the designer has done her job well. There are two main ways to move beyond the frame.

Use Experimental Materials
Experimental materials and production methods can introduce a sculptural, dimensional element to your design. Stefan Sagmeister is a master of this practice. He designed a pop-up business card with a logo that expanded into 3D space. He designed a lenticular business card that changed when a person tilted it, like a Cracker Jack prize. He designed a spinning business card with alternate letters of the logotype printed on opposite sides of the card, and the only way a person could read the logo was by spinning the card on an attached string. In all cases, the experimental materials advanced the conceptual goals of the project. The business cards were for creative agencies. The cards immediately sent the message, "We're unique, and we're able to get people's attention in unique and memorable ways." Unlike most business cards, which get thrown away immediately, Sagmeister-designed business cards are often kept for years.

Sagmeister designed a CD package with holes punched into the actual case for an album called *Fantastic Spikes Through Balloon*. He designed another CD package with an enclosed cigarette in the transparent spine of the case for a musician who loved to smoke. For the band Aerosmith, he even designed a Christmas card that plays as a record. Again, in each of these cases, his use of experimental materials was directly related to the concept of each project. Sagmeister is not an industrial designer. He's not designing furniture or cars. He's still essentially a graphic designer. He has just expanded the parameters of graphic design to include sculptural elements.

Use Experimental Delivery Mechanisms
Experimental delivery mechanisms (promotional strategies) can be used to introduce a performative, relational element to your design. The circus is the classic example of this approach—it is entertainment and marketing all wrapped up in a microcosmic, immediate package. You watch a group of performing clowns while another clown walks through the crowd selling clown T-shirts. Of course it's marketing, but there is nothing sneaky about it; it's all enjoyably integrated into a classic, multisensory experience. (Sometimes I'm inclined to agree with artist and Catholic nun Sister Corita Kent: "Damn everything but the circus.")

Once again, Stefan Sagmeister is the contemporary master of this kind of design. In Vienna he was hired to make posters advertising a fashion event, to be placed on famous advertising columns in the middle of the city. Sagmeister decided to dress the columns up in fashion gowns as part of the promotion, but the media buyers failed to reserve the columns in time. Undaunted, he made replicas of the columns and dressed them up in gowns. Furthermore, his fake columns were mobile. He hired students to stand inside the columns and move them around town.

Some students developed a technique of standing still long enough for people to start reading the posters, and then they would suddenly move and freak the people out. Other students would chase people down the street. The project got tons of press and was a success. A nonperformative designer thinking "inside the frame" never would have arrived at that solution. She would have simply designed the 2D poster deliverables and turned them in. The details of their implementation would have been somebody else's problem.

Aren't these experimental delivery mechanisms just marketing and promotion rather than graphic design? Usually. But when the nature of the promotional campaign is directly related to the literal form and content of the graphic design, this constitutes performative design. By dressing these very officious-looking columns in the fabrics of fashion, Sagmeister brought them to life, quite literally. In so doing, he mirrored the way in which this fashion event brought the historic city of Vienna to life.

The delivery mechanism was directly related to the concept of the project.

The only way this kind of design/marketing integration can be achieved is for the designer to be involved in the creative process from the beginning. If the graphic designer has no influence over the marketing of the product, performative design is not likely to occur.

INSCRIBE A TRACE OF THE PERFORMANCE WITHIN THE FRAME

In addition to pushing your design outside the frame of the page and into the performative realm, you can also bring the performative realm into the boundaries of the frame. You accomplish this by inscribing into your design the evidence of some real-world performative act.

Once again, Sagmeister provides the quintessential examples. For his AIGA Detroit poster shown in Chapter 3, he had the ad copy carved directly into his own skin (just the kind of thing a performance artist would do). His torso was then photographed, and the photograph became the advertisement. The trace of the performance was inscribed within the frame of the 2D design space. You can't look at this poster without thinking about the performative event.

In Sagmeister's monograph *Made You Look*, his own handwritten notes appear in the

IF PERFORMATIVE DESIGN STRATEGIES WORK FOR YOUR CLIENT, THEN THEY WORK.

WHO CARES IF THEY ARE MORE LIKE MARKETING THAN "PROPER" DESIGN?

margins of the book. Because the notes are handwritten, it feels like each copy of the book was previously owned by the designer himself. It makes the entire reading experience feel more immediate and intimate.

DON'T MISS IT
Contemporary design historians have had an awkward time categorizing Sagmeister's work because most design historians evaluate what exists within the frame of the document border. But Sagmeister's poster for the fashion columns alone hardly represents the genius of that overall campaign.

If performative design strategies work for your client, then they work. Who cares if they are more like marketing than "proper" design? You don't need to adhere to the established boundaries of graphic design—you just need to solve the problem.

The next time you are stuck on a project, try thinking beyond the frame of your medium. Performative design may be just the strategy to help you overcome the project's roadblocks.

Allure vs. Clarity

This dichotomy is closely related to form versus content. Design should be inviting and interesting, but it also has to be understood. Allure increases audience interactivity and involvement, but at what cost? If the design is so mysterious that it is undecipherable, then allure turns to confusion and defeats its own purpose.

Magazine designers understand "allure versus clarity" in terms of "readability versus legibility." Experimental designer/educator Dan Friedman explains, "Legibility (a quality of efficient, clear, and simple reading) is often in conflict with readability (a quality which promotes interest, pleasure, and challenge in reading)." In other words, you could design an article to be so safe and plainly legible that it becomes boring and unreadable. Designer Herbert Lubalin concurs: "Sometimes you have to compromise legibility to achieve impact."

Of course, there is no reason a design can't be both alluring and clear. Each project requires its own particular balance, and finding that balance is one of the main challenges of graphic design.

Samples and Examples (Emulation) vs. Principles (Formalism)

Emulation and formalism are two different ways to learn design. The emulator looks at a bunch of work by other people, gets the general intuitive idea, and then proceeds to design. The formalist learns a bunch of principles and then proceeds to design based on those principles. Here again, neither method is "right." Emulation and formalism should always work in conjunction with each other. Examples illuminate principles; principles illuminate examples.

Handmade vs. Machine-Made

This particular dichotomy is inseparable from human history and culture. In general, people prefer whichever design approach is rarest in their own era. The Celtic monks of A.D. 600 valued symmetry. They thought it was an attribute of God. Their technology was such that they couldn't make their designs absolutely symmetrical. They prized the precision of machine-made design (compasses and rulers were their machines) because it was rare in their era.

Contrarily, in the late 1800s, England was oversaturated with shoddy, machine-made goods. In reaction to this, William Morris spearheaded the Arts & Crafts movement, which valued a return to handmade craftsmanship in design.

Fast-forward to the rave/techno design movement of the 1990s. Computers were cool, new, and still relatively rare, so machine-made design was all the rage.

As I write this book in 2006, computer-aided design is commonplace. Consequently, there is a revived interest in hand-drawn illustration, hand-drawn "vernacular" lettering, and the physicality of analog textures. We now desire evidence of human imperfection in our design.

Whichever approach you choose, be sure it logically relates to your project. You don't want to use irregular, hand-drawn lettering to advertise a precision-engineered automobile simply because hand-drawn lettering is "in."

Design Cycles: Minimalist vs. Ornate vs. Chaotic

To grossly oversimplify, graphic design throughout history cycles in and out of three main phases—chaotic, ornate, and minimalist. Chaotic design phases are full of free-form experimentation and a lack of interest in universal rules and principles. Ornate design phases are full of filigree, gilding, and ornamentation. Minimalist design phases are marked by a concern for rigorous principles and a desire to impose on the content as little as possible. These phases sometimes overlap, and they don't follow each other in any predictable historical order.

Here is a chronological sampling of phases from the mid-1800s to the present:

- Victorian (chaotic)
- Art nouveau (ornate)
- Dada (chaotic)
- Bauhaus (minimalist)
- Art deco (ornate)
- International style (minimalist)
- Psychedelia (ornate)
- Punk (chaotic)
- Neo-modernism (minimalist)

This list is by no means comprehensive or even terribly accurate, but it illustrates my point.

Which type of movement is the best? I offer a single quotation in defense of each:

- Minimalist design: "Less is more" (Ludwig Mies van der Rohe)

- Ornate design: "GLORY be to God for dappled things—/ For skies of couple-colour as a brinded cow; / For rose-moles all in stipple upon trout that swim; / Fresh-firecoal chestnut-falls; finches' wings" (Gerard Manley Hopkins)

- Chaotic design: "I am the world's forgotten boy / the one who searches and destroys" (Iggy Pop)

Now that each side has had its say, I offer a word in defense of plain old wisdom: Choose the approach that best suits your project. Design statesman Milton Glaser offers a wise rebuttal to van der Rohe's modernist dictum "less is more." Glaser says, "Just enough is more." Whatever approach it takes to come up with a great design, that's the best approach.

Contemporary vs. Timeless

Is it possible to create design that speaks to your own era and is also timeless? Design must at least be contemporary, or it will not be remembered long enough to be judged as timeless. Perhaps the best a designer can hope for is to remain in dialogue with changing culture, practicing a career of evolving relevancy that accumulates in the creation of what will eventually be judged as timeless work.

Interview: Milton Glaser

Milton Glaser has been designing for over half a century, and he's still producing relevant contemporary work. I asked him how he reconciles the differences between contemporary and timeless design.

In your speech "Ten Things I've Learned," you said, "Anybody who is in this for the long haul has to decide how to respond to change in the zeitgeist. What is it that people now expect that they formerly didn't want? And how to respond to that desire in a way that doesn't change your sense of integrity and purpose?" Personally, how do you do it?

You mean from the perspective of a practicing graphic designer?

Yes.

Because the answer is quite specific. It differs vocationally. If you're an architect, the answer is not the same because your work lasts longer and is less ephemeral.

But when you're dealing with questions of communication that are deeply rooted in ideas of style or change (our economy is driven by this idea of change and obsolescence)—when stylistic idioms change, you have to reflect on your relationship to that change.

Advertising is most susceptible to change because it has to be cool and appear current. Advertising is driven by making people dissatisfied with what they already have. That is an economic engine of our economy. It has to do with this idea of replacing what you have and buying more of what now seems to be cooler or hipper or more useful or whatever. So somebody in advertising must be very conscious of the fact that when the voice begins to change in the culture, when some element becomes more visible, you have to accommodate that change and drive it.

As a designer, you're in a middle ground between marketing and sales and certain ideas about aesthetics—beauty, form, and so on. It's always hard to get that balance between what is driven by marketing and fashion, and what is driven by an idea of aesthetics and beauty.

Was there ever a time where you felt your own work was perceived as dated?

It's inevitably true that once you become identified with a particular moment in time, it's very hard to disentangle yourself from that moment, especially if you become successful early. I suspect that some of the work I did, like the Bob Dylan head, will pursue me to my grave. But as I once said, "Better to be to remembered for something that you no longer do than not to be remembered at all."

But I don't think that single Bob Dylan poster describes your career.

No, it doesn't. But I've been extremely conscious of this issue from the very beginning. My orientation has always been not to use what is going on at the present as the root of my work, but to use the continuity of history and the continuity of art as the basis for it. When we started Push Pin Studios [in 1954], I became very much identified with a certain kind of style—psychedelic, working with flat colors and tints and all that. But I was also very conscious that I would be parochialized forever if I continued doing it, so when I left Push Pin, I started what you might call the second phase of my life, where the work was much less identified with the Push Pin period. My work was also more stylistically neutral—the style really came out of the intent of the piece. I was careful to try to achieve a general rootedness in the disciplines of typography, color, drawing, and so on; so whatever the stylistic moment, I had enough mastery over the form to be able to move in it.

Students are susceptible to investing in the style of the moment. Then when that style passes, they have no resources except to rethink what it was they should have learned earlier. It is a real vocational problem when

"STUDENTS ARE SUSCEPTIBLE TO INVESTING IN THE STYLE OF THE MOMENT.

THEN WHEN THAT STYLE PASSES, THEY HAVE NO RESOURCES EXCEPT TO

RETHINK WHAT IT WAS THEY SHOULD HAVE LEARNED EARLIER."

Milton Glaser's iconic poster of Bob Dylan from 1966 encapsulated an era of psychedelic design, but it didn't limit Glaser's development of a versatile, boundary-crossing design practice.

people think that the style of the moment has any "truth" to it. The style of the moment is only a vernacular that you must master—if that's what you're doing at the moment—with the understanding that "this too shall pass."

In your post–Push Pin phase, have you ever done work for clients who came back to you and said, "This isn't 'Milton Glaserish' enough"?

That sometimes happens, but not frequently. I did something for Starbucks some years ago which was very much in the manner of work I had done 20 years earlier. When it's done that way, it's like any other job where you use a historical reference; except in this case I was my own historical reference. But generally speaking, I haven't worked that way. I endorse the idea of redefining the client's expectation. Since my approach is rooted in solving the client's problem (or reestablishing the nature of the problem), clients don't usually want me to repeat myself.

The current "slow design" movement proposes that there should be less change over time. Do you think it would be better ethically or aesthetically if stylistic design cycles changed less? Maybe that ties into economics?

I think it does. Our culture is based on dissatisfaction and the idea of the search for the new—the search for new opportunities, the search for a new life, the search for a new car, and all the rest of it. It's very hard to resist that dissatisfaction if you are part of the system—if your role is to convince people that they should have these feelings and that there is something new on the horizon. The "new" itself is intrinsically more interesting than what has passed. Our obsession with the new and emerging has hurt the culture enormously on every level imaginable. And it is driven by television and advertising, and everybody is susceptible to it. Every day you're told that the way to achieve happiness in America is to have a better home, better furnishings, a better car; and that becomes the central objective of many, many people. And if you are in the world of advertising particularly (but it certainly doesn't exclude design), there is almost no way you can remain immune to those forces.

As you approach a new project, do you always use illustration, or do you let the project dictate?

I love illustration. Basically, I love to make things. My instincts are: Whatever it is, I want to make it. The act of making is really thrilling to me. A lot of people don't have this same instinct, and for a lot of design you don't need it. What you need is a conceptual strength to link ideas. So there are two kinds of satisfaction, both of which I enjoy very much. One is to find the hidden answer contained within the question. (Every question presumes its answer, and finding that answer is thrilling.) And the other way I love to work is to physically make something—a drawing or collage or something.

And I would guess that the physical act of making things informs the conceptualization of your design solutions as well.

Very much. In fact, one of the things that distinguishes my work is the fact that I use drawing so frequently as an element. As you know, a lot of designers don't draw at all, and to some degree, it isn't essential to the process of design.

So a designer can skip the process of drawing altogether and simply cut, paste, and collage on a computer?

I think you can. I think you can be a designer without being able to draw a stick figure. But again, there are two things we're talking about. One is vocational possibilities: You can get a job. The other is expressive possibilities: If you don't have a sense of form, you're out of luck. This is one reason things look so horrible now—people don't have primary training in form, color, typography, and whatever else they do. They only have opportunistic training—learning the programs and assembling material that already exists. Assembling things that already exist is very different from making things. You are always the victim of the software somebody has already prepared for you. Undoubtedly these tools can be used inventively. I'm having a terrific time working with the computer because I'm trying to make it do things that are not customarily considered appropriate— getting texture into digital work, and complexity, and overlaying, and all this. It's great, but it's also because I have a sense of form.

How are you going to say whether something's too big or too small unless you've gone through the experience of comparing big and small a thousand times in drawing? There is no better educational instrument for developing sensitivity to shape, edge, and color than drawing. It affects the neurological system so that you begin to integrate this information into an aesthetic. Where is your aesthetic going to come from if you don't have that experience?

I want to talk a bit about modernism. It sought to be timeless, but it wasn't. Although Müller-Brockmann's work is lovely, it now represents a distinct visual period. What is still valuable about modernism, and what did they get wrong?

They didn't get anything wrong. There was the hubris of believing in an ultimate solution to the question of what art could be or what life could be. I mean, you have to be a little more modest about that. And so they said art should be reductive and clear and simple and uniform and unornamented—they had their litany of all the things. Modernism came out of a historical context and was essentially a religious movement in its earliest manifestations. It had (and has) that manifestation of belief: "We have finally found the messiah, and here's what it is." And it was sped forward by the fact that you could teach it, unlike many manifestations of art which are not teachable. The rules and ideas about modernism were easily integrated into academic programs.

Do you think that's why it had a longer run than art nouveau?

I think so, because you could literally say, "Here's what you must do." And like religion itself, when you give people a lot of rules they have to follow, it keeps them off the street. So finally everybody thought, "I know how to do it. I can make design and here's the answer." And once you provide that as a kind of mechanism to young people, it becomes their reality. It's very seductive to feel that there is an answer to anything—to life or to art. [Art historian] E. H. Gombrich said, "There is no art; there are only artists." And I think Gombrich had it right. There is no design; there is no art. It's only what happens at a particular moment in time where people invent what those things are. You invent what design is.

Modernism had a long and useful run. It cleared away a lot of deadwood. It did give people a way to start. And it is a terrific way to start. You can start with the idea that education needs to start with the principles of modernism. Just don't believe modernism is "true." Modernism is kind of a workout. You get yourself a muscular system.

One of my pet criticisms of modernism is the elimination of ornament. I mean, that's silly. Why should you eliminate one of the fundamental, most historically powerful instruments of communication? So those kind of silly ideas, which are linked to other persuasive ideas, became a kind of methodology. At a certain point, what was most obvious to me was the fact that you cannot speak to all people with the same voice. The "fact" that sans serif flush-left Helvetica was the way to say anything you were saying was silly.

At Push Pin, did you intentionally set out to reintroduce a more Arts & Crafts approach as a conscious opposition to modernism, or is that just how you were working at the time?

I don't know. I think I personally just got bored with modernism. It was a great starting point, and we were all modernists because that was our training. But I had gone to Italy on a Fulbright. I saw Baroque architecture, which is supposed to be bad stuff, but I'm looking and I'm thinking, "You know, this ain't so bad!" I got a more historical view of what design was, what form was, what architecture was. Also, I

"ONE OF MY PET CRITICISMS OF MODERNISM IS THE ELIMINATION OF ORNAMENT. I MEAN, THAT'S SILLY. WHY SHOULD YOU ELIMINATE ONE OF THE FUNDAMENTAL, MOST HISTORICALLY POWERFUL INSTRUMENTS OF COMMUNICATION?"

realized how parochial and stupid I was for not understanding the visual history of the world. And I just said, there's another way to look at all this stuff—a broader and more interesting and more complex way. The nice thing about rules is that they protect you from failure. The downside is that they also prevent you from going beyond the boundaries of what is already agreed upon.

Are aspects of modernism and grid design inherently related to corporate identity systems?

Identity is driven to some degree by technical issues: A good identity has to be reduced to one-fourth inch in a newspaper and still be understood. So by that fact alone, identities can't be complex. They have to be coherent; they have to be simple. All those kinds of technical

Milton Glaser's 17-foot cloud wall for the Rubin Museum of Art, designed in 2004. As much a work of art as a piece of interior design, its motif is inspired by clouds from Tibetan art.

demands set the stage for what you can and cannot do. But I always thought that the camel on Camel Cigarettes was as good an identity as you could ever find because it sticks in the mind, you remember it, and there's a sense of incongruity. So when you talk about identity, designers have a kind of geometric stylization mode for identity, but I think it can be more interesting than that. Also, now all the identities are so much in the same camp that they become impossible to differentiate.

To return to the original quotation, "Anybody who is in this for the long haul has to decide how to respond to change in the zeitgeist." Are there any crucial pieces of advice that you would give to a design school graduate who is going to be doing this for the next 50 years?

The first thing is: Don't make up your mind too soon about what it is you want to be doing. You have to wait a long time to find out what really interests you. One of the big problems that young people have is that they get stuck too early in an inadvertent career path. They take the first job they have, they spend six months doing it, and either they move or they stay. If they stay, they get better at it, they get higher pay, and before you know it, that's their career. Quite by accident they got a job in editorial design, then after five years they discover they don't like editorial design. But they can't move out of editorial design because now they have a kid and a Manhattan apartment, they're

earning a good living because they are doing something they're good at, and they're doomed.

Stay loose for the first five, ten years of your work life until you have enough skill and understanding to make a choice that you can stay with for the rest of your life. After all, as you said, you may be doing this for 50 years. The worst thing you can do is find yourself in a job that you're not particularly interested in for 40 of those years.

Travel a bit. For Americans, going to Europe and getting out of American culture is another good thing to do—to realize there's another universe with different beliefs that may affect your view of yourself and what you do.

Once a designer has done her ten-year trial period and she knows she's in it for the long haul, by that time will she know all she needs to know?

Quite the contrary. The great thing about my life is that I come to work every day with the possibility of learning something I don't know. In this particular field, there is always more to learn than you know. You never get there. There is a universe that you have not even encountered, and the possibilities for getting closer to that universe exist, even at this "ripe old age." I just did something for the Holocaust Museum in Houston, and I think it's the best thing I ever did. It's just different, and it takes off from a different place and a different assumption. And I'm thrilled by the fact that I can still learn new tricks.

Milton Glaser's reverently redemptive poster for the Holocaust Museum in Houston, designed in 2006. The text is from the Viktor E. Frankl's book *Man's Search for Meaning*.

ONE DAY, A FEW DAYS AFTER THE LIBERATION, I WALKED THROUGH THE COUNTRY PAST FLOWERING MEADOWS, FOR MILES AND MILES, TOWARD THE MARKET TOWN NEAR THE CAMP. LARKS ROSE TO THE SKY AND I COULD HEAR THEIR JOYOUS SONG. THERE WAS NO ONE TO BE SEEN FOR MILES AROUND; THERE WAS NOTHING BUT WIDE EARTH AND SKY AND THE LARK'S JUBILATION AND THE FREEDOM OF SPACE. I STOPPED, LOOKED AROUND, AND UP TO THE SKY – AND THEN I WENT DOWN ON MY KNEES. AT THAT MOMENT THERE WAS VERY LITTLE I KNEW OF MYSELF OR OF THE WORLD – I HAD BUT ONE SENTENCE IN MIND – ALWAYS THE SAME: "I CALLED TO THE LORD FROM MY NARROW PRISON AND HE ANSWERED ME IN THE FREEDOM OF SPACE." HOW LONG I KNELT THERE AND REPEATED THIS SENTENCE MEMORY CAN NO LONGER RECALL. BUT I KNOW THAT ON THAT DAY, IN THAT HOUR, MY NEW LIFE STARTED. STEP FOR STEP I PROGRESSED, UNTIL I AGAIN BECAME A HUMAN BEING. THE WAY THAT LED FROM THE ACUTE MENTAL TENSION OF THE LAST DAYS IN CAMP (FROM THAT WAR OF NERVES TO MENTAL PEACE) WAS CERTAINLY NOT FREE FROM OBSTACLES. IT WOULD BE AN ERROR TO THINK THAT A LIBERATED PRISONER WAS NOT IN NEED OF SPIRITUAL CARE ANY MORE. WE HAVE TO CONSIDER THAT A MAN WHO HAS BEEN UNDER SUCH ENORMOUS MENTAL PRESSURE FOR SUCH A LONG TIME IS NATURALLY IN SOME DANGER AFTER HIS LIBERATION, ESPECIALLY SINCE THE PRESSURE WAS RELEASED QUITE SUDDENLY. THIS DANGER (IN THE SENSE OF PSYCHOLOGICAL HYGIENE) IS THE PSYCHOLOGICAL COUNTERPART OF THE BENDS...RIGHT TO DO WRONG, NOT EVEN IF WRONG HAS BEEN DONE TO THEM. WE HAD TO STRIVE TO LEAD THEM BACK INTO THIS TRUTH, OR THE CONSEQUENCES WOULD HAVE BEEN MUCH WORSE THAN THE LOSS OF A FEW THOUSAND STALKS OF OATS...BUT FOR EVERY ONE OF THE LIBERATED PRISONERS, THE DAY COMES WHEN, LOOKING BACK ON HIS CAMP EXPERIENCES, HE CAN NO LONGER UNDERSTAND HOW HE ENDURED IT ALL. AS THE DAY OF HIS LIBERATION EVENTUALLY CAME, WHEN EVERYTHING SEEMED TO HIM LIKE A BEAUTIFUL DREAM, SO ALSO THE DAY COMES WHEN ALL HIS CAMP EXPERIENCES SEEM TO HIM NOTHING BUT A NIGHTMARE. THE CROWNING EXPERIENCE OF ALL, FOR THE HOMECOMING MAN, IS THE WONDERFUL FEELING THAT, AFTER ALL HE HAS SUFFERED, THERE IS NOTHING HE NEED FEAR ANY MORE – EXCEPT HIS GOD.

Milton Glaser

TEN YEARS: REMEMBRANCE. EDUCATION. HOPE. HOLOCAUST MUSEUM HOUSTON, EDUCATION CENTER AND MEMORIAL.

The Human Element: You

After all this talk of paradigms and forms, modernism and deconstruction, performance and semiotics, balancing and reconciling, it may seem as if design is just a series of theories and opinions. Nothing could be further from the truth. The art of creative design ultimately relies heavily on the individual personality of the designer. Otherwise, anyone could follow basic modernist principles and be as good as Josef Müller-Brockmann. Anyone could follow his own untrained intuition and be as good as David Carson. This is not the case. Rules and paradigms can help, but they don't instantly transform mediocrity into greatness. The trick is figuring out ways to apply these approaches to your own personal practice.

The "way" to greatness is through work. The only way these paradigms and formal systems can get worked into your working design is through work. Experiment with asymmetrical balance. Experiment with adding a semiotic layer of commentary. Experiment with performative design. Only by applying these abstract concepts to your work can you begin to truly own them.

■ ■ ■

WHATEVER YOUR HAND FINDS TO DO, DO IT WITH ALL YOUR MIGHT.

—ECCLESIASTES 9:10

CONCLUSION
TAG. YOU'RE IT.

Art historian James Elkins wrote a book called *Why Art Cannot Be Taught*. In it, he contends that since art is so unlike other academic subjects, such as mathematics and science, it is very difficult to teach in a straightforward manner. In a similar way, design is difficult to teach. You can learn the rote, rudimentary rules of graphic design in a few years, but it takes a lifetime to develop these rules into something resembling a creative practice.

In *The Thinking Eye*, Paul Klee meditates on the difficulty of teaching art and design at the Bauhaus:

> Education is a difficult chapter. The most difficult. The education of the artist above all. Even if one supposes it to be continuous, even if one supposes that there might be a certain number of real educators, many remain within the realm of the visible, because it is enough for them. Few get to the bottom and begin to create. Most stick rigidly to theories because they are afraid of life, because they dread uncertainty.

INITIALLY, THE APPROACHES IN THIS BOOK WILL FEEL UNCOMFORTABLE, AND YOU'LL WANT

TO RETURN TO YOUR SAFE, KNOWN PRACTICE. BUT IF YOU ARE WILLING TO EXERCISE

NEW DESIGN MUSCLES, YOU WILL EVENTUALLY BECOME A BETTER DESIGNER.

To teach design effectively is to risk an element of uncertainty. The exercises and approaches in this book are not a color-by-numbers recipe for success. Like Brian Eno and Peter Schmidt's Oblique Strategies, they require intelligent and tailored application on your part. Which parts of this book are most applicable to your process and how will you incorporate them into it? Only you can answer those questions for yourself.

Furthermore, practice does not guarantee success or even growth. Edward de Bono tells of the two-fingered typist who never got appreciably faster at typing. According to de Bono, "If you practice poor thinking for years you will become an extremely good poor thinker." Likewise, if you practice mediocre graphic design for years, you will become an extremely good mediocre graphic designer.

I play the guitar. I used to pick with three fingers rather than five. I was OK, but there were certain things I simply wasn't able to play. Adding my other two fingers made everything worse for a while. It felt really uncomfortable. But eventually I got used to it, and my playing markedly improved. The same will be true with some of the exercises and approaches in this book. Initially, they will feel uncomfortable, and you'll want to return to your safe, known practice. But if you are willing to exercise new design muscles, you will eventually become a better designer.

This book is by no means the final word on design creativity. My hope is that it will lead you to further develop your own creative strategies. Create your own exercises. Experiment with new production methods. Send yourself back to school, so to speak.

Graphic design can be understood as a set of formal rules to be followed, but the best graphic design is always a step beyond mere adherence to formal principles. The greatest designers are in communication with the problem, the client, and the audience. They are translators, finding the essence of a design challenge and articulating its answer in a compelling, clever, appealing way.

Designer Stefan Sagmeister's lifelong client Hans Gratzer, former director of the theater in Vienna called Schauspielhaus, said this about Sagmeister: "He understands the problem, circles the subject, grabs it, turns it around, rips out its secret, separates it, forms it into a picture, and gives back the secret." (Would that all our clients had such an appreciation of our work!) Design at this level requires passionate dedication to the creative process and faith that we designers are more than wage-labor commercial flunkies.

If this book is able to inject some joy, play, and fulfillment into your commercial practice, then it will have served its purpose. May you apply yourself passionately and intelligently to your craft so that the world becomes a more beautiful, livable, functional, enjoyable place.

■ ■ ■

Exercises

The last thing a busy designer has time for is rudimentary design exercises, yet they can help keep your ax sharp in the midst of a potentially ax-dulling workload. Given that, don't feel obliged to do these exercises on a regular basis, or even at all. They are simply ways to experiment and grow outside of your commercial practice.

Time-Limited Exercises

- Completely design a CD cover or poster in 3 hours.

- Completely design a CD cover or poster in 30 minutes.

- Draw 30 sketches in 60 minutes (2 minutes per sketch). Don't judge their value. Move on to the next sketch immediately. You are going for quantity and creative stamina over actual sketch quality.

- Draw 30 circles (1 inch in diameter) 2 inches apart on a newsprint roll. In 5 minutes (10 seconds per circle), draw sketchy details around each circle to make it a unique image (Saturn, a baseball, a teapot). Again, the emphasis is on creative stamina rather than sketch quality.

Style and Genre Exercises

- Design two solutions for the same design problem in two similar historical genres (for instance, art nouveau and art deco). Focus on similarities and nuanced differences.

- Design two solutions for the same design problem in two contrasting historical genres (for instance, Swiss grid Modernist and postmodern grunge). Focus on differences and nuanced similarities.

- Design three solutions for the same design problem. For the first solution, adhere strictly to a grid system. For the second, use the same grid system but try to deconstruct it, breaking the rules of the grid and pushing it to its limits. For the third, abandon the grid altogether and simply compose your design in free space using intuition. Use the same typefaces, copy, and colors for each design, relying solely on layout and composition for your expressive differences.

- Design an advertising campaign in different media for one product. For example, design a billboard, a poster, a newspaper advertisement, and a 30-second video spot for the same jazz band performance.

- Design a poster supporting a political cause, then translate that same cause into a more tactical medium—one that relies less on a physical design object and more on a cleverly implemented performative concept.

- Design an advertising campaign for the same product in two visual styles: machine-made and handmade. Make the machine-made style as digital and futuristic as possible. Make the handmade style as analog, nondigital, physical, and organic as possible.

Perspective Exercises

- Advertise the same product to different demographics: teenagers, yuppies, retirees, and so on.

- Translate a real-world design project into an experimental art project. Ask yourself, "If there was no client, how would I proceed?"

Conceptual Exercises

- Design an advertising campaign for the same product in two modes: contemporary and timeless. Make the contemporary design as trendy, hip, and cutting edge as possible. Make the timeless design as classic and style-agnostic as possible.

- Design an advertising campaign that appeals equally to teenagers and senior citizens.

- Design an advertising campaign for a political cause that appeals equally to conservatives and liberals.

- Design an advertising campaign supporting a cause you support.

- Design an advertising campaign supporting a cause you oppose.

- Design five different advertising campaigns for the same product. Each campaign should focus heavily on one of the five design realms from Chapter 9. For instance, the first campaign should focus heavily on the realm of media constraints; the second, on the realm of audience needs; and so on.

- Stefan Sagmeister suggests using the following four-part, multiple-perspective technique, which he adapted from ad executive James Young's 1939 manual *A Technique for Producing Ideas*:

  1. Think about the project from any point of view—your mom's, yours, color, form. Write each response down on an index card.

  2. Spread the index cards out on a big table and see if you can find the relationship between different thoughts.

  3. Forget about the whole thing.

  4. The idea will strike you miraculously when you least expect it.

- Begin with someone else's advertising campaign that you admire and try to improve it.

- Choose the most exciting hypothetical design project you can imagine (Radiohead album cover, Pixar feature film trailer, whatever) and implement it according to very stringent production requirements.

- Choose the most boring, rote hypothetical design project you can imagine (adult diapers packaging, medical insurance Web site, whatever), and implement it with absolutely no production requirements at all.

Of the two projects above, which did you enjoy more? Which was the most successful?

These are just a handful of exercises. Feel free to invent your own. The idea is to pose challenges that cause you to analyze your particular way of working. Then take the lessons you've learned and apply them to your commercial projects.

■ ■ ■

Selected Resources

Rather than list all the resources I've consulted in writing this book, I've selected the ones I think will most benefit the designer who wants to read further on these topics. Some of the resources are available online as of the time of this book's publication, but they may not be there by the time you read this book. These resources are divided per book chapter and section, beginning with a list of general resources.

General Resources

Michael Bierut, William Drenttel, Jessica Helfand, and Rick Poynor (editors). *Design Observer*. www.designobserver.com (Web log).

Kenneth Clark. *Civilisation—The Complete Series*. BBC Warner. 2006. (Television series originally aired in 1969.)

Kees Dorst. *Understanding Design*. Gingko Press. 2004.

Steven Heller (editor). *Voice: AIGA Journal of Design*. http://voice.aiga.org (online magazine and community).

Armin Hofmann. *Graphic Design Manual*. Arthur Niggli. 2001. (Originally published in 1965.)

Kaliber10000 (The Designers' Lunchbox). www.k10k.net (online community).

Paul Klee. *The Thinking Eye* and *The Nature of Nature*. Lund Humphries Publishers Ltd. 1992. (Originally published in English in 1961.)

Ellen Lupton. *DesignWritingResearch.org*. www.designwritingresearch.org (personal Web site).

Bruce Mau. *Life Style*. Phaidon Press. 2000.

Marty Neumeier. *The Brand Gap, Revised* (New Riders). 2005.

Newstoday. www.newstoday.com (online community).

Introduction: What This Book Is and Is Not About

Hermann Vaske. www.whyareyoucreative.com (online project).

Chapter 1: A Process Primer

Hillman Curtis. *MTIV*. New Riders Press. 2002.

Jesse James Garrett. *The Elements of User Experience*. New Riders Press. 2002.

David Siegel. *Secrets of Successful Web Sites*. Hayden. 1997.

Chapter 3: Four Ways to Bypass Inertia

EXPLORATORY SKETCHING

James L. Adams. *Conceptual Blockbusting* (4th Edition). Perseus Books Group. 2001.

Edward de Bono. *De Bono's Thinking Course*. Facts on File. 1986.

Robert McKim. *Experiences in Visual Thinking* (2nd Edition). Brooks/Cole Publishing Company. 1980.

Nicholas Roukes. *Design Synectics*. Davis Publications. 1988.

OBLIQUE STRATEGIZING

Gregory Taylor. *Oblique Strategies*. www.rtqe.net/ObliqueStrategies/ (online resource).

Chapter 4: Mining Art and Design History

Michael Bambini. *The Look of the Century*. Dorling Kindersley Publishing. 1996.

Steven Heller, Mirko Illic. *Genius Moves*. North Light Books. 2001.

Steven Heller, Julie Lasky. *Borrowed Design*. John Wiley & Sons. 1992.

Steven Heller, Seymour Chwast. *Graphic Style*. Harry N. Abrams. 2001.

Richard Hollis. *Graphic Design: A Concise History* (2nd Edition). Thames & Hudson. 2002.

Owen Jones. *The Grammar of Ornament*. DK Adult. 2001. (Originally published in 1856.)

Philip Meggs. *Meggs' History of Graphic Design* (4th Edition). Wiley. 2005.

NL DESIGN (Mieke Gerritzen et. al.). *Catalogue of Strategies*. Gingko Press. 2001.

Colin Rhodes. *Outsider Art: Spontaneous Alternatives*. Thames & Hudson. 2000.

Chapter 5: Vary Degrees of Derivation

Thomas Riedelsheimer. *Rivers and Tides: Andy Goldsworthy Working with Time*. New Video Group. 2004 (DVD).

Chapter 6: How I Stopped Worrying and Learned to Love the Edit

Edward de Bono. *Six Thinking Hats*. Back Bay Books. 1999.

C. McNair Wilson. www.mcnairwilson.com (personal Web site).

Chapter 7: Software and Systems

GENERATIVE SOFTWARE

Joshua Davis. *Flash to the Core*. New Riders Publishing. 2002.

GRID SYSTEMS

Robert Bringhurst. *The Elements of Typographic Style* (Version 3.0). Hartley and Marks Publishers. 2004. (Chapter 8 deals with the Golden Ratio in great detail.)

Willi Kunz. *Typography: Macro- and Microaesthetics*. Arthur Niggli. 2004.

William Lidwell, Kritina Holden, Jill Butler. *Universal Principles of Design*. Rockport Publishers. 2003.

Müller-Brockmann. *Grid Systems in Graphic Design*. Arthur Niggli. 1996. (Originally published in 1961.)

Timothy Samara. *Making and Breaking the Grid*. Rockport Publishers. 2005.

Chapter 8: Maintaining a Personal Design Playground

Rural Studio. http://ruralstudio.com (online gallery and resource).

Chapter 9: The Five Realms of Design

THE REALM OF MEDIA CONSTRAINTS

Jørgen Leth and Lars von Trier. *The Five Obstructions*. Koch Lorber Films. 2004

Scott McCloud. *Understanding Comics*. Harper Paperbacks. 1994.

THE REALM OF AUDIENCE NEEDS

37 Signals. *Getting Real*. http://gettingreal.37signals.com (online book).

Gerry De Mol. "Quantum Cats and Mosquito Hunting." www.ogilvy.be/images/MANIFESTO_UK.pdf.

Christopher Locke, Rick Levine, Doc Searls, David Weinberger. *The Cluetrain Manifesto*. Perseus Books Group. 2001 (online at http://cluetrain.com).

THE REALM OF CLIENT NEEDS

Clement Mok. "Designers: Time for Change." *Communication Arts*. May/June 2003.

Mark Oldach. *Creativity for Graphic Designers*. North Light Books. 2000.

Paula Scher. *Make It Bigger*. Princeton Architectural Press. 2005.

Steven Tolleson. *Soak, Wash, Rinse, Spin: Tolleson Design*. Princeton Architectural Press. 2000.

THE REALM OF PROFESSIONAL ETHICS

"AIGA Standards of Professional Practice." www.aiga.org/content.cfm?contentalias=standards_of_practice.

Guy Debord and Gil Wolman. "A User's Guide to Détournement." www.bopsecrets.org/SI/detourn.htm.

First Things First 2000: A Design Manifesto. www.xs4all.nl/~maxb/ftf2000.htm.

Greil Marcus. *Lipstick Traces: A Secret History of the 20th Century*. Harvard University Press. 1990.

Dan Ollman, Sarah Price, Chris Smith. *The Yes Men*. MGM. 2005 (DVD).

THE REALM OF AESTHETICS

Paula Scher. "The Devaluation of Design by the Design Community." *AIGA Journal of Graphic Design*. Volume 11, Number 4, 1993.

Chapter 10: Balance Forms and Reconcile Paradigms

BALANCE FORMAL ELEMENTS

Christopher Alexander. *A Pattern Language*. Oxford University Press. 1977.

Mark Stephen Meadows. *Pause & Effect*. New Riders Press. 2002.

RECONCILE OPPOSING PARADIGMS

Milton Glaser. "Ten Things I Have Learned." www.miltonglaser.com/pages/milton/essays/es3.html.

Ellen Lupton, Abbott Miller. *Design Writing Research*. Phaidon Press. 1999.

Rick Poynor. *No More Rules*. Yale University Press. 2003.

Stefan Sagmeister, Peter Hall. *Made You Look*. Booth-Clibborn. 2001.

■ ■ ■

Figure Credits

Images not credited below were made by the author.

Introduction
Bread photograph by Anthony Otte.

Chapter 1: A Process Primer
Source apple photograph by Rafael Rigues, modified by the author.

Fresh Styles for Web Designers cover design mockups. © Segura Inc. info@segura-inc.com

Diagram of the Five Elements of User Experience. © Jesse James Garrett.

Chapter 2: Basic Creative Wisdom
Absolut Vodka advertisements under permission by V&S Vin & Sprit AB (publ). ABSOLUT®VODKA. ABSOLUT COUNTRY OF SWEDEN VODKA & LOGO, ABSOLUT, ABSOLUT BOTTLE DESIGN AND ABSOLUT CALLIGRAPHY ARE TRADEMARKS OWNED BY V&S VIN & SPRIT AB (publ), ©2005 V&S VIN & SPRIT AB (publ).

"Infinity" advertisement for BIC. Created by TBWA Hunt/Lascaris (South Africa).

First page of Genesis from the *Doves Press Bible*. The Rosenwald Collection, Library of Congress.

Citi logo. © Paula Scher/Pentagram.

"War Is Madness" poster. © Seymour Chwast, The Pushpin Group, NY.

Chapter 3: Four Ways to Bypass Inertia
Open graphic design studio identity exercises. © Michael Levy (www.michalevy.com).

Open graphic design studio posters. Michael Levy (www.michalevy.com).

AIGA Detroit poster, 1999. Art direction: Stefan Sagmeister. Photo: Tom Schierlitz. Client: AIGA Detroit. Size: 27.5 x 39 inch.

Chapter 4: Mining Art and Design History
"Best of Jazz" series poster. © Paula Scher/Pentagram.

Page from Kelmscott Press *The Works of Geoffrey Chaucer*. The Rosenwald Collection, Library of Congress.

Tughra of Sultan Sulaiman the Magnificent. C. 1555-60. Ink, paint, and gold on paper, removed from a firman and trimmed to 20 1/2" x 25 3/8" (52 x 64.5 cm). The Metropolitan Museum of Art, Rogers Fund, 1938 (38.149.1). Photograph (c)1980 The Metropolitan Museum of Art.

Moska. Aubrey Beardsley, *Moska*, ca. 1895. Pen and black ink on wove paper, 15.8 x 17.2 cm (sheet). Fine Arts Museums of San Francisco, Gift of Dora Donner Ide, 1986.2.3

Poster for *The Man with the Golden Arm,* Saul Bass (c) Judith Miller / Dorling Kindersley / Posteritati

Album cover for *This Is The Day… This Is The Hour… This Is This* by Pop Will Eat Itself. 1989. Made In The Designers Republic.

Toulouse-Lautrec centenary poster. © Paula Scher/Pentagram.

Portal at Chartres Cathedral. Photograph by Eixo.

Nude Descending a Staircase, No. 3. Marcel Duchamp. (c)2006 Artists Rights Society (ARS), New York / ADAGP, Paris / Succession Marcel Duchamp.

Cranbrook Graduate Design poster. 1989. © Katherine McCoy.

Fourth International Browserday brochure. 2001. © Mieke Gerritzen.

AIGA New Orleans poster, 1997. Art direction, design, illustration: Stefan Sagmeister. Additional Illustration: Peggy Chuang, Kazumi Matsumoto, Raphael Rüdisser. Photography: Bela Borsodi. Paint Box: Dalton Portella. Size: 26.5" x 37.5" (67.3 x 95.2 cm).

Chapter 5: Varying Degrees of Derivation

Untitled, Paris, 1995 © Marshall Soules.
In a Foreign Tongue, Rome, 1995 © Marshall Soules.
Castro, San Francisco, 1997 © Marshall Soules.
McDeal, Kenora, 2004 © Marshall Soules.

Chapter 7: Software and Systems

MEEK 4.0 Typographic Synthesizer interface. © Rob Meek 2001-2006 (robmeek.com).
Zinc Magazine cover. © Joshua Davis (joshuadavis.com).
BMW promotional prints. © Joshua Davis (joshuadavis.com).
Screenshots of www.once-upon-a-forest.com. © Joshua Davis (joshuadavis.com).
Atlantic Center for the Arts poster. © David Carson.

Chapter 8: Maintaining a Personal Design Playground

The Yancey Tire Chapel. Sawyerville, Alabama. Photograph by Timothy Hursley.
testpilotcollective.com splash pages. © Joe Kral.
hellmedia.com type studies. © S. Bradley Askew.
trueistrue.com. 2002. © Mike Cina (www.weworkforthem.com).
soulbath.com. © Hi-Res (www.hi-res.net).
requiemforadream.com. © Hi-Res (www.hi-res.net).
upsod.com. © Dustin Hostetler.
Four band posters. © Dustin Hostetler.
BPM Magazine cover. © Dustin Hostetler.
trueistrue.com. © Mike Cina (www.weworkforthem.com).
prate.com. © Jemma Hostetler.
oculart.com. © Geoff Lillemon.

Chapter 9: The Five Realms of Design

www.k10k.net. Cuban Council (www.cubancouncil.com)
www.coudal.com. Coudal Partners.
www.south.co.uk [*With The Tides* site]. Design: Monkey Clan (www.monkeyclan.com). Illustration: Karen Ingram.
Ilya Web site. © Hi-Res (www.hi-res.net).

Chapter 10: Balance Forms and Reconcile Paradigms

Architectural Association poster. 2006. Designer: Zak Kyes.
nOulipo (after Georges Perec) conference poster. 2005. Designer: Zak Kyes. Client: Roy Edna Disney / CalArts Theater (REDCAT).
Contribution to *Crossfields* magazine. 2005. © Zak Kyes.
"Shipping & Receiving" exhibition invitation. 2005. Designer: Zak Kyes with Tahli Fisher. Client: Armory Northwest, Los Angeles.
DVD cover for *On The Edge: The Femicide In Ciudad Juarez* (a film by Steev Hise). 2006. Designer: Zak Kyes. Released by Illegal Art.
Specialten Magazine cover, Issue 15. 2006. Editorial Design: Zak Kyes. Photography in collaboration wih Tim Brotherton.
Bob Dylan Poster. 1966. © Milton Glaser.
Rubin Museum of Art cloud wall. 2004. © Milton Glaser, Inc.
Holocaust Museum Houston Poster. 2006. © Milton Glaser, Inc.

■ ■ ■

INDEX